The Which? Guide to Computers

About the author

Since working for a decade in the software industry Richard Wentk has been a freelance writer, computer trainer and consultant, with a particular interest in making computer technology accessible to non-technical people. He is also the author of *The Which? Guide to the Internet* and *The Which? Guide to Computers for Small Businesses*.

The Which? Guide to Computers

Richard Wentk

 CONSUMERS' ASSOCIATION

Which? Books are commissioned and researched by
Consumers' Association and published by
Which? Ltd, 2 Marylebone Road, London NW1 4DF
Email address: books@which.net

Distributed by The Penguin Group:
Penguin Books Ltd, 27 Wrights Lane, London W8 5TZ

First published September 1995
Reprinted January, March 1996
Revised edition September 1996
Reprinted September, October 1997
Revised edition May 1998
Reprinted November 1998
Revised edition September 1999
Revised edition October 2000
Revised edition October 2001

British Library Cataloguing in Publication Data
A catalogue record for this book is available from the British Library

ISBN 0 85202 877 6

For a full list of Which? books, please write to Which? Books, Castlemead,
Gascoyne Way, Hertford X. SG14 1LH, or access our web site at
http://www.which.net

With thanks to John Docherty, Sara Edlington, Caroline Ellerby, Ivor Garfinkle,
Martin Harney, Jacqueline Hewitt, Fionna Johnson, Ian Kilminster, Marie Lorimer,
Bruce Tober, John Wheelwright.
Illustration on pages 10–11 Kevin Jones Associates as used in *PC Guide* (Future Publishing)
Issue 1, July 1995
Cover photograph Tony Stone Images/Nicholas Veasey
Cover and text design by Kysen Creative Consultants
Typeset by WPG Ltd, Welshpool, Powys
Printed and bound in England by Clays Ltd, Bungay, Suffolk

Contents

Introduction

During the last decade the role of the computer has shifted from complex technical tool and occasional plaything in the home to virtually essential consumer item. Where once information technology could be purchased only after protracted negotiations with teams of professional salespeople, now much-improved and much cheaper versions of similar technology can be bought by anyone – in the high street, in retail parks and even in large supermarkets. The speed with which computers have become everyday items is phenomenal. According to a survey in 2001 by ICM, a market research company, computers have become a major topic of conversation outside work hours. Almost half of all pub conversations and one-third of dinner party discussions are now about computer technology. The survey also found that nearly three-quarters of the respondents would rather swap technical hints than talk about holiday plans.

Basic computer skills are now as fundamental in everyday life as the ability to use a telephone. The astonishing success of the Internet, which relies for its growth on access to affordable computer technology, has made it possible for people with little or no technical expertise to shop, chat, manage their finances at any hour of the day or night and even create new careers for themselves by trading or advertising goods and services electronically. World Wide Web addresses and the letters 'www' are now commonplace on radio, TV, in newspapers and magazines and even in the advertising of very small businesses. Far more information is now transferred electronically than by more traditional paper-based methods. Email has become as widely used for social purposes as the telephone, and more widely used than the letter or postcard. Music, photographs and even videos are moving on to the Internet, where they can be swapped and discussed more conveniently than ever before, by those who have access to the technology. A typical mid-price computer today, costing £500, is far more powerful than a £1-million machine of the 1980s. More expensive, but still affordable, machines are beginning to exceed the speed and power of what would have been known as a 'supercomputer' a decade ago.

For all the technological advances, however, the biggest obstacle facing anyone thinking of buying a computer is still the dearth of simple, easy-to-understand consumer help. This lack of accessible information, both at the initial purchase and as ongoing support, can lead to problems for both home and business users. A 1999 survey by MORI showed that over 50 per cent of the people interviewed felt very stressed by computer problems. 'Computer rage' – the physical or verbal abuse of computers which are not working properly – is a common occurrence, especially in the workplace. Another source of frustration is the time it can take for suppliers to rectify problems. While some technically literate buyers are able to undertake their own repairs, many find that they have to rely on the technical support skills of dealers and engineers, and the level of service provided often falls short of the claims made at the time of purchase. For beginners, the likelihood of coming to grief – when faced with dubious sales tactics and outright dishonesty on the part of a small number of unscrupulous dealers – is still much higher than it should be.

Certainly there are risks involved in buying and using a computer, and a number of businesses have run into serious problems by misjudging their computer requirements. Such risks can be minimised, however, and the potential benefits are enormous for those willing to ignore the hype and base their choice of computer on a realistic assessment of their needs. This is a key part of the buying process, but it remains one that many small businesses either spend too little time on, or overlook altogether.

Similarly in the home, families which take the time to think about what they really want from a computer before buying one will find that they have acquired something that is a superb arithmetical aid, a reference library, an extra dimension to any hobby or interest, and a provider of entertainment to children.

This book has been written for the non-technical person, who wants to know how a computer will perform as a practical tool, not as a grey box with an attached set of performance statistics. The pages that follow include simple explanations of what a computer can do for you at home and in your small business, how to choose between competing products, how to estimate the real costs of a computer system, and – perhaps most importantly – how to make sure that you and your business are protected if things go wrong. Suggestions are made to help you guard against the common pitfalls of computer purchase, together with hints and tips on how to save money by negotiating better prices and buying wisely. Many of the common jargon words are explained, to enable you to read and understand advertisements and articles in computer magazines. Also covered are the pros and cons of the Internet and other electronic information services, the legal implications of maintaining a computer system, especially in the light of the Data Protection Act 1998, advice about how to finance your purchase, how a computer affects your tax position, and how to ensure that continuous use of computer equipment and accessories will not damage your health.

If you are to get the best from your investment, your computer system has to be matched to your individual requirements. The information presented here will help you clarify what you want, and give you the knowledge and confidence to deal with computer dealers competently. Whether you are running a business or simply looking for a tool to write letters, do your personal accounts, and educate and entertain your children, this book offers everything you will need to help you choose a computer system and use it effectively.

Anatomy of a personal computer

Keyboard
The keyboard and the mouse are still the main way of telling your
computer what you want it to do. The keyboard is very much like the
standard typewriter keyboard with an extra set of keys for numbers on
the right-hand side and various other special keys which are used by
some software.

Screen/Monitor
The screen is where information is displayed, and you can see what your
computer is doing. Screens vary in size, but even the smallest are
capable of displaying photographs clearly.

Speakers
Many computers now come with speakers which are used for playing
music and adding sound effects to software. These have serious uses
beyond entertainment. For example, voice recordings can be added to
computer documents, and video clips can have sound included.

Mouse
The mouse sits under your hand with the connecting lead at the top under
your fingertips. As you move it around, a pointer on the screen follows
your motions. You select on-screen options with the mouse buttons, which
are also under your fingertips.

Joystick
This optional extra is used solely for games.

Base unit
This is the part of the computer that does all the work. All the extras plug into the base unit. Base units come in different shapes and sizes. Some stand upright on the desk, and some are designed to stand on the floor. All modern computers include a fan to keep the insides cool.

Expansion slots and connectors
All modern computers have a set of sockets on the back for essential extras such as a keyboard, screen and mouse. These are designed so that you cannot plug the wrong item into the wrong socket.

Chapter 1

What a computer can do for you

A computer is the perfect tool for manipulating information. In the office it can be used as a typewriter, a very fast adding machine, a record-keeper and address book. In the home it can help educate and entertain both children and adults with games, music and video, provide access to the Internet, manage home finances and help with writing letters.

However, any modern machine, even a modest one, can be used for much more than this. In fact a computer can be used to help with almost anything, from automating a bakery to keeping track of stock in a bookshop or showing customers examples of different hairstyles, with their own features superimposed electronically.

'Information' is a very wide term; it covers words, sounds, holiday snapshots, video clips and numbers. Images such as maps and technical drawings can easily be stored and manipulated on modern computers. Less familiar uses, such as photographic editing and retouching, interior design and automated route planning are just some of the sophisticated applications now widely available.

A computer is a sizeable investment. Used wisely, it can streamline the running of any business and make home life more entertaining, creative and enjoyable. But it can also become more of a problem than a solution. You can cripple a business by making the wrong decision about purchasing and using a computer system, or spend a fortune on a home computer that provides nothing but trouble. Using real-life examples this book illustrates the sorts of mistakes people make regularly and how you can avoid them.

CASE HISTORY: Jenny

Jenny Shipway, who runs a clothing business, was looking for a computer to help with business administration.

'A friend suggested I got a computer to help with the books. This sounded like a great idea, so we started to look around at what was available and eventually decided on a PC.

'So I got the computer first. Now I know that was my first mistake – I should have got the software sorted out and then found the right computer for it.

'I had an idea that somehow the computer on its own would make everything easier. I hadn't even thought about software for it at all. There was some free stuff that came with it, but it didn't seem to do much. It certainly wasn't what I wanted.

'At my friend's suggestion I had a look round some of the computer shops in Tottenham Court Road, London. In a lot of them the sales people leapt on you the second you walked through the door. I felt pretty intimidated.

'Eventually I found one shop that was slightly more relaxed. I explained that I was running a business and needed some software for it. I was steered in the direction of a software package described as an "office suite", which I was told was perfect for businesses. Exactly what I was looking for. It cost nearly £450. That sounded a lot, but I thought that if it did the job it would be worth it.

'It didn't do the job, and it wasn't worth it. I found it was much too complicated. I eventually got the word processor and the electronic organiser working, but the rest of it was beyond me. It wasn't what I wanted at all. I'm sure if I were running a big company it would be just the thing, but for my kind of small business – doing the sales, bought ledger and VAT – it just wasn't right.

'In desperation I bought a few computer magazines. I didn't understand much of the editorial content, but I saw what I'd just bought being advertised for £250! That was the going rate, because of something called a "competitive upgrade". I'd paid the full recommended retail price, when I could have saved myself nearly half of that, never mind that it didn't do what I wanted anyway!

'Of course I was furious, but there was nothing I could do. I realise it was my own fault, as I wasn't clear about what I needed and I didn't think things through. Computers have this aura of infallibility, and it's easy to feel intimidated and make decisions you'd never dream of in another context.

'I tried contacting the shop, but of course they said they couldn't take the software back. I'd broken the seal and started using it, and that, as far as they were concerned, was that. I even contacted my lawyer, but he said that in the circumstances I'd be pushing my luck trying to take action.

'I think that was the worst moment. At that point I'd spent the best part of £2,000 and had nothing to show for it, apart from some letters printed out more stylishly than I could have achieved on a typewriter and a slightly better organised address book. Someone suggested I tried ringing around computer consultants listed in Yellow Pages. A few were off-hand and said that they only dealt with larger companies. One or two simply didn't return my calls. But eventually I got through to someone who very patiently listened to what I wanted, gave me some options, and we settled for a proper accounts system. It cost all of £100, and it does everything – accounts, tax, VAT, PAYE, the lot. He even helped me get it working, showed me how to use it and helped me sell the "office suite" to someone else. Apparently I hadn't registered it, so I wasn't even the official owner. We were lucky – we managed to get nearly £100 for it. Unfortunately, that money went on his fee. That hurt a bit, but I do think it was worth it.

'I realise now that it's easy to waste a fortune in this game. If I was doing it all again I'd make damn sure I did my homework, or I'd get real expert help from someone who's been down the same path. That's just so important – otherwise I'd have wasted the best part of £2,000 and been left with nothing to show for it at all.'

Software first

A quick look through some computer magazines shows that most advertising concentrates on hardware. Computers are sold as boxes, rather than useful tools. The industry works on the basis that hardware is exciting – doubly so if it works faster than last year's hardware. Software (which is what turns the hardware into a useful tool) appears to be something of an afterthought.

When deciding on a computer system, it is important to approach things from the other end: software first, then hardware. You have tasks that need to be carried out; a computer may be able to help you with them. So take a look at the software available and decide which package you might find useful for which tasks. Then find a computer that can run your chosen software.

Leisure uses

Since the late 1980s the home computer has gradually been integrated with other home-entertainment and leisure products. All modern computers can play music CDs through attached speakers or through headphones. Music can also be copied from the Internet, often for free, in the form of **MP3 files** – a system created to distribute music electronically directly between computers without any need for tapes, CDs or other physical recording media.

Many home computers can now also play videos in the form of **DVDs** (Digital Versatile Disks). These are a replacement for VHS video tapes. They are the same size as a CD, but hold ten times as much information, which is enough for a complete film with much better picture quality than that available from video tapes. They often also include extra background information, such as interviews with actors and directors and 'behind the scenes' clips. DVDs are now widely available and are rapidly making traditional VHS tapes obsolete.

Software is sold on both CDs and DVDs. **Multimedia** software includes pictures, sounds and video clips, and is typically used to provide education and entertainment. The available range of topics covered is huge, covering home and garden design, animated children's software, home encyclopaedias, and other educational materials covering science, art, history and so on.

Leisure uses also include a range of creative applications. Software for music, art, animation and even video editing is now widely available at relatively reasonable prices. This means that interested amateurs can experiment without having to invest a huge amount of time or money in acquiring basic skills or buying expensive tools or materials. Another advantage is that mistakes can easily be corrected.

But perhaps the most popular leisure use of computers remains game-playing. Players can now explore hugely detailed virtual worlds set in a variety of locations, from alien planets to World War II. They can also link up with other gamers for competitive or co-operative play, either over the Internet or over a telephone line.

Managing your money

A computer can be an invaluable tool for managing your money. At its simplest it can help you balance the books and perform cheque-book reconciliations. With its help you can keep a history of all your transactions that is at least as detailed as that kept by your bank. This can make domestic budgeting easier – you can, for example, keep a detailed record of heating and lighting bills on a quarterly basis, and be ready for the next set of bills well before they arrive. Another possible use is to check annual percentage rate and mortgage calculations, so that you can work out exactly how expensive a loan will be and find the most cost-effective way to pay it off.

CASE HISTORY: Steven

Steven Adams works from home as a freelance journalist. Before he got a computer, he had problems keeping on top of his financial situation.

'I'm not a very organised person. I love working from home, and also having the opportunity to get out there and chase stories rather than being stuck in an office. But I always used to get my accounts in late, and I'd usually be charged interest by the Inland Revenue. I was hopeless at keeping track of invoices, too; sometimes I wouldn't even bother sending them in. But that's a bad habit to get into, as you have no idea where your money is coming from or who owes you what. It was getting so bad that my accountant took me to one side at one point and politely suggested that I needed to get my act together.

'Even though it should only take maybe half an hour a week to sort out all my expenses, somehow I just couldn't seem to find the time. So I started to wonder if my computer could help. I knew that all I needed was some software.

'The first thing I tried was a spreadsheet. This wasn't what I wanted at all. For a financial whizz it would be perfect, but for me it was just too involved. It was too open-ended and I didn't fancy having to program it myself before I could start using it.

'So I had a good, long think about what I needed. I decided it had to be something that was designed from the start to do the things I wanted. It should be able to track my invoices and then remind me when payments were late. I also needed help keeping track of the expenses that come up on each job. If I don't note these down I end up paying tax on the money that's refunded to me. Then I needed some general accounting and bookkeeping help, and also something that could work out expenses incurred as part of my job in a more general way, like petrol, phone bills and so on. Finally I needed something that was easy to set up and use. I'm not VAT-registered, so that wasn't a problem, although a VAT option would be useful.

'The next step was to go into a newsagent and buy a pile of computer magazines. Most of the adverts were hardware-based. But there were a few software products listed too.

'Eventually I tried a demonstration copy of some bookkeeping software that came free with a magazine. It was a limited version, but I tried it out and found that it did almost everything the way I wanted it done. The full version was only £100, so I got that, and got organised. I bought the version with the VAT option, and, now that work is picking up, I don't have to worry about hiring an accountant every so often to sort things out. It's great, because the software paid for itself right away.'

Bookkeeping

For most businesses keeping the books is something of a chore. A computer can automate the work, as well as producing professional end-of-year accounts. Keeping up with VAT calculations can also be made much less time-consuming. It is relatively simple to automate VAT accounting, including any rate changes and zero-rated items. It is also possible to produce a single printout at the end of the accounting period which can be sent straight to HM Customs and Excise with a covering letter. At the time of writing (April 2001) both the Inland Revenue and HM Customs and Excise now offer trial schemes that allow electronic submissions of both returns and payments over the Internet, and even include a small discount for returns made this way. By 2005 it is likely that these will have become standard, and the paper returns will no longer be as widely used as they are today. In the 2000 Budget tax breaks were announced for companies that switched to electronic submissions. The latest details of these will be available from your local Inland Revenue and HM Customs and Excise offices.

CASE HISTORY: Stella

Stella Beck runs a stationery supply company.

'Bookkeeping has never interested me, but it's never seemed cost-effective to employ someone to do it. I used to be very disorganised about it, and sometimes I'd lose bills and forget to chase payments.

'I bought a simple accounts and money-management package, and it has really helped. I'm disciplined enough now to make sure that all the sales and payments go through the system, and at the end of the day it tells me exactly where I stand. It's been a godsend for the VAT, because that used to take forever. Now, I just have an electronic record I can send directly to the Customs and Excise people. They're happy because they don't need to hassle me, I'm happy because it takes an hour to sort everything out instead of a couple of days of panic. The business is happier too. I have more time to deal with people, which is the part I really enjoy.'

Sole traders can use a computer to keep track of their creditors and debtors. This can be combined with invoice- and cheque-printing systems to provide an all-in-one cash flow control system. It is possible to set up a system whereby bad debts are chased with letters, as well as making sure that bills are paid as late as possible to help with cash flow. One advantage of a system like this is that it enables you to estimate accurately the financial position of your business a month or two ahead, based on sales projections.

Advanced accounting systems can handle credits and debits in foreign currencies, and allow for exchange-rate fluctuations. Of current interest is the ability to deal with transactions in Euros; at the time of writing some businesses have to accept payments in Euros as well as pounds, and suitable software can make it easier to maintain a summary of these transactions. The job of calculating payroll contributions is also relatively straightforward. The computer can be made to allow for budget and tax changes and even refer to them on a year-by-year basis. Keeping track of payroll outgoings, PAYE and National Insurance contributions becomes much simpler.

Financial planning

For financial planning the spreadsheet is now an indispensable tool of the trade. It presents you with a grid of boxes, called 'cells', each of which contains either a number or a formula. You can specify something as simple as 'add up all the numbers entered above and print the total here', or as complex as calculating the total payment for a loan, based on a principal, a period and an interest rate.

CASE HISTORY: Martin

Martin Smith, a chartered accountant, was wary of computers until one of his clients showed him a spreadsheet in action.

'I was hooked. It was just the perfect tool for the job. Most people who use spreadsheets don't have a financial background, so they only use simple applications like profit and loss accounts. I found I could do much more than that, because it's easy to do things like profit management, payback analysis and answer other 'what-if?' questions.

'Most of my work used to be tax-based. Now I get a fair bit of work helping with business plans. With the spreadsheet I can track interest rates and currency exchange rates and watch what effect they'll have on a new project. New businesses can be very sensitive to these, so I can warn clients just how much of a risk they're taking. The fact that I can draw graphs helps as well – they can put a message over in a very direct, accessible form.'

As Martin's story shows, spreadsheets are ideal for speculative calculations. It is easy to set up a table of potential income against interest payments and then vary the interest rate to see what happens. Without a computer you would have to recalculate each entry. With a computer you can change a single number (in this case the interest rate), and the spreadsheet does the rest. The information can be presented graphically as well as in tabular form. This is useful for trend-spotting and can also help with producing financial reports for directors and shareholders.

Money on line

All the main high-street banks now offer electronic banking over the Internet, although only a few (such as Barclays) offer an equivalent service to business customers.

In general banks appear to be moving towards cutting back on both branches and staff, pushing customers wherever possible towards taking care of transactions electronically. Some banks, such as Smile and Egg, only exist in electronic form, although they are still associated with high-street banks and post offices which can handle payments and credits the traditional way. With the equivalent of twenty-four-hour opening and no queues, the advantages for customers are obvious; but there are also disadvantages, such as the complications involved in making deposits by post, the problem of dealing with cash, and the time and effort involved in setting up regular payments to payees such as credit cards and utilities. An increasing number of banks are also offering loans, mortgages, insurance and other financial services over the Internet. Electronic share-dealing is another option that is becoming increasingly widely used. Again, this can be done directly and almost instantaneously over the Internet, either through a bank or an on-line share-dealing house.

For businesses, the situation is less straightforward. Older technologies can be used to confirm balances, arrange automated payments, and authorise money transfers at home and abroad. But as yet only some banks have integrated these services with the possibilities offered by the Internet.

Stock control

For applications that require a more in-depth approach to information management, the best available tool is the database. A database can be used to keep track of any kind of information and pick out trends and details from it. For example, when managing a sales team it is possible to collate sales by area, by product, by salesman or by season.

Keeping track of hundreds of different items in a warehouse while working out the optimum use of space is something of a challenge by hand. But a database can be used to tackle the problem easily, as well as making it possible to play with 'what-if' scenarios.

CASE HISTORY: George

George Becker runs a car spares service. He uses a computer to keep track of stock levels and to manage his inventory in an intelligent way.

'I got someone in to set up a database for me. It keeps track of all the parts I sell, warns me when stocks are low and reminds me to reorder. It's not foolproof – every so often we'll get a run on some part or other out of the blue, and I run out. But it's made my life a lot easier.

'The reports are great. I can keep track of exactly what the stock is worth and cut down on slow-selling lines so I don't have goods lying around taking up space.

'It helps with the selling too. It's all been marked up so that if one part needs an extra, that comes up on the screen. We don't get people coming back a day later saying "Can I have one of these as well?" any more.'

Another efficient use of a database is in personnel. It is easy to set up a database of employees, with photographs, to include all the details of appraisals and indications of an employee's work record. This makes it possible to arrange a 'skills bank' that can be used when employees are being selected for new projects.

Managing personal information

An electronic personal organiser can completely replace a paper one. It is a convenient way to store information such as 'to-do' lists, anniversaries, currency-conversion factors, appointment and meeting reminders and general notes. Electronic organisers can also be set up to provide an audible reminder or alarm at a certain time, and to keep links between different kinds of information. All the contact details of everyone involved on a certain project can be kept together, and appointments can be linked with telephone numbers so that any changes can be communicated quickly and easily. Typically, these details can be transferred from a desk-bound computer to an electronic organiser, or even a mobile phone, so that they can be used when out of the office (see page 272).

CASE HISTORY: Trevor

Trevor Knight sells advertising for a magazine publishing company. He used to use a paper 'organiser' but recently switched to a computer-based system.

'I can honestly say it's changed my life. Now everything – appointments, follow-up calls, names, addresses, phone numbers, fax numbers – are all systematically stored away instead of being in an overstuffed ring-bound notebook with pages and business cards spilling out of it. The computer can find anything in a fraction of a second. The fun part is getting it to dial the phone numbers and log the calls for me too.'

Communications

A computer can also be used to transmit information as well as storing it. With the addition of a simple and affordable extra called a **modem**, your computer can dial telephone numbers for you (see Appendix II). This turns a computer into an automated telephone book which can save you hours during the course of a working week.

A modem can also be used to send and receive faxes. These can be read on screen and printed out only if necessary for future reference. While many budget fax machines still use fax paper which is prone to curling, fading and yellowing, computer-printed faxes are always printed on plain paper. Finally, modems remain the most popular way to connect to the Internet (see below).

CASE HISTORY: Ryan

Ryan Williams is a freelance journalist with a particular interest in learning how computers can be used to communicate.

'Originally I bought a modem to send and receive faxes. Most of what I sent came straight from my computer anyway, so I didn't need to print it out.

'Then, a few years ago, one of my editors told me about electronic mail. The company already used an internal mail system and was enlarging it so that outsiders could send mail as well. It meant I could send copy straight to the office without even faxing. The text would go directly from my computer to the office system. This has made life much easier for everyone, as any work sent to an editor is immediately accessible, and they can make changes very quickly and easily.'

Within an office, computers can be connected together on a **network**, so that information and messages can be passed among them. **Electronic mail (email)** can take the place of paper memos, and the network can also be used to share resources such as printers and external fax machines. The biggest advantage of a network is that it makes it easy to keep track of people and make sure that everyone works together smoothly.

The **Internet** offers the same kinds of facilities but on a much larger scale. The Internet is an international computer network that allows mail to be exchanged with any computer anywhere. For example, you can mail someone on the other side of the world with a list of prices and services. Unlike ordinary mail, the information arrives almost instantaneously. Costs are based on local call charges, and are sometimes free no matter where the destination. Collaborative projects can also be managed and undertaken across the Internet.

The Internet can be an excellent source of computer support and advice. Aside from Internet connection charges – usually quite reasonable – this support is free and is provided by experts or enthusiastic amateurs. Many other pastimes and interests also have their own communities of experts and enthusiasts on the Internet which are almost always open to everyone. The Internet can also be an excellent source of reference material for almost any subject imaginable, both technical and home- and hobby-oriented.

Presentation

Business presentations play an important role in many corporate environments, and here too the computer can offer effective help.

As with desktop publishing tools and word processors, many presentation applications offer a range of templates that can be used to add impact to a presentation. They also include libraries of graphics and symbols. The most sophisticated tools offer simple animation features, which include video effects such as dissolves and cross-fades, and also animated graphs and symbols. Pre-recorded music clips, sound effects and even video recordings can also be used to add emphasis and interest to the presentation.

Until the 1980s all stationery was printed by professional printers. However, with the advent of desktop publishing, pioneered by the Apple Computer Corporation with its Macintosh range, it is now possible for a business or an individual to produce professional-quality leaflets, flyers, posters, advertising material, business cards and so on. Desktop publishing software is available for all makes of computer, and in many cases is sold with off-the-peg design templates. These guarantee professional results and help to overcome the lack of design and layout skills which blighted many early amateur desktop publishing efforts.

CASE HISTORY: Sally

Sally Griffiths runs a computer training company.

'A big part of the job is getting information across as clearly as possible, and computers can be really good for that. Today's software makes it easy to design striking presentations, and we use those to communicate with as much impact as possible. It helps our clients to pick things up more quickly. They're also impressed when they see what a computer can do.

'We tend to work a lot with corporate teams, and they often need to use the same technology themselves. So it's a bonus that presentation software is one of the easier kinds of software to use. They can get superb results very quickly. It helps with confidence – some people are still a bit intimidated by computers – and it helps them practically too.

'We also consult on presentation and image in general, and there are some very interesting things that businesses can do with a simple black and white laser printer and pre-printed stationery'.

The automated mailshot is another useful facility that can help with presentation. This takes a standard letter, a list of addresses and other relevant details and automatically produces a string of personalised letters (complete with printed envelopes). Targeted carefully and used creatively, mailshots can be very effective.

At the moment, budget colour printers are very affordable but cannot yet compete with the quality and sharpness of black-and-white printers. Over the next few years high-quality colour printers will become more widely available and affordable, but for now it is still possible to produce strikingly professional results by using pre-printed paper. These offer graphic backgrounds as an effective backdrop for text that can be added later. They can be used to produce professional-looking leaflets, letters and business cards from your own home or office for a much smaller outlay than something that has been designed and printed by a print house.

Electronic presentation is becoming increasingly popular. Instead of creating paper reports, many larger businesses now place information on local computer networks, called intranets, where they can be read and searched by anyone who needs them. Apart from saving on printing costs, electronic presentations can include animations, sounds and video, and can also be produced in colour.

Businesses can use the same kinds of facilities to promote themselves internationally on the World Wide Web (known simply as the Web) – a popular part of the Internet. This kind of electronic presentation has now become commonplace, and in some cases will even have taken the place of paper-based presentations. An advantage of the Web is that it can also handle electronic sales – a feature known as ecommerce. A full discussion of ecommerce is beyond the scope of this book, and doing ecommerce well is usually a job for a paid specialist. However even small businesses can now offer electronic order-taking and credit card payment facilities. Your bank or credit card company will be able to provide you with information about the latest costs and details.

Professional tools for specialist work

Computers can also be used to help with specific professional applications. Job-specific software is readily available for a wide range of professions, including law, medicine, architecture, design and various kinds of engineering.

CASE HISTORY: Fionna

Fionna Johnson works from home as an illustrator and graphic designer.

'Like a lot of creative people, I was very wary of computers. To be honest I thought they were rather dull. But when a friend demonstrated what he could do on his computer with graphic-design software, I was smitten. Now I have similar equipment, it enables me to try out all sorts of different approaches in a fraction of the time it would take to produce alternative designs conventionally. So I can supply a far better, more flexible service to clients at a low cost.

'I now use a graphics tablet and stylus instead of a pen and paper, and "draw" into the computer directly. I can simulate any kind of brush – airbrush, water-colour, pencil, whatever – and even make the "paper" as wet or dry as I'd like. The range of colours is all but infinite. And it's easy to add extras such as fragments of photographs or news clippings, and then, if you want, distort them to produce a special effect.

'I've had a huge amount of extra work as a result, and it's really freed me up creatively. I can do things I never even dreamed of doing with ink and paper, and I still haven't reached the limits of what I can do. I don't even need to worry about mistakes. I can backtrack through various changes I make, and the computer takes me back to where I was before.

'The only problem is getting things printed. Detailed full-colour artwork can cost a small fortune to print out if you use a bureau, but more and more publishers now handle designs sent in over the Internet. For more detailed work where this isn't practical, I can burn my work onto a CD at home and send that through the post.

Computer-aided design (CAD)

This software can be invaluable for visualising two-dimensional and three-dimensional objects. CAD software is rather like an advanced version of the traditional drawing board, except that it can be used to design in three dimensions as well as two. The drawings – which can include mechanical parts, buildings, items of furniture and so on – are held inside the computer's memory. They can then be viewed on the screen from any angle and altered quickly and easily. CAD can help with engineering, architecture, interior design and any other kind of work that can benefit from the chance to look at a plan or layout before it is drawn or built. Advanced CAD tools can be used to place computer-generated images of items on a photographic background. This is ideal for architectural work, enabling the effect of a building on its surroundings to be assessed before the building is built.

Image manipulation

More and more artists and graphic designers are using computers. Many advertising hoardings now carry work that was designed – at least in part – on a computer, and computer animations are routinely used in television advertising, including spectacular 'morphing' effects, where one object appears to change into another. Computer animators such as William Latham are working with the branch of mathematics known as fractals to create intriguing new images. Computers offer designers many advantages over conventional media, including the ability to create new special effects that are not possible any other way.

27

Other examples

Computer technology is also influencing photography. Photographers have always used studio and darkroom techniques to enhance their work, but with a computer such adjustments or image manipulation can be made more easily using **photographic tools**. The best tools – such as Adobe's Photoshop – make it possible to do virtually everything it's possible to do with a conventional darkroom, and much more besides. Because all the processing is done inside the computer, a light-free environment and expensive, unpleasant chemicals are not required.

For haulage firms and countless businesses for which getting from A to B is an important consideration, one of the most useful computer tools of recent years has been the **electronic route-planner**. This works out a route between two places based on a number of criteria (shortest, cheapest, quickest, and so on). The route can be tailored to take into account typical speeds and miles-per-gallon ratings of different vehicles. Planners for roads in Europe and the United States are also available.

Another practical application is the preparation of **timetables for schools**. In the past this has been an onerous and time-consuming task, but a computer can keep track of all the information with ease.

Legal firms can now access case histories and precedents electronically. **Legal databases** are available that detail previous judgements and make it easy to track related cases. This can save many hours of research.

Even **catering and hotel management** can benefit from computerisation. Many hotels now use computers to keep track of room bookings, maintain a list of their guests' spending and calculate an itemised bill at the end of their stay. In fact almost any business will be able to be find suitable software listed in the relevant specialist magazines.

Choosing the right software for the job

Software comes in two types. The first is the dedicated application, specialised for a single job: for example, an accounts package, which is designed to keep the books and cannot be used for anything else. To use this kind of software you just type in your information. All the setting up has already been done for you.

The second is the general-purpose package, which gives you a framework in which to work. These have to be tailored to your needs before you can use them. In this group are all the large business software packages. A spreadsheet can be used not only for accounts but for tax, financial projections, balance sheets, and mortgage and loan calculations as well. Before you attempt any of these tasks, however, you have to create a template for each one. This kind of software gives you two jobs instead of one – first you create a framework for the information, and then you add the information itself – but it has the advantage that you can organise information to suit specific needs. However, setting up the software will take extra time.

The type of software you choose will depend on the kind of work you want to do. If you want a specific job done or if you are worried about the amount of time it will take you to master a computer, then a tailor-made package is a good choice. This will give you a return much more quickly and will be easier to use and set up in the short term.

If you would like to explore what a computer can do for you in a more general way and would prefer a more flexible approach, then one of the larger business packages, such as Microsoft's Office 2000 or XP, may suit your needs better. Some of these are very powerful indeed, and there is often some overlap between the applications they include. For example, you could work out quarterly sales figures by geographical region using either a spreadsheet or a database. Neither is 'right' for the job; you will simply approach the problem in two different ways, depending on which you use.

If you decide on the second type of package you will have the added advantage of integration. These applications are often designed to work with each other, so you will have the ability to move information from a database to a spreadsheet, and perhaps create some charts which could then be 'pasted' into a word processor for a business report.

A computer at home?

For home use the situation is less complicated, as you will be more likely to buy a general-purpose machine that will work with a range of software, rather than buying a specific product. Today's computers are so powerful that almost any new machine costing around £1,000 will be powerful enough for most software. If your main interests are limited to writing letters and occasionally experimenting with the Internet, then you can comfortably spend even less: a system costing around £700 (including the printer) should be satisfactory. For very demanding work, including the latest games and serious home video editing, models costing £1,500 and £2,000 will be ideal. Spending less will give you a machine that is still very usable, but you may find that games do not perform at their very best, and video editing will involve a certain amount of waiting.

Is a computer essential?

Every year the computer industry spends millions of pounds in an attempt to persuade you to buy its products. For all this, you may find you do not need a computer at all.

CASE HISTORY: Jill

Jill Taylor runs a small newsagent's shop. She considered getting a computer to help manage the accounts and organise paper deliveries, but decided against it.

'We don't make a fortune, so we didn't have much to spend. We made a few enquiries and looked at a few computers, but in the end decided it just wasn't worth it. My husband has been doing the books for years, and he is quite happy with the way things are. He might get them done more quickly with a computer, but he says he enjoys the work. And he double-checks everything, so mistakes aren't a worry.

'As for the paper round, that takes half an hour a day to sort out. I have to write all the addresses on the papers by hand anyway, and it wouldn't be a lot quicker to use printed sticky labels. Keeping track of the payments is a bit of a chore, but I've been managing the job for a long time now and I'm used to it.

'Once we thought about it, it was obvious that we could get by without a computer. We'd have to spend over £500 to get something that was up to the job, and there seemed better things to spend the money on. In the end we just decided to leave it – and I can't honestly say I've regretted that.'

It is tempting to buy a computer 'just because'. If you look at your needs closely, however, you may decide that you do not need one at all. If you have less than £500 to spend and intend to use your computer mainly for writing letters, then it may be better to look at some of the all-in-one word processors currently available. These cost between £200 and £400, and offer you many of the features of a computer-based system. They have the advantage of being easier to use, easier to move from one place to another and easier to learn.

If you want to dabble in the basics of computing, but are not concerned about doing any serious work or keeping up with the very latest developments, then consider a second-hand machine. These are adequate for light-duty work, will introduce you to all the basic concepts and can cost as little as £100. They will not be able to work with the latest software and hardware, so you should assume that you are buying a closed system. In other words, what you buy is what you get. Adding extras later is not an option. For someone on a strict budget a second-hand machine can prove an excellent, low-risk introductory buy.

If you are planning to use your computer for more business-oriented tasks, you can expect to pay £500 for a basic modern machine to over £5,000 for a no-expense-spared system. In general, you get the best compromise between cost and performance at around £1,000 to £1,500, for a complete system including printer and software. This will give you a modern machine that you can expand as your funds grow and will have a life of two to three years. (At the end of that period it will still be useful, but you will need to reassess your needs in the light of technological advances.)

When it comes to looking at the individual facets of your business, the best approach to computerisation is to ask yourself how much time you spend on certain activities and how organised you are already. If you are perfectly happy keeping addresses and phone numbers in a card file, then you should think long and hard before buying an electronic system to replace them. In general, activities that you perform occasionally are best done by hand. Activities that are time-consuming, repetitive and a chore are best done by computer, but if you have a system that works for you now without a computer, there is no good reason why you should feel any need to buy one.

As a rough guide, you can start by working out how much time you waste over the course of a year on tasks that add nothing to the value of your business. Next, calculate how much this time is worth at a suitable hourly rate. Estimate how much time these activities will take if you get a computer to help you. For some kinds of work — VAT, payroll calculations and so on — this should be relatively straightforward — you can guesstimate how long it would take to type the relevant information into the computer, and then add a week or so as 'learning time'. Other kinds of work will be much harder to quantify, and you may need to arrange a demonstration at a reputable computer store before you can get an idea. Once done, you can work out the time and cost saving of installing a computer by comparing time saved against the total time.

This is only useful as a rough guide. The installation of a computer sometimes results in improved productivity and new business opportunities which are not always foreseeable. Sometimes it doesn't. By doing this comparison, you will at least have some idea of whether you are buying on a whim or taking a calculated risk.

Now that you have an overview of what is possible, it is time to look at your options in more detail and examine more closely what you should look for when considering each one.

Chapter 2

Buying a computer – an overview

To get the most from a computer you need to remember that you are buying not just a collection of gadgets and widgets but a complete system – something that is very much greater than the sum of its parts. Computer advertising often tries to lure novice users into spending more than they need by tempting them with vague promises of speed and power. In practice, these factors can have surprisingly little to do with long-term usefulness and reliability. Buying the fastest computer in the world is a waste of time and money if you spend all your time struggling with it. Similarly, a computer that breaks down or leaves you baffled can be more of a liability than an asset.

To avoid this kind of difficulty, it is important to leave the glossy advertising to one side and look realistically at the different elements of a computer system.

Hardware describes the physical parts of the computer – keyboard, screen, main system unit and any other extras you decide to buy. Think of it as an extension to your office. Inside the computer's case you will find the equivalent of a filing cabinet for storing information and a desk-like area where you can choose from a selection of useful tools. The more you spend on hardware the more quickly these tools will do their work for you, and the more room there will be in your new 'office' for both tools and information. There are many different kinds of computer, but the two most popular lines are the IBM-compatible PC (known as the PC) and the Apple Macintosh (known as the Mac).

Software describes the tools or programs which run on the hardware, and more often than not you will need to buy them separately. There are hundreds, perhaps even thousands, of different software products available today, all tailor-made to help you with specific kinds of work. For example, if you want to write letters or create text you need to buy word-processing software; to keep track of finances, you buy an accounting package.

Software, much more than hardware, determines how productive your computer will be. Good software is so easy to use that you forget that it is there. It is also easy to learn (**user-friendly**), which means you can start doing useful work with it very quickly. Bad software can be a hindrance, and will force you to work around it rather than work with it. It can also cause difficulties when you start to use it: for example, when your computer does something unexpected and you are left floundering and confused, with no idea what to do next.

For business or professional use it is important to *choose your software first*. This is one of the golden rules of computer buying. Work out what you want to do, decide which software will work best, and find the hardware to match. For home users, this is less important, and any mid-priced general-purpose machine will be suitable for games, the Internet, and letter writing, and should have a working life of between two and four years.

It is important to note that while the hardware and software are the most obvious parts of a computer system, there are a number of other options you also need to consider.

Support means help with maintenance and problem-solving. If you rely on your computer on a daily basis, you need to be sure that the support will be efficient and quick – being left without your computer for a week or a month can be disastrous.

The other kind of support is needed for those times when you are unable to work out what to do next. You may perhaps be using a word processor that claims you can print lettering in italics, but, even though you have looked at the instruction manual, you still can't see how to do this. At times like this it is a very good idea to have someone or something you can refer to – otherwise you can find yourself wasting a lot of time or using your software at a tiny fraction of its potential.

Training is closely related to support and provides you with the help you need to get started. There are numerous training resources available, some very affordable. Courses or personal tuition can prove expensive, so you may want to consider books, videos and computer-based training software. Magazines can also be a supplementary source of introductory hints and tips.

Insurance is vital to ensure that if something goes wrong, you have the financial resources to put it right. If your computer fails or is stolen, you may be left without access to the information essential to the running of your business. In the short term such a loss can be crippling; in the long term it can be catastrophic. Fortunately, you can protect yourself from these kinds of risks. You can insure your system to protect the information as well as the system itself. You can also keep the information safe by making regular safety copies or backups.

Security becomes an issue when your information is confidential, or you are not the only person with access to it. There are also legal considerations to be aware of if you start to collect information about your customers or your employees (see Appendix XI). There are ways to protect information and ensure that it can be read only by selected users.

The other kind of security is much simpler and cruder: you need to protect your computer against theft. This is a serious problem, especially for businesses based in large towns and cities. Again, there are basic steps you can take to make sure that your equipment is as unattractive to thieves as possible. This is discussed in Chapter 11.

Space Is there sufficient or a convenient space in your existing work area? Computers, like children, can be more demanding than anyone expects. If your existing office is not adequate to cope with a large new arrival, you will need to budget for extra space or furniture to cope with it.

The buying process

Once you have decided what you need and looked at the options, you can start the buying process. Don't rush into it, however. There are good ways and bad ways to buy a computer. Briefly, you are likely to have the following options:

- hire a consultant
- buy a complete package from a dealer or by mail order
- do the research and buying yourself
- buy a second-hand system
- ask a computer-literate friend or colleague to guide you through the process.

A consultant

The expense and time required mean that hiring a consultant is not an option for most home users. But for the larger small business this can be the easiest and the least time-consuming way to buy and install a computer system. It should also – in theory, at least – give the best results. Unfortunately, in the short term it is by far the most expensive approach.

Consultancy fees can vary from £25 to £300 an hour; the rate depends on the consultant's experience and the size of the project. Computerising a sole trader's business is relatively straightforward. Computerising a medium-sized company which has offices in different parts of the country requires a much higher level of expertise.

A good consultant should be able to:

- talk to you in detail about your requirements
- analyse your needs
- let you know if your expectations are unrealistic and discuss alternatives
- choose the best and most cost-effective solution, and settle on a firm price
- install a fully tested and working system
- provide training and advice on how to use the system most effectively, or make recommendations on the best sources for training from outside
- be on call to provide support if anything goes wrong, or arrange for professional support from another source.

One of the best ways to find a consultant is by personal recommendation. Ask friends and colleagues. (Remember, however, someone who works well with a friend may not be the right person to work with you.)

If you need to start 'cold', you will find that some consultants advertise in the trade press and *Yellow Pages*. They may also run shops and small dealerships of their own. Your local dealer may know of a tried and trusted consultant.

Unfortunately, there is as yet no professional organisation that can guarantee a level of service. This means that when you are looking for a consultant you are largely on your own, and you need to apply the same instincts you would use when hiring any employee.

These are some points to consider:

Professionalism You need to feel confident that your consultant will keep appointments, be professional and be on call at any reasonable time. A few consultants are technically brilliant but can be abrasive with those less knowledgeable than themselves. Avoid them unless you specifically need the services of an unusually gifted specialist.

Some parts of the computer trade can be quite informal; if the consultant turns up to your first meeting dressed casually, do not assume that he or she is not professional. Don't allow first impressions to put you off – if your consultant is able, it will show in the references and attitude, not necessarily in the choice of clothes.

Honesty and directness There is a small chance that you will be your consultant's first client – which he or she should divulge in any initial interview. In this case it is advisable to be especially attentive to your consultant's previous work record. A good consultant will be happy to offer credentials.

It is prudent to discuss exactly what the terms of your working relationship will be and, if possible, draw up a full contract, so that, if there are any problems, you are covered legally, and both of you know exactly where you stand.

Previous work experience A good consultant will be happy to provide details of previous clients who can offer references. Asking for these will give you an idea of the consultant's capabilities and personality – both from the answers you get to your questions and the stories previous clients have to tell.

You should also ask about the consultant's areas of expertise. A specialist may not have the skills needed to take on more general work.

Communication skills A good consultant should be able to speak plain English and not intimidate you or make you feel that you are working at cross-purposes. The consultant should demonstrate a clear grasp of your requirements. Be very wary of someone who tries to blind you with science, or talks entirely in computer jargon.

The words 'feasibility study' should also be treated with suspicion. Putting together a computer system for a small business to handle accounts, payroll work, word processing and some desktop publishing does not require a feasibility study – although computerising a medium-sized country-wide business might. If in doubt, get a second opinion.

Although a consultant can be expensive – perhaps doubling the price of your computer system – the long-term benefits could justify the initial outlay. If your computer is vital to the efficient running of your business and you are unsure of your own technical abilities, then a consultant can be a very cost-effective option.

Buying from a dealer

Buying from a dealer can be a risk. Computer dealers range from small shops run by enthusiasts to large multinational companies. They also vary widely in terms of quality of service, reliability, professionalism and support. The ideal is a friendly local dealer who has a strong interest in retaining your business, enjoys working in the trade and has plenty of experience to draw on.

Unfortunately, some dealers are less than scrupulous – it is no exaggeration to say that a handful are little more than used-car salesmen who, aware of the potential of a new market, have been quick to take advantage of it. If you fall foul of one of these you can find yourself being deliberately misled by someone who wants to off-load obsolete stock at an inflated price and has no interest in your needs or long-term custom. Worse still, when you go back a short time later to complain or ask for help, you may well find that the business has disappeared without trace.

To find out whether you are dealing with a saint or a shark, simply visit your local dealer in person, explain roughly what you are looking for and listen closely to the response. Vague sales pitches such as 'This is the very best', 'Everybody uses this one' or 'Really fast machines, these' should be treated with suspicion. Try applying the same criteria as you would when assessing a consultant. Does there seem to be a genuine understanding of what your needs are? Is there a wide range of options to choose from, or are you being steered towards stock that is piled high in the shop front? Does the shop assistant demonstrate knowledge of the subject and a professional attitude? If you feel confident about the level of aptitude and service, then you have probably found your source. You may pay more than you would from the cheapest possible casual seller, but you may also find yourself with a free source of help and advice – both of which can be invaluable for inexperienced users.

Buying by mail order

If you are unable to find a good local dealer, you have the option of buying by mail order from computer magazines. Take the same approach again – telephone the computer company, talk to the sales department, explain what you want, ask a few awkward questions and note down the replies. The tone, precision and usefulness of the responses will tell you a lot about the way that particular dealer does business. You cannot realistically expect the same level of service from a mail-order dealer – especially a large one – as you would from a small local shop. And, of course, the larger mail-order companies sell only their own brands, and so cannot be expected to offer impartial advice on choosing between their brands and others.

It is tacitly acknowledged in the industry that the high-street consumer electronics stores are likely to offer you the worst of both worlds. Prices are often significantly higher than elsewhere, and the level of support and help that the staff can offer tends to be minimal. At best you may be steered towards big-name products that happen to be in stock at the time. At worst you may find that you know more about the computers than the staff on the other side of the counter. Some high-street retailers offer telephone support – at a price. If you want help (and if you are new to computers, you will), you will probably be asked to pay for it by the minute on a premium-rate number. This can be stressful and expensive, and you have no guarantee that your problem will be solved. Worse still, a small number of less scrupulous companies will deliberately mislead you by covering up inadequacies in their products or trying to persuade you that problems that should be covered by a warranty are actually your fault.

High-street stores often charge a much higher annual percentage rate (APR) than a bank or other credit source might. As a result, you could find yourself spending the kind of sums that might have bought you the services of a consultant, and yet still be left with something that you cannot use properly, that does not quite do the job you want, and that you do not understand.

Since 1988 computers have also been available in larger supermarket stores, following a trend set by Tesco with a range of computers made by Fujitsu. Sold this way, PCs become something of an impulse purchase, and, realistically, this is often the worst possible way for beginners to buy. A more effective approach is to evaluate these 'deals' in the same way as all the other computer-buying options – with the difference that checking on after-sales service and support becomes even more important than usual.

Do it yourself

Doing the background research and buying a computer yourself is the most time-consuming option and the most demanding in terms of your personal resources. Buying a computer 'blind' with no research at all is very unlikely to get you a good deal. In fact, it may not even get you something you can use effectively. While this is less of a problem now than it once was, if you have the time it can be worth learning the basics of the subject from the hundreds of books, magazines and courses that are available. This can be a good investment, as dealers tend to respect knowledgeable customers more than complete novices. The difficulty is that not everyone has the time, inclination or interest needed to master the field.

This approach can only be recommended if you are not in a hurry, if your computer is not going to be central to the running of your business (or is for casual home use), and if you feel you have the ability to take on the subject in depth. The rewards can be high, however. You will be able to save on hardware costs, because you will know how and what to buy and and how to get it at a much lower price. You will also be less dependent on outside help. Just like someone who knows how to repair his or her own car, you can enjoy the benefits of cost-saving and independence. The disadvantage is that it takes time to learn all you need to know to reach this standard.

It is worth noting that magazines often include comparative reviews, which can make buying decisions more straightforward. Although some reviews are quite technical, even relative novices should be able to read between the lines and make some progress towards an informed buying decision. For those with Internet access, Which? Online (www.which.net) regularly publishes user satisfaction surveys, which also provide valuable background information. As a very rough rule of thumb, mail-order companies tend to provide better value for money than the larger high-street stores. But they also typically demand a higher level of knowledge and technical experience, which makes them less appealing to the complete beginner.

Buying second-hand

At first sight, the second-hand approach may seem appealing for several reasons. You will be buying a tried-and-tested system which someone else has already been using. In theory, all the teething troubles should have been sorted out, and you will be able to work with something that does the job straight away.

However, there are a few caveats. It is important to remember that computer equipment depreciates quickly. This means that second-hand 'bargains' are rarely what they appear, and in many cases you will be able to buy a new, much better system for the same price as a second-hand one.

Another problem is that for legal reasons software cannot usually be sold to a third party, even when it has been paid for in full by the original owner. This means you will not be eligible for any help the manufacturer may offer to users, and you will not be able to take advantage of any improved versions (**upgrades**) of the software that the manufacturer decides to release, unless you buy them at the full price.

Finally, you cannot be sure that someone else's system matches your needs. Another person's set-up may be perfect for him or her, but it may not be right for you.

Second-hand computer equipment does have its uses, though. If you are working to a very tight budget – a few hundred pounds, perhaps – then you will have to buy second-hand. In this part of the market the equipment has depreciated as much as it is going to, making it less of a long-term risk, but there are still pitfalls to watch for. The most worrying is that spare parts and consumables may no longer be available. Before buying, check that you can still get these for the second-hand machine. You may well find that it will be difficult to buy replacement parts for any machine more than a couple of years old. A good source of help with repair questions can be a small local computer store, and it can be worth making some notes about the technical specification of a second-hand machine before buying, and asking them if they will be able to support you if problems occur.

With a little help from your friends

In theory this is the best and cheapest way to get help. In practice, you should make absolutely sure that your friends and colleagues fully understand your computer requirements and have set up a similar system for themselves before you act on their advice. Unless you have a friend who is prepared to help you put a system together from start to finish, you should treat the advice of friends and colleagues as a source of useful, but not definitive, information.

Latest is not always best

Innovation is a permanent feature of the computer industry. If you are doing your own research and making your own purchasing decisions you may encounter **advance product announcements**. The product may look worth waiting for but, as a rule of thumb, it is best not to wait. *Be wary of any major innovation.* If a product has been on sale for less than a year, there is still a chance that there may be something wrong with it. Many new products simply are not reliable. This may sound incredible, but time and again it has proved to be the case. Manufacturers of both hardware and software are under great pressure to keep ahead of their competitors, and products are often released before they have been fully tested in the field. If your computer needs are conservative, and you need reliability far more than the very latest, fastest and best of everything, then it is prudent to avoid becoming a manufacturer's guinea-pig.

If you do need the very latest and best – and particularly if you are likely to lose work to your competitors without it – then you may need to take the risk. This can put you in a more vulnerable position than someone who is buying established technology. To minimise your risk, hold out as long as you can and watch for any problem reports in computer magazines.

Another reason to avoid waiting for new products is because sometimes they simply fail to appear: this phenomenon is known as

vapourware. A typical piece of vapourware is announced; it misses its first release date, its second, and perhaps even its third and fourth. A year or more may have passed since the first announcement. Sometimes vapourware does eventually appear as a genuine product, but not invariably. There is no way of knowing in advance how it will turn out.

Computer manufacturers have been known to use colourful and creative tactics to put the competition at a disadvantage, and advance product announcements are among these. Manufacturer A is about to release an impressive new product. Manufacturer B, whose sales will be hurt by this, hears about the new product and immediately announces to the world that a brand-new B product is better and will be available very soon. Some buyers wait for product B. The release date comes and goes. Manufacturer B announces that there are a few problems. However, not only are these being sorted out, but the extra time is being used to incorporate some exciting new features. The second release date passes. Buyers are now confused – should they buy product A, which is known to work and is available now, or product B which sounds much more impressive but is not yet available?

A product that you can use now is worth more to you than one that is not yet available – no matter what claims are being made for it. As a small business or home user your needs are modest, and you can safely ignore the scheming, plotting and salesmanship. If in doubt, get something that is known to work. If it does what you want, and you are confident you will be comfortable using it, then buy it. If something better comes out later you can always change it – if you still need to.

GREAT EXPECTATIONS?

However you buy your computer, assume that you will not be able to work with it straight away. The software and the hardware both require a learning curve – a period of time which you will need to familiarise yourself with the system.

It is a good idea to start with simpler software, such as a basic word processor, to gain basic experience and confidence before moving on to more complicated packages. It can be very helpful indeed to spend some time on a basic training course before buying, so as to familiarise yourself with the bare necessities of computer use. These courses are often available free at your local college. (For more details on training see page 176)

Chapter 3

Presentation, DTP and graphics

The quality and visual appeal of your stationery can tell those with whom you correspond a lot about your business. With a computer it is possible to produce print-shop-quality results at a fraction of the price. The production of letters, diagrams and leaflets can be streamlined so that they can be created to order much more quickly. What follows is an introduction to the possibilities offered by computer-based word processing, desktop publishing and presentation software.

Basic word processing

Why use a word processor when a typewriter will do? If you have been using a typewriter for many years without problems, why pay the extra for a word-processing system? For some kinds of work a typewriter is still perfectly adequate: a cheap, reliable way to produce high-quality letters. For something more versatile, however, it is worth considering a computer-based word-processing system.

The chief advantage of electronic systems is that you can correct mistakes before you print them. You can make as many changes as you like in the document before the print touches the paper. Paragraphs are managed automatically. If you delete a word in a sentence the remaining words move to fill in the gap.

Word processing also gives a range of broader editing options. Words, sentences and paragraphs can be moved around. Text can be copied from one document to another. Footnotes and headers can be added and pages can be numbered automatically. You can also keep electronic copies of your work, so that letters can be stored inside the computer or on floppy disks and reused later with minor changes. It is also possible to build up a library of blank letter headings addressed to different clients, which will save typing in their details every time.

A very useful word-processor feature which has been available for some time is the **mail merge facility**. Mail merge works by taking a standard letter with carefully ordered blanks, and then filling in the details from a separate list. It is possible to include simple individual details which can make a letter look more personal. It can also be used to print envelopes.

Layout

At the next level of sophistication, a word processor gives you detailed control over the visual appearance and layout of the text. Lettering has always been available in different styles (called **fonts**) and sizes (measured in **points**). Most word processors are supplied with a selection of basic fonts, and extra fonts are available as libraries, almost always at additional cost. The main text of this book is typeset using a font called Bembo with letters that are 10½ points in size. Other examples of fonts and point sizes include:

This is 9 point Times

This is 12 point Arial

This is 14 point Zapf Chancery

This is 16 point Garamond

Fonts can add extra impact to a piece of work when used with restraint and discretion. For letter-writing it is more practical to use a single font, although you may want to add a letterhead in a different style to make the letter more eye-catching. The addition of font styles such as **bold** or *italic* can emphasise points in the text and make headings distinctive. <u>Underlined</u>, superscript and subscript lettering can also be used.

For example, a standard letter could be improved by using different lettering styles and sizes: the name and address of both the sender and the recipient could be in bold text, and the name of the signatory could be underlined. All of these details could be stored in the computer with the text of the standard letter.

Professional word-processing software includes a set of *style sheets* for applications such as memos, faxes, business letters and presentations. These contain no text – only the information needed to lay out the different areas of text on the page. They are easy to use, and excellent results are possible.

Spelling and grammar checkers

Spell check is a facility on most word processors. It scans a document and queries unusual words. Most have a dictionary option, so that you can add words of your own. Spell checkers are invaluable but not infallible. They have no way of noting common mistakes, such as misspelling 'their' or 'there' for 'they're', where the words are spelled correctly but the proper use depends on context.

It is important that you get a checker with an English dictionary. Early examples used American spellings ('color' for 'colour', and so on), and these proved more of a hindrance than a help for UK users. Most professional packages on sale in the UK now include UK spellings, but if you buy a cheaper package it is a good idea to check this.

Many word processors also include a **thesaurus**. This works like the paper equivalent, except that it can benefit from the computer's speed and suggest alternatives more quickly. Computer-based spell checkers and thesauruses are limited in the number of words they have in their vocabularies; most contain as many words as a small dictionary. A computer version of the *Oxford English Dictionary* is available – but it is expensive, and the current version does not integrate seamlessly with any of the popular professional word-processing packages. A recent development is an online version for Internet use, although again this is expensive, and also rather awkward to use.

Grammar checkers are more subtle and often less useful tools. A grammar checker scans a piece of text for grammatical errors, such as split infinitives and dangling participles. It gauges the impenetrability of the prose according to a variety of measures, one of which is estimated reading age. Grammar checkers are entertaining to play with and can offer some advice on how to improve writing style. However, the subtleties of the English language are still beyond the grasp of even the most powerful computer, and many of the suggested 'improvements' will be irrelevant, misleading or hilarious.

Outline managers and other text tools

Professional word processors also offer options which make the management of text much easier: for example, they can literally count the number of words in a document. Other information, such as the document creation date, is also likely to be available.

Outline managers can transform a list of notes into a neatly laid out outline that can form the skeleton of a writing project. The word processor can also prepare a contents list or an index, maintain a list of revisions, or keep track of a table of authorities for listing references in a legal or other professional context.

Macros

Most professional word processors include a **macro** facility. This provides an easy way to automate regularly repeated actions. A macro is a recorded set of actions that can be 'played' manually at any point in the editing process, or automatically when you start using the word processor. If, for example, you want the last two documents you were working on to reappear on screen when you start up your word processor, you can create a macro that loads and displays them for you. You can also create letterheads and other standard layouts, tidy up punctuation, and so on.

Macros can be as basic or as complicated as you care to make them. Most word processors are supplied with a range of macros that add extra features to the package. For example, the Lotus Word Pro word processor comes with around 200 macros that can be used for cross-referencing text, clearing the screen, finding old documents and so on.

CASE HISTORY: William

William Henley, who writes for a national magazine, recalls his first encounter with a powerful word processor.

'As a writer all I have to worry about is the text, and it's the production editor who looks after the layouts and the graphics. But even basic editing has been made a million times easier with a word processor; it's really useful to be able to go back and rewrite and add to work after it's been typed in.

'The magazine has contributors who supply their work by email over the Internet, or (very rarely now) on floppy disks or home-made CDs. One problem is the number of different formats, so the production department asks for plain uncoded text – known as ASCII [American Standard Code for Information Interchange] – which is the lowest common denominator and doesn't include extras like italics, but will work on any system. Even then there are compatibility problems. Sometimes there are strange characters at the start of each paragraph and so on.

'To sort this out I use a macro that goes through a document and deletes everything that isn't standard. I used to do this by hand, and it could take minutes to go through a piece and delete the stuff that wasn't wanted. Now it takes a few seconds. I also have other macros which help with basic layouts, so I can produce copy that doesn't need much fiddling around with when it's laid out. And the word-count tool is a godsend; we have to write to length, and it makes that a whole lot easier.'

Voice dictation systems

A recent development in the word-processor market is the voice dictation system. Instead of typing your words, you speak them into a microphone. You can make words appear on the screen, and to a limited extent you can also control your computer this way.

Current voice-based systems are moderately sophisticated. Prices have fallen dramatically, so that a 'continuous-speech' system that can recognise spoken English with no unnatural gaps costs between £50 and £200. Accuracy is variable. Most systems have to be 'trained' first – a time-consuming process that typically requires the reading of a set text. Vocabularies are usually large enough for general use. Systems that can work with more specialised professional vocabularies are sometimes available to order, at extra cost.

Perfect accuracy is still some way off. Current systems make regular mistakes, which need to be corrected afterwards, and punctuation still needs to be spelled out in full, rather than understood implicitly. But people who are used to dictating, or who find typing awkward, will still find that these systems can save time overall. Some also offer voice control of the computer as a whole, so that other software can be started, documents can be printed, and so on.

Desktop publishing

Whereas word processing is text-oriented and ideal for letters, memos and faxes, **desktop publishing (DTP)** is used whenever text and graphics have to be laid out on a page. Typical uses include newsletters, price lists, advertising flyers and posters.

DTP continues where top-end word processors leave off, by adding features such as the ability to split text between columns and pages, to make it flow around complicated shapes, to print it upside down, sideways, at an angle or along a curved line, and to include photographs and other images on the page. Font handling is much more sophisticated, making it easy to produce banner headlines, paragraph headings and quote boxes. Lines, ovals, boxes and frames can be added to draw attention to areas of text, and textures and borders can be created to make a document look more ornate. Unlike word-processing software, which is almost exclusively used to print black letters on white paper, all but the very cheapest DTP software can work with colour, although you will need access to a colour printer to print out the results.

Even a budget DTP package is capable of far more striking results than a word processor. The two are often used together, with the latter providing basic text-editing features and the former more sophisticated page-layout facilities. Most DTP software includes filters which can import text directly from a range of popular word-processing packages. This ensures that special effects such as italics are maintained.

Graphics can be imported in a similar way. These can be clip art (see below) or graphs or tables that have been created using other software.

Two examples of clip art.

Medicines to help you stop smoking

Treatment Notes

An independent view from Consumers' Association

About 1 in 4 adults in the UK smoke cigarettes. And around 120,000 people die each year as a result. So it's not surprising that about two-thirds of smokers say they'd like to give up. But the nicotine in tobacco is very addictive, and stopping smoking without help can be extremely difficult.

This issue of *Treatment Notes* explains nicotine addiction. It also looks at the medicines that can improve your chance of quitting. These are nicotine replacement therapy, such as gum or patches, and a newer non-nicotine treatment.

Included inside

- Why it's so hard to quit
- Nicotine replacement therapy
- Bupropion (Zyban)
- NRT or bupropion?

▶

DTB Treatment Notes was created on Word 97 and laid out using Quark XPress (Mac version)

Clip art is a selection of basic cartoons, images, drawings and sketches that is often supplied with a DTP package. As with fonts, extra images are available at additional cost. Note that clip art collections with hundreds of thousands, or even a million or so images are now widely available. While this may seem impressive, consider that it may take you hours, or even days, to search through a collection like this. When looking at these collections, it is worth checking whether or not they have any kind of search facility to make it easier to find a specific type of image.

Remember, too, that installing a very large number of fonts in a computer can slow it down significantly, especially when it starts up. Even commercial designers tend to limit the number of fonts they work with – perhaps 200 – rather than keeping thousands of different fonts available simultaneously.

CASE HISTORY: Jessica

Jessica Macbeth is a teacher and personal skills trainer who also works as a writer. She uses her DTP system to produce limited editions of books which she sells at her classes.

'I use a laptop computer with Adobe PageMaker DTP software to work on my books. I also have a scanner and a cheapish bubble-jet printer. You can get books of clip art with all kinds of different images, and I scan these in and use them to add spice to my work. For the page layouts, I have about 50 different fonts installed, although I tend to use the same handful again and again. They have a huge effect on the look of a page.

'The results I get when I print them out are good enough to take to a printer. He scans in the pages and prints them out using a professional printing press. I supply the artwork double-sized, and he reduces it. This reduction takes away some of the rougher edges. For my next project I've found a printer who can take my work over the Internet.

'It's a lot of fun and very satisfying too. Anyone who has basic layout skills can do it. This is what DTP was supposed to be about, before it was hijacked by the corporate world. It doesn't have to be used for business reports – people can have fun with it too.'

Hypertext and multimedia

Today, most documents are produced on paper. However, for some users words and graphics are not enough. Many top-end word processors now include a facility which allows sound and video clips to be added, though they can only be viewed on another suitably equipped computer. These multimedia documents are an indication of how information will be exchanged in the future, when words, sounds, pictures, video clips and other information will be integrated seamlessly.

Multimedia documents lend themselves to the creation of **hypertext**, which does not follow the traditional linear format of the printed page. A typical hypertext document includes areas of the screen that respond to the user's enquiries. Some words may be highlighted: when selected, further information on the topic in question is revealed. These 'hidden' pages may contain links of their own, and so on. The result is an 'intelligent' document that can be browsed through, following words and ideas that take your interest, rather than as a linear sequence of words that has to be read from start to finish.

One application of hypertext is the electronic CV (curriculum vitae), which has proved popular in creative fields such as advertising and design. As well as plain text, an electronic CV can include voice clips, photographs, examples of previous work and snatches of music. This lends itself to all kinds of intriguing creative possibilities.

A more mundane application of hypertext is the creation of computer-based help for computer users, which has become the standard for new software. Users are presented with a list of basic options, from which they select the 'help' option. From here, they can explore different topics in more detail. Because these are linked to each other in an intelligent way, there will always be a list of relevant options available on screen at any point in the process.

Some companies in the United States now present their annual reports as a hypertext document which is distributed on CD and includes video clips of the directors and animations showing the financial results. The non-linear nature of hypertext makes it easy for investors to access the information they want.

A company called Adobe has worked hard to establish its Acrobat system, which is a computer-independent way of presenting electronic documents. The Acrobat reader software is available free, and allows users of any kind of computer to read documents prepared with the

Acrobat editing tools. Documents can contain text, graphics and other information. Acrobat is an indication of the likely direction of electronic publishing in the medium term.

Apple computer users have had access to a hypertext product known as Hypercard since the late 1980s. IBM-compatible users have access to OLE (Object Linking and Embedding), which was developed by the Microsoft Corporation. Both of these products can handle the demands of a full hypertext system. OLE takes hypertext a stage further by including links between applications, as well as information. Because all the links are maintained automatically, it is possible for different people to contribute to the same document. One person can be responsible for graphics, another for text and a third for sound. They can work independently, but whenever one person makes a change the document as a whole is updated.

Hypercard has not been available since the mid-1990s, and OLE has turned out to be less flexible and useful than Internet-based technologies such as HTML (see below). HTML and Acrobat have become the standards for electronic publishing.

Electronic publishing on the Internet

Because it is now easy for anyone to publish information on the Internet, a range of packages has become available to help with this. Many word processors include an Internet-ready option that can convert a page of text into HTML (HyperText Markup Language – despite its fearsome name, this is simply the special code that is used to lay out pages of information on the Web). Word processors that create HTML are very easy to use: the user simply chooses a 'Save as HTML' option, and the word processor does the rest of the work. To make the information appear on the Internet, it is copied to a special computer called a server. Many Internet Service Providers (the companies that allow home and small business users to use the Internet with a small computer) offer these servers, and will frequently allow work to be placed on them for Internet-wide viewing for free.

One drawback with this approach is that word processors are still best at word processing; even the best examples lack the more sophisticated tools (such as various Internet-specific page layout options, and options for animations or other special effects) that are needed to create a really professional-looking electronic document. So buyers also have the option of using a web-page editing package instead. These offer much cruder word-processing facilities, but are designed to make all the other tasks involved in creating pages for the Web much more straightforward. In the end they, too, create HTML, but users have much more control over the way their pages are laid out and are better able to manage the link-words that are a vital part of the Internet's HyperText facilities.

Dedicated enthusiasts can create web pages armed with just a simple text editor and a manual describing how HTML works. While a knowledge of HTML is often useful to fine-tune page layouts, this approach is not recommended for beginners. In fact, even experienced users are likely to find it heavy going.

Business presentations

Presentations have become an accepted part of the business scene over the last few years, whether for asking a bank for money, pitching for business or investment, or passing on information within a company.

Computers can play a major role in the preparation of a presentation. Apart from word processing and DTP, which can be used to produce high-quality handouts and slides, there is a set of tools specially developed for presentations. These packages are geared to creating punchy images with banners, slogans and other details, and most can support graphs, charts, video-like animations (such as cuts and cross-fades between pages), sound effects and video clips, as well as straight text. Like word processors, most of these packages include templates that make it easy to build a complete presentation. They also contain libraries of backgrounds, foregrounds, clip art and other graphics which can be used to customise the presentation. A complete beginner can produce a professional presentation within a day or so; experienced users can do the same much more quickly.

You can make presentations directly from your computer. A useful, if expensive, option is the overhead projector screen. This plugs into the back of your computer and fits over a standard overhead projector base. The screen is translucent, and whatever appears on it is projected in the usual way. As a result, you can prepare a presentation on your computer, and then project it to your audience while controlling the presentation from your computer's keyboard (remote control options are also available, allowing you to walk around the room and make your presentation at the same time). Portable computers, discussed in Chapter 10 and Appendix VII, are often used for this purpose. With the addition of some speakers, or access to a small PA system, you can use your computer to create a full sound and video experience.

Since the late 1990s an alternative has been available in the form of portable projectors, which can display images created by a computer on a wall or screen. These are less bulky and cumbersome than overhead projectors, but they are also currently very much more expensive – costing between £2,000 and £10,000, depending on image quality and brightness. Using a single simple connection, the projector displays an exact copy of what appears on the computer's screen, whether it is a laptop or a desktop machine. A presentation can then be made in the usual way.

Pre-printed paper

Unless you work with hypertext, text and pictures are designed to be printed. To be able to do justice to the physical appearance of any work you produce you need to use the right kind of printer (see Appendix II). Even with a cheap printer there are things you can do to make your work more attractive.

CASE HISTORY: Isabel

Isabel Davis, who works for a firm of accountants, was given the job of producing an information pack for new clients. She considered using printed colour brochures designed on a DTP system, but discovered there was a cheaper way to create a similar effect.

'Someone sent us a catalogue of pre-printed papers, and I was very impressed. They come in a huge selection of colours and designs, and some even come with templates you can use with your existing software.

'I sent off for some samples and decided on a basic style, which is available for various formats – business cards, letterheads, presentation covers, and so on. I used the DTP system we have to add some fancy lettering, and saved that as a letterhead. Now, whenever anyone prints a document, the heading appears at the top, fitted into a blank space on the special paper. It looks very eye-catching.

'People have started to look at us as a dynamic company that gets things done, so we've had quite a bit of extra business.'

Pre-printed paper is available from specialist outlets (see Addresses). At its simplest it can be used as a striking background for posters and other displays. Commercially produced paper that is designed specifically to be used in a business setting – folded flyers, letterheads, business cards and compliments slips – is not customised: areas are left blank so that details of individual businesses can be added. Some

---

PACKAGES TO WATCH FOR

The word-processing market is dominated by Microsoft Word. Word has become a de facto standard, and many business communications are sent as Word-compatible emails. For home use Lotus WordPro and Corel's WordPerfect are worthy competing products, much cheaper or sometimes given away free by magazines. For Apple Mac users, Word is again a popular choice. Among voice dictation packages names to watch for include Dragon Dictation Systems and IBM's ViaVoice system.

DTP is dominated at the budget end of the market by Microsoft's Publisher and Serif's PagePlus. Both packages are under £100 and very easy to use, although they lack truly professional features. At the top end, the choice is between Quark Xpress and Adobe's InDesign. Xpress is used by many magazines as a professional page-layout tool, but at around £800 is very expensive. InDesign is a relative newcomer but has better support for web publishing, includes many of the same features and is available for around half the price.

For electronic publishing Adobe's Acrobat system can be used to produce electronic documents that can be read on the Internet or distributed to other computers without any worries about incompatibilities. The editing tools cost around £200. On the World Wide Web, Adobe's Page Mill is a good beginner's choice, although very similar budget packages, such as HotMetal Pro and the Namo Web Editor, are often given away free by magazines. For professional use Macromedia's Dreamweaver includes more sophisticated page layout as well as support for animations and special effects, and costs around £300.

For business presentations Lotus Freelance and Microsoft Powerpoint are the standard tools. Both are very quick and easy to use, even for a complete beginner.

---

companies also supply templates that can be used with the most popular word processors. This makes it even easier to design high-quality output on screen, before committing it to paper, and at a very low cost.

For some kinds of work, however, only the very highest quality is acceptable. Professional-quality colour printers are available from around £1,000. These prices will come down over the next few years, but at the moment are out of reach of all but rich individuals and businesses with a substantial colour printing requirement.

Print bureaux

Print bureaux can take text and graphics created on the computer and print them on commercial-scale machines. One possible application is the creation of slides for a business presentation, although colour printers are now so cheap that this option is only used where pin-sharp quality is essential. Print bureaux can also produce very high quality colour output, and are also useful for situations where documents require tens or even hundreds of copies. (Small computer printers are not designed for this kind of workload.)

Chapter 4

Keeping track of your money

Repetitive and tedious chores such as accounting, bookkeeping and VAT are perfect tasks for a computer. It will make the dull jobs easier, thus saving you time, and it can help you be more organised.

CASE HISTORY: Ray

Ray Thomas recently decided to computerise his business, a garage and used-car dealership, having found that keeping up with PAYE, tax, VAT, billing and other financial matters was getting beyond him.

'We were just coming out of the recession at the start of the 1990s. We'd survived pretty well, and I'd kept all my mechanics. Business was picking up again, but I was spending more time on paperwork than I wanted. I used to employ someone to come in and do the books and sort out everyone's pay at the end of the month. But he retired, and getting anyone else in would have been costly. I started to wonder whether a computer might help me out.'

Ray was able to get help by asking his local TEC [Training and Enterprise Council] for details of someone who could put a system together for him. They also suggested he went to the local college to get some basic training.

'I was worried about this, but it wasn't nearly as bad as I thought. It took a while to work out what was what, but by the end of the course I'd got the basics under my belt. The TEC also suggested some names of people who could help me out. We bought the kit from a local firm, and they've been really good about the problems we've had – but there haven't been many. Gary, one of the mechanics who knows a bit about computers, sorted out the software side of things with a bit of help from them. And now it works like a dream. The computer does everything my old accountant used to do. It looks after the VAT returns, works out all the PAYE deductions – and so on. It even prints the cheques. We use stationery that works with the software. When the tax codes change and allowances change, Gary just keys in the new ones. It takes a couple of hours, and we're set for another year.

'Gary suggested doing some leaflets on the computer. It hardly cost us anything because he used some software that came free with a magazine. And when we did a leaflet run locally it got us some new trade.

'All told, I think the system cost about £2,000 to set up. Now that's a one-off payment, but we were paying the accountant more than that each year. I'm thinking of opening a car-hire business now, so we've started working out how the computer can help with that too.'

Buying financial software

There is no lack of suitable software for managing money, as the advertisements in computer magazines show. Many excellent packages are available at very reasonable prices, and, unless you are running a very large business, you should be able to pick up a system that does everything you need for £500 – much less if you are a sole trader.

Most **accounting packages** contain a minimum of purchase ledger support, sales ledger support with account tracking (so you can watch for late payments), cashbook calculations to look after petty cash and double-check bank statements, VAT tracking, balance sheets and profit-and-loss reports, and support for multiple bank accounts. An important feature is error correction – if you discover a mistake you should be able to correct it without having to retype every entry. Security may also be important, and some packages include password access. They may also offer the facility to design individual invoices, as well as support for different kinds of invoice (pro-forma, quotation and so on). One useful feature is the ability to set up discounts for individual clients.

As well as keeping track of employees, their hours and their payment schedules, **payroll software** should also cope with special circumstances such as one-off contracts, sick pay and maternity leave. It should be possible to set up regular payment schedules – weekly, monthly, four-weekly and annual – and rearrange these to deal with variable hours and payment rates. Good support for overtime calculations is essential. Some packages can deal with National Insurance (NI) payments for directors and the way in which company cars can affect NI and tax. You should also be able to produce a single

59

report of PAYE details for the Inland Revenue and print this information directly on to the relevant forms.

Stock control software is more specialised. Features to look for include advance warnings of low stock, tracking of the total value of different items and a report of the total value of the stock as a whole. The software should be capable of optimising stock levels as well as keeping track of them; a range of simple analysis options and reports will help you with this. Useful extra features include the capacity to add additional information to the stock description of each item – so that, for example, items which need to be sold together can be flagged as such at the counter – and a measure of the amount of warehouse space taken by different stocks.

Some packages are tailored to the needs of specific businesses. These are advertised in trade journals and offer a comprehensive all-in-one solution for the typical small business user. They tend to be more expensive than off-the-shelf products and can also be less flexible. On the other hand, they are written specifically for a certain market and incorporate terms and concepts with which that market is already familiar. Such packages do one kind of job very well indeed and require less setting up. In general, however, standard business packages can do the same kind of work for less money.

As with other products, it is useful to check for specific features when deciding which software to buy. With financial products watch out for the following:

Ease of use Software should not be hard to use. There is no need to follow the conventions of accountancy – such as double-entry bookkeeping – if you find these confusing and they do not fit your requirements.

Professional recommendations A product that is recommended by an official body, such as the Institute of Chartered Accountants, or the Inland Revenue and HM Customs & Excise, is more likely to be productive. The Inland Revenue will accept direct printouts from certain brands of software, and this may avoid the need for the further services of an accountant.

Printing facilities and stationery Some packages offer their own printed stationery, including cheques and invoice forms. Others support stationery from other sources, such as printed P35 annual returns. Since it is your computer's job to save you time, the more pre-printed stationery you can buy, the better – otherwise you may be left with software that produces results on the screen, but leaves you to write out 200 cheques by hand at the end of the month. Check which stationery you can use, how much it costs and how easily you can get hold of it.

Features Most of the common accounts packages offer all the basics you need. However, if you run a medium-sized business that trades overseas and has many different bank accounts you will need to check for extras such as multi-currency support and cross-account calculation options. In general, it is advisable to make a checklist of tasks – for example, taking account of maternity leave for PAYE calculations – and ensure that your software supports all of these. Good software will also offer further options; for example, support for BACS (Bankers' Automated Clearing Service), which can pay money straight into a recipient's account (see below). Euro support is also an important option to consider, as is support for electronic tax and VAT returns.

When checking features, make sure you ask what kinds of reports are available. As well as a balance sheet and a profit-and-loss statement, you will also need to be able to track customer accounts, flag late payments and track creditor payments. As before, you should assess your needs carefully and make sure that the software can produce all the reports you need.

Support As with all software, you should check to see what kind of support the manufacturer or main distributor offers. Will you be able to telephone with queries if you get into difficulties?

Price Some sophisticated financial packages cost thousands of pounds. These are aimed at finance professionals and larger businesses and may not be ideal for the smaller trader. You should be able to get a very good package for much less than this.

Options Some packages integrate with other software from the same manufacturer and make it easy for you to share information between them. Some features – such as tax returns, invoice-tracking and financial analysis – are available as options. Make sure you get details of every product each manufacturer offers, so you can plan ahead for options. For example, you may not need to worry about VAT now, but if the business takes off you may be forced to start including this in your bookkeeping. It is always a good idea to plan ahead and get software that can cope with anything that might happen.

Updates Some financial software is available with an annual update option which contains the latest information on tax codes, allowances and other details. You can add this information yourself, but if your time is valuable check to see if your software includes these updates.

Internet support This is useful both for getting software updates, and for filing, and perhaps also paying tax and VAT returns electronically. Banks do not as a rule allow software to talk to their computers directly – you can look at and change your balance over the Internet, but the information has to be copied to your accounts software by hand. Check to see which Internet features are available, and how closely linked they are with the information that your bank makes available online.

Personal finance software

There are a number of financial packages aimed specifically at the home user. These include features such as:

- bank statement reconciliation
- mortgage and loan planning
- credit card reconciliation
- bill-minding
- budgeting
- calculating expenses by category
- simple investment management
- overall net worth calculations.

These packages are recommended if you like to keep a tight rein on your finances and oversee exactly how your money is being spent. They are also an efficient way to check for bank and credit card errors.

For sole traders with a modest turnover, a personal money manager can be an excellent alternative to a larger accounts package. It will handle all the information you need to keep track of your income and expenses. The latter can be itemised according to category, so you can keep track of your spending and produce a single printout at the end of the tax year with all your expenses shown in detail. Categories are user-defined, so you can go into as much or as little detail as you like, and you may be able to supply the printout as part of your tax return.

Sophisticated money managers allow the user to track late payments and list when creditors should be paid. Some can even handle VAT – usually on the accrual system, which means that VAT becomes due when an invoice is issued, not when payment is received.

If your business needs are modest, it is a very good idea to look at these personal finance packages first rather than the larger business accounts packages. Many of the former include business-ready features such as invoice-tracking and VAT calculations. They are easier to set up and use than their larger siblings, and are often less intimidating to work with – which means you are more likely to take the time to keep your finances up to date. They may well be cheaper too.

For domestic use, these packages can take quite a bit of your time. To keep an accurate record you have to make each transaction twice – once in the real world and once in your computer. If, like many people, you use standing orders, direct debits, automated credits, debit cards, credit cards, cheques and cash to move your money around, you might find that the time you need to spend to maintain an accurate picture is not worth it. This is something that depends on personal preference – some people like to keep track of every last penny; others have an instinct for how much it is safe to spend and when, and are not concerned about the details.

Perhaps the most useful features of a personal money manager are bill management, loan estimation and cheque-book reconciliation. With accurate financial records it is easy to work out which bills are due and how much they are likely to be. This can give you warning of cash-flow hiccups. Cheque-book reconciliation checks the figures in case your bank has made a mistake. Loan estimation can help you work out interest payments in unusual situations not covered by loan agents' tables.

CASE HISTORY: Terry and Sarah

Terry and Sarah McGinnes use a money manager to help them plan their long-term spending.

'We've been using it to work out whether or not we can afford to go on holiday somewhere exotic this year. Terry has been promised a salary rise, and we've been looking to see how that affects how much we can spend. He won't get the rise until we get back, so we're planning to take out a long-term loan now, and to pay it back more quickly than we would normally. We can get the loan because we can afford the monthly payments now, but it will cost us less when we pay it off quickly.'

Tax planners

A useful extension to the idea of the domestic money manager is the tax planner. These packages are updated every year and include all the details you need to fill in your tax return. The results can be printed on ordinary plain paper. Some packages have Inland Revenue approval for this, which means you can send in the sheet with a covering letter and do not need to copy the numbers across to your tax return form.

Tax planners can be a good way to estimate your tax liability, but they cannot give you the same level of advice as a trained accountant. If your tax affairs are straightforward they can make the task of filling in your return much simpler. For the self-employed, some of whom will need to check whether specific expenses are deductible, it can be worth spending the money on hiring an accountant.

Portfolio managers

The management of stocks and shares is a task that is tailor-made for a computer. Not only can it keep track of prices, earnings and dividends, it can also analyse market trends and make 'buy' or 'sell' suggestions based on proven analysis techniques.

In the past there were a handful of portfolio management programs available, but these have now been almost entirely replaced by Internet share-dealing and management services, which can offer all the same facilities together with the power of instant buying and selling. These services can provide market quotes, histories, graphs, charts and other information almost instantly. They can also make it possible for adventurous traders to buy and sell on exchanges outside the UK, such as the New York Dow and the NASDAQ technology index. Rates of commission are usually very reasonable. Details of these services often appear in magazines for investors.

Spreadsheets

A spreadsheet is a general-purpose calculation tool. It provides a grid of cells that you can fill with information: a number, a date, a word or a formula. Most cells contain a number, but they can also contain a formula that works with the numbers – a total, an average, a percentage

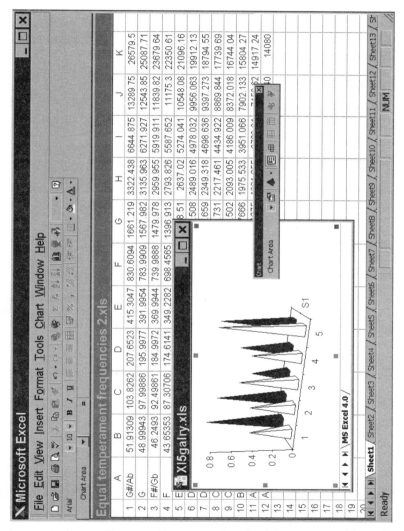

An example of a spreadsheet created using Microsoft Excel and illustrating some of the graph-drawing capabilities

and so on. The formulas can be simple or complex. Many spreadsheets are used as adding machines, providing a total for a set of figures in a column and then a grand total for the row of subtotals across the bottom. The range of possibilities is huge, however, and covers everything from simple arithmetic to complicated financial calculations such as loan repayment schedules, pricing based on profit margins, and useful figures such as the internal rate of return. Some spreadsheets include formulas to help with statistical analysis and engineering, and can handle general mathematical problems such as matrix manipulations and equation-solving.

The biggest advantage of a spreadsheet is the ease with which it can recalculate results. If one entry is changed in a column, the total at the bottom changes. No matter how complex or convoluted the calculations, the spreadsheet will keep track of all the links between the numbers and formulas entered and work out the final result.

If you decide you need a spreadsheet, it is a good idea to look first at those included as part of an 'office suite'. These all-in-one packages include a spreadsheet, word processor, database and other optional extras, such as presentation software and perhaps a personal information manager or a contact manager. A suite-based spreadsheet gives you *integration* between these different programs, so that information can be exchanged between them all quickly and easily.

Many spreadsheets can also present information graphically. Pie charts, bar charts, line graphs and maps are all common. So, for example, you could prepare the financial aspects of a business plan in a spreadsheet, and then transfer the graphs and tables over to a word processor or DTP package to present them professionally.

CASE HISTORY: Laurie

Laurie Leonard used a spreadsheet to help him create a business plan for his new business and was able to use some of the more advanced features to good effect.

'I started off knowing nothing about business plans and less about accountancy, but after reading a few books I started to get an idea of what my bank manager was going to ask me when I asked for the loan.

'The best thing about the spreadsheet I used was the way that many of the measures I had to calculate, like gearing and the internal rate of return, were already included as formulas. It was easy to estimate sales figures, guess interest rates, work out loan repayments and so on. I could also play with the numbers to see what would happen if interest rates suddenly went up.

'I did a printout of the results, and took along my portable computer as well. Because of the "what-if" features I was ready for the difficult questions, and I got the computer to recalculate the new figures on the spot. I think my bank manager was impressed that I'd done my homework – and even more impressed at the built-in safety margins I was offering – and I got the loan I needed.'

Your money on line

Many banks are now offering on-line services. These are advertised widely, and counter staff should be familiar with them. These services can be a useful way of keeping track of your money, especially out of normal business hours, and can also save you time by eliminating the need to make regular trips to your branch. Some banks have used this as an opportunity to close less heavily used branches, handing over paper transactions to post offices.

A related phenomenon is the Internet-only bank. Banks such as Smile and Egg have no physical branches at all. They are worth considering, as they have sometimes been able to offer competitive loan and savings rates compared to the traditional high-street banks. Post Offices are typically used to pay in and withdraw money, and current account facilities are otherwise similar to those offered by the major High Street banks

Internet banking works by way of a bank's web site. You are given a pass code which lets you 'log in' to the site. Once in, you are effectively connected to the bank's own computer network, and can check your balance and make transfers and payments in the same way that a branch cashier can. Some banks still offer 'computer banking', which requires special software and offers improved security because it connects via a modem-to-modem direct link rather than through the Internet. Business users may also be issued with a 'smart card' and a reader which acts as an extra security check. When considering these services, it can be worth asking if they are compatible with any financial software, such as Microsoft's Money or any of the popular accounting packages.

Business users with more demanding banking requirements have a number of other options, although these only become cost-effective once more than 150 payments are made regularly every month. This makes them ideal for payrolls, although once in place they offer all the usual electronic banking advantages as well. There are two fund-transfer schemes operating in the UK: BACS and CHAPS.

BACS (Bankers' Automated Clearing Service) offers an on-line cheque payment service. Instead of writing out a cheque, the details are supplied to the bank in some other way, but the transaction is treated as a cheque and suffers from the same delays. Unlike a cheque, however, the money is not *debited* from your account until it is transferred. BACS is ideal for payroll use, and with an on-line BACS system you can completely automate payroll payments and make all those end-of-month salary cheques redundant with a single phone call.

Some banks offer a simpler, non-electronic version of BACS called BOBS (Branch Oriented BACS Service), which works like a semi-automated standing order. You supply the bank with a list of people whom you pay regularly. Then, once a month, you supply a list of amounts to be paid to them. This can be presented as information on a floppy disk, as a computer printout or even as a handwritten slip. The bank then transfers the money according to your instructions. BOBS doesn't rely on modems and remote computer access, but it is slower and more cumbersome than purely electronic forms of transfer.

FINANCIAL PACKAGES TO WATCH FOR

For the small business TAS Books (Megatech Software), Quick Books (Intuit), Sage Instant Accounts (Sage), Money Manager (Connect Software) and Pegasus Solo Accounting (Pegasus) are all excellent accounts packages. Many of these can be combined with extra modules to add features such as full reporting, job costing and so on.

For domestic users the most popular packages are Money (Microsoft), Quicken (Intuit) and Moneybox (MoneyBox Software).

Popular tax planners include QuickTax (Intuit) and Consumers' Association's own tax-planning software, TaxCalc, which is updated annually.

The most widely used spreadsheets include the immensely powerful Lotus 1-2-3 (Lotus) and Excel (Microsoft).

CHAPS (Clearing Houses' Automated Payment System) is a same-day version of BACS. CHAPS payment requests go directly to the inter-bank clearing network and are usually credited (and cleared) on the day the request is made. In effect, CHAPS offers an electronic banker's draft service.

Some on-line banking schemes also include options that allow payments to be made abroad. Most UK banks subscribe to the international SWIFT (Society for Worldwide International Financial Telecommunications) network. On-line payment requests can be routed through this network to move money out of the country. Some countries are not on the SWIFT network, and payments made to these will be transferred by telex message. You may also come across TAPS (Trans-continental Automated Payment Service), which is another international network.

Access to the CHAPS, SWIFT and TAPS networks is useful for larger businesses that regularly trade abroad, and for anyone who needs to make guaranteed payments quickly. Most smaller businesses will not need to use these features, but for those that do access to on-line payments can give a competitive edge.

On the whole, all banks offer a similar selection of services across a comparable fee-scale. But some add extras which can make a choice easier. Barclays, for example, includes options which give you details of current exchange and interest rates. Others, such as the HOBS (Home and Office Banking Service) scheme from the Bank of Scotland, give you access to a special high-interest deposit account. By storing surplus funds in this account overnight you can gain extra interest.

For online share dealing, services such as e*trade (www.etrade.co.uk) and Self Trade (www.selftrade.co.uk) offer a useful starting point, although many banks and building societies now offer similar services, which are also worth looking into. Magazines such as *Investor's Week* often include an up-to-the-minute directory of suitable services.

Chapter 5

Keeping track of information

Small business courses traditionally emphasise the importance of bookkeeping and cash flow. But keeping track of information can be just as important to a business as keeping track of money. By using and storing information effectively you can benefit your business. For example, if you are dealing with hundreds of people, you can use your information store as a memory-jogger to add personal details to a conversation, or you can keep track of what each conversation was about, and use the computer to remind you when another call is due. Computers excel at this kind of work and offer a much more efficient way of organising information than pen-and-paper-based methods.

Personal information managers (PIMs)

A Personal Information Manager is a computer-based version of the popular ring-bound paper organiser. To some extent PIMs have been superseded, or at least augmented, by mobile phones and electronic organisers, and especially by products that combine these two tools. These will typically do everything a PIM does, but in a small portable package that can be used as a phone as well. However, for office-based work PIMs remain useful, even though in the long term they are likely to be replaced by small mobile devices.

A typical PIM will offer you:

- an address book
- an appointment diary
- a 'to-do' list
- a year planner
- a space for general notes, useful tables and other information.

The computer-based PIM makes it a lot easier to keep the information up to date. Maintaining a list of addresses requires no messy alterations. When someone's address changes, you simply type in the new one (if you're likely to need the old one later you can always keep a safety copy).

Another very useful option is an **auto-dialler** feature. If you have a modem (an electronic phone-line link discussed in more detail in Appendix II), some PIMs will automatically dial a telephone number for you. Support for dial prefixes (such as 9, for an external call through a switchboard, or 132 to access the NTL network) is also provided. Unfortunately, this support can be rather basic. You will be able to specify your local STD code, so that local numbers are dialled without it, but usually NTL users will need to keep track of local codes (which do not require the 132 code) by hand.

Another useful feature is the telephone log. Most organisers maintain a list of calls made using the auto-dialler. This can be helpful in estimating a telephone bill or in charging someone by the hour. Incoming calls can also be logged in a similar way – although this is a slightly more clumsy process, as the logging has to be started by hand when the call comes in.

Many PIMs include an alarm feature. You can set up your computer so it gives an audible reminder of an appointment before it happens.

The latest PIMs are beginning to include network-related features. (Networks are covered in Chapter 6.) This means everyone's appointments can be linked together. Team members can schedule appointments with their colleagues automatically, or you can use the network to find a time when everyone is free for a meeting. Another popular use is task assignment – a group manager can assign jobs to team members. The team leader can leave the fine points of the work to the team members and concentrate on scheduling a project as a whole.

CASE HISTORY: Kenneth

Kenneth Hesket discovered PIMs five years ago and has never regretted it.

'I got my PC way back when, and someone told me about a program called Sidekick. I tried it out and loved it right away. For the first time I could keep all my information organised in the PC and get at it in any way I could think of. I no longer keep a pile of scrap paper for addresses next to the phone. Now it all goes into the PIM. I've got into the habit of using the "to-do" lists as a memory jogger and, all told, I get about half as much again done now as I used to. I don't spend time looking for things and I'm rarely late for appointments any more. It's one of the most useful productivity aids I've ever come across.'

Choosing a PIM

Some PIMs are simply electronic versions of paper organisers; others take a much more free-form approach and let you organise information as you wish. It is important to choose the PIM that suits your way of working.

Here is a list of features to look for:

Flexibility You should be able to design your own address book pages and specify what kind of information you want to include. You may, for example, want to allow space for home and business contact details for some clients, and perhaps electronic mail addresses as well. Some PIMs are inflexible, and the information must be entered in a set way. Others are more open-ended, and you can decide which details to include in the different sections. An extreme example of this is InfoCentral, which can store any kind of information and make any kind of connection between each item.

Connections between sections If you enter an anniversary or a birthday, it should appear in the diary section as well. Items put into a 'to-do' list should also appear on the diary pages.

Display options You should be able to switch between one day per page to at least one week per page.

Priorities You should be able to schedule tasks according to priority. Tasks that are overdue should be flagged in some way and carried over to the next day.

Specific dates As well as birthdays and other important dates, you should also be able to specify dates such as 'the third Wednesday in every month' or even just 'the third of every month'. If the third happens to fall at a weekend, then the PIM should warn you or move the date to the following Monday.

Alarms and tickles Alarms are to remind you of meetings. Tickles are reminders that a task is due for completion. You should be able to set the alarm to go off at a given time *before* an event.

Time logging Some PIMs include features to help you keep track of the time you have spent on different projects or talking to clients. Some of these can even produce a final billing record. Phone logs can be used to track both incoming and outgoing calls.

Search options PIMs tend to handle address information inflexibly. They often lack the option of setting up a company contact name and address and then listing other contact details, such as internal exchange numbers, for the people who work there. A search feature can work around this by giving a list of people who work for the company, even though their names and addresses may be scattered around your address book.

Security Some information in your PIM will be personal, some you may need to share with colleagues – and some may be changed by colleagues too, who may need to reschedule an appointment for you or add a task to your list. A PIM should include security features which control access to different areas. Most PIMs use a password system – one for you, one to grant *read only* access for colleagues, and public access for those areas that are public and can be changed by anyone.

Communication features An auto-dialler is very useful if you have a modem. If you use email, then records of email address details will also be essential. Check also that the PIM can be organised to cope with multiple addresses.

Workgroup features These are most useful for sharing information within a team but redundant for those who work alone at home.

Speed and reliability The PIM should be able to get results quickly and reliably. It should have the capability to search for and present contact names quickly. Some PIMs may offer useful features, but if it

---

PIMS to watch for

Lotus Organiser (IBM) has scored consistently high marks in usability studies. It is very similar to a paper organiser but includes some simple linking, so that, for example, an entry in the 'to-do' list can call up a relevant telephone number. One drawback with Organiser can be that it is very structured (although some users find this reassuring – they can start using it right away). Symantec's ACT! is another popular product.

Packrat (Action Computers) is a do-it-all PIM with more features than you could ever need. All information templates can be customised, and there is full network support. Packrat also includes features which overlap with larger and more expensive project managers. It can even be integrated into other pieces of software, so that Packrat's options appear on screen when you are using your word processor or other software.

InfoCentral (Corel) is a different kind of PIM. Instead of the usual address book and calendar format, InfoCentral works more like an

---

takes minutes for the information to appear on screen you might as well be using a pen and paper.

Support for hardware PDAs The information in some hardware organisers (see page 272) can easily be shared with their software equivalents, while others are completely incompatible. It is useful to check whether your hardware organiser includes support for your chosen software.

Contact managers

PIMs tend to be calendar-oriented, with an address book section that is kept separate. Contact Managers (CMs) integrate these two kinds of information more closely. If you need to keep track of the letters, faxes or memos you have sent to different people, a CM is a better choice. A good CM can produce reminders when you need to get in touch with someone again, and can also produce personalised letters and faxes from the information you store in it. This can save you the task of typing out the same letter hundreds of times with only minor changes.

outliner. You can enter any kind of information and then build links between different items. This approach takes some getting used to, but users who make the effort to learn it are enthusiastic about what it can do for them.

Microsoft's Outlook and Outlook Express are widely used; the latter is a part of Windows 98 and is also often installed with Microsoft's Internet Explorer – which in turn is the free software provided by many Internet Service Providers. As an organiser, Outlook works perfectly well, and superficially the fact that it also includes email facilities makes it an attractive choice. In practice, though, Outlook has an appalling security record and is very vulnerable to picking up and transmitting Internet viruses. To prevent virus-related problems it is well worth considering alternatives – such as Lotus Organiser as a PIM and Eudora Pro for email. Even though they may not be as well integrated, the reduced security risk more than offsets any inconvenience caused.

CMs can be very useful in a larger company that uses a computer network. The CM allows each department to share the same information, but in a different way. For example, if a customer calls technical support and is put through to sales, his or her details can be transferred at the same time, and every aspect of the call can be logged. An advanced CM includes features such as sales forecasting, support for price lists, instant profit calculations, and 'meeting generators' for use on networks (you specify a list of attenders, and the CM compiles a list of times that they are all free).

When choosing a CM you should look for the following:

Fax support Fax communications should be integrated seamlessly.

Network support You should at least be able to schedule meetings with colleagues on the network. Support for email both inside and outside the company is another option.

History logging This is vital for a good CM. You should be able to log all your actions, together with the responses they generate, and also be able to schedule reminders for yourself.

Document support and mail-merge These enable you to prepare standard letters, personalise them automatically and print them.

Query generation and reports You should be able to list information by company, by area and by any search criterion you choose. You should also be able to generate reports summarising your work.

Palmtop support Some CMs are designed to integrate well with palmtop computers. You can manage all your appointments on a big desktop computer, and then use the palmtop when out on the road. (For more information on palmtop computers and electronic organisers see Appendix VII.)

Databases

Databases are used to organise information in a user-defined way. They are powerful, complex programs and can be used to extract summaries of information as well as keeping it together. Databases are completely open-ended, so you can organise your information in any way you like. You can also filter the information in different ways by presenting the database with a query. This produces a broad picture, known as a **report**, which conveniently summarises the facts and can help you spot trends, anomalies and other patterns. If, for example, you are maintaining a list of sales, you can create a report which totals the sales you have made to each customer. You could also total sales by geographical area, by specific towns, or even identify all those to customers whose surnames begin with 'W'. It is this flexibility that makes databases so powerful and useful.

Basic databases allow you to keep track of any kind of information that can be represented as text or numbers, such as client contact details, sales records and so on. More advanced databases can also handle graphics – including photographs – and other kinds of information. There are two kinds of database:

Flatfile databases store information in a single 'table' and are more or less the computer equivalent of a card index. The 'cards' can be very complicated, with hundreds of entries on each one, but each card uses the same template for the information.

Relational databases spread information across different tables, while maintaining links between them, so you do not need to copy information unnecessarily. To understand this better, imagine a series of orders, each of which includes a customer's name and address. A flatfile database would require you to type in the name and address *for every single order received from that customer.* With a relational database you can assign each customer a number or code instead. The customer's details are kept in one place, and the order details make a reference to them. If the customer moves, you only have to type in the new address once. This is obviously quicker and more likely to be accurate than retyping the same information every time.

An important feature to look for when choosing a database is *referential integrity.* This means the software ensures that you never enter information without all the details filled in (for example, you cannot create a purchase order without a set of customer details to go with it). Not all databases check for this, and without this feature you can experience problems as links between different kinds of information become confused.

Relational databases can be used for much more than maintaining names and addresses and keeping track of sales.

Database DIY

Unlike PIMs and CMs, databases need to be set up before you can use them. You have to decide what kind of information you want to keep and then create the templates (known as **forms**) needed to keep it. This can be a challenging task, especially for a beginner. Not only will you need to work through the software so that you understand what it does and how to use it, you will also need to think clearly about how to organise the information.

If your needs are fairly simple, then form design will be obvious. Most database products include examples to help you, and you should be able to modify these.

Creating a more complex database, however – one which keeps track of sales, accounts and other information for a medium-sized company – is a job for a specialist programmer. Database design is one of the few instances where it will not be possible to buy something that is right for the job straight off the shelf.

Some databases include their own versions of a programming language, which is usually based on the popular BASIC (Beginners

All-purpose Symbolic Instruction Code). This allows you to make detailed changes to information after it has been stored in the database.

Database systems that work on a network of computers are proving popular with medium-sized businesses. They are sometimes integrated with a range of other networked options such as email, and perhaps even conversion systems which allow small personal computers to be connected easily with more powerful business-oriented machines.

CASE HISTORY: Andrew

Andrew Kemble runs an advertising agency and uses a database to keep track of sales leads.

'We used to use a card-index system and a set of diaries, and we had problems all the time. The system didn't work well if someone ran more than one company, but had one account with us. That kind of thing caused confusion. Organising follow-up calls was a pain too. If someone was off sick we couldn't always make sense of what they'd written in their diary.

'We got someone to install a database for all this. Now we can search for people by their personal details, company name, or any other way. It's a lot easier to keep track of what they've used us for in the past. We can include details of the kind of work they've had from us in the past and build up a picture of what they'll be interested in in the future.

'But it's the follow-up calls that have really paid for the system. Now we just use the computer to print out a list of all the calls that need to be made that day. And it was a godsend last Christmas – it printed all our envelopes for Christmas cards.'

Choosing a database

In the same way that a spreadsheet is often sold as part of an 'office suite', databases are usually integrated with other products from the same manufacturer. It is possible to create your own collection of business applications from different manufacturers, but this is a much more expensive option and makes it much harder to exchange information effectively between the different applications. Unfortunately, it is highly unlikely that you will be able to get hold of a demonstration version of a database from the larger manufacturers. Some databases are available

An example of a form design within a popular database

as shareware, but in the main you will need to rely heavily on reviews in computer magazines. Features of a database to consider include:

Ease of use Watch out for reviews that emphasise usability, preferably with untrained or only slightly experienced users. Read their comments to get an idea of how well you might do when trying to use the software. Older databases are text-based, and these are harder to use. The latest examples allow you to design forms by moving boxes and other options around on the screen. These are much easier to use and usually produce better results too.

Flatfile or relational? The larger and more popular database packages are relational. You can use them as a flatfile if you want to, and explore the relational features later as you become more confident. You cannot work the other way, however: a flatfile system cannot be expanded to give you relational features. You will have more space and room for expansion with a relational database.

Form design options If you need to include photographs or graphics, ensure that the database can handle this. Some products include options to make forms look more appealing on screen, such as fonts and graphics which are purely decorative. Others take a much more workmanlike approach. If you need your forms to look good – and remember they can be printed, as well as appearing on screen – then check what kind of presentation control features you can use.

Speed Watch out for speed ratings (sometimes these are known as *benchmarks*). If you buy a slow database because it is easy to use, but need access to thousands of records, you may need to invest in hardware that is faster than average.

Hardware requirements Some databases are more demanding than others. Make sure that your computer has enough memory and disk space to be able to handle the database efficiently.

Help features Most modern software comes with help that you can access while working, so you will not need to refer to the manual once you have mastered the basics. But watch out also for templates and design hints to make your job easier, especially when you are just starting out.

Query features How easy is it to get information out of the database?

CASE HISTORY: Mary

Mary Hardwick is network manager for a telesales company.

'We now have hundreds of thousands of telephone numbers in our database. Originally I developed a system that would change over the numbers for Phoneday. But now that BT has taken to changing area codes on a more regular basis – and more changes are planned – my bosses decided it would be useful to extend that work to create a more general tool. Quite a few places are still using five-figure numbers, and these are gradually being updated to six-figure ones.

'We're still using the same database system, although it's a new version of the software. The system includes a simple programming language that can be used to alter any or all of the information we hold in an intelligent way. All I have to do is write a simple program that looks at the numbers and makes the modifications. So in the case of the original Phoneday it was easy to change all the 0181 numbers to 0208 automatically. For the others we either get details from BT beforehand, or in some cases our reps tell us when an area code has changed. In either case it takes a few hours at most for all the information to be updated. It would take far longer if it had to be done by hand.

'In the near future it looks like we won't have to do this any more; BT will sell us their own number database. But as we started out targeting specific customers rather than selling to the general public, we've had to develop in this rather awkward way.'

PACKAGES TO WATCH FOR

Microsoft's Access is currently the most popular and highly rated database product on the market. It includes cue cards that make it easy for you to design forms from scratch, even if you have minimal experience. Access is supplied as part of Microsoft's Office 2000 Suite.

Other office suites, including Lotus Millennium and Corel's Wordperfect suites, include databases of their own. For less demanding work these are perfectly adequate.

Do I need a database?

If all you need is a simple contact list, then a PIM or a CM is a better – and cheaper – solution. However, if you need to do any of the following, a database will be more appropriate:

- include photographs and diagrams along with text and numbers
- create one-to-many links between information, and be able to list the details in different ways – for example, list all patients assigned to a certain doctor, or all patients taking medication bought from a certain company
- analyse information in many different ways – for example use sales figures to work out the most profitable product lines or geographical areas
- customise the way information is stored to suit your own special needs.

Chapter 6

Exchanging information

If you are planning to use more than one computer, you should consider installing a **network** – a system that allows your computers to exchange information with each other and also to share printers and other facilities. Small business networks are sometimes known as LANs – Local Area Networks. This distinguishes them from WANs – Wide Area Networks – such as the Internet, which are not located in one place.

Networks

Networks come in three forms. The cheapest is known somewhat irreverently as 'sneakernet'. Sneakernet is not a true network. Information is transferred manually on floppy disks from one machine to another. This is time-consuming and disruptive and can result in more than one version of the same information. In an office where everyone is working on different parts of the same document, information needs to be carefully managed to prevent this. Despite its disadvantages, 'sneakernet' is still used in some offices, where work is rarely shared and someone takes responsibility for preventing multiple versions.

Sneakernet works best if all the machines are the same type. It is now possible to transfer information between PCs and Macs quite easily; this was not always the case though, and if you have older machines you may be faced with compatibility problems.

Printer-sharing problems can be overcome with a **printer switch** that connects one of a group of computers to one or more printers. This is a simple and cheap solution. More complicated versions are available which can be switched remotely from the computer itself.

For groups of between five and twenty computers, the best option is the **peer-to-peer network**. This connects all the machines to each other, but no one machine is more important than the rest – hence the 'peer' title. Each computer has a special 'public' area for information, and any computer on the network can read or write data to this area. This makes it ideal for situations where work needs to be passed from place to place. Security is maintained because only the public areas are shared. Private work can only be accessed from each individual machine.

A peer-to-peer network allows extras, such as backup systems and printers, to be shared between a group of users. Its biggest drawback is the disruption that can occur when new software is added to the system. The software has to be installed on each machine, which can prove very time-consuming.

For larger work groups a **file-server system** is more efficient. This is built around a single central computer which serves as a repository of all the information in the company. The information on the server can be accessed by each satellite computer, which may or may not have its own hard disk, depending on the kind of work it is expected to do.

Server systems are complex and need to be installed by experts. They also require formal office organisation. A designated network manager ensures that the system runs smoothly and efficiently and that sensitive information is not available to all users.

Peer-to-peer networks and file-server systems rely on **network cards** – plug-in circuit cards that can link computers together – which need to be connected with a suitable cabling system. The details vary from system to system, but a common standard is **Ethernet**, a reliable high-speed connection that can be used to link together all the computers in a large building. More recently **wireless networks** have become available. These use radio links to replace cabling.

Any network that is used exclusively by a single business is now becoming known as an **intranet**. In theory an intranet offers business users the kind of facilities available on the Internet (see later in this chapter for more about the Internet), but with a scope that is limited to the business itself. In other words, electronic mail and other information are passed freely from computer to computer within the company, irrespective of whether the computers are in the same building or in different countries, but the information is disconnected from the rest of the Internet for security. A true intranet is more efficient and secure than the Internet, but it is also more expensive to set up, especially for multinational companies. However, this new jargon word is now often used to describe any inter-office network, irrespective of the facilities it offers.

A recent development is the Virtual Private Network (VPN). This uses the simplicity and convenience of an Internet connection to link different offices, perhaps in different countries. Information is sent over the Internet in code, so that it can only be read by authorised recipients. While Internet connections are still expensive, they are very much cheaper than a completely private international network linking parts of the same organisation.

An even more advanced option is an all-in-one network that uses similar technology to provide internal and external telephone services. Many phone companies are now using Internet-like systems for their own networks, and this makes it easy and cheap for a large company to create a single integrated network which can handle computer information, telephone calls, voice mail and fax messages. The details of these systems are outside the scope of this book, but they are mentioned here because by around 2005 the same technology is likely to start becoming available for domestic users.

Network software

To get the most from a network you need to use the best possible software. Some software options become possible only once a network has been installed.

File sharing – the ability to share documents and other information with co-workers – and printer sharing are two of the most basic possibilities offered by a network. File sharing can eliminate much of the paper blizzard that used to dominate many offices. Printer sharing makes it possible for an office to rely on one or two printers, which are kept out of the way. Some printers are designed to plug into a network without needing a computer – they have network connections and suitable hardware and software already built in. These are a more useful (if also more expensive) option than printing from a computer that is already being used for other work. Employees using a computer that is serving the printing needs of an entire office are likely to find that their machine is slowed down considerably.

Another useful tool is **email**. Messages are typed on one computer and appear almost instantaneously on the screen of another. Email is an excellent way to improve office efficiency and is beginning to replace paper memos as the standard way of passing information between computer users.

CASE HISTORY: Howard

Howard Hawker works as a programmer for a small company that produces computer games, and he found that the email system was ideal for communicating with his colleagues.

'We use email for a variety of things – to schedule meetings, pass on company news and deal with queries. It's a lot more immediate than typing a memo, but not as intrusive as making a phone call. People can read their email when they feel like it, so it doesn't clamour for attention in the same way the phone does or interrupt concentration and work flow. It's helped our project to progress, and everyone seems to be getting a lot more done. Now I'm not sure I'd want to live without it.'

Networks are ideal for group management. Colleagues can contribute ideas and comment on projects without having to spend time in meetings. Some PIMs now include network-ready functions (see page 70).

A network is also an ideal tool for formal project management. (Chapter 8 includes a brief introduction to project management software, and many of the available software packages include integrated network features.)

In a large company it is common for customer details to be stored in a single database that anyone can access. Customer correspondence, however, will usually still be scattered around different departments, and it can take a whole morning of telephoning around to track down one letter. Lotus Notes, a document database system, was designed to solve this problem by maintaining a list of all the relevant documents used in a company no matter in which department, building or site they are. The system is fully network-ready, so that if, for example, a customer sends a fax, the fax itself – with accompanying notes, if necessary – is stored in the database. In multi-site audit work, for example, different teams can build up a complete audit picture by using the package to integrate their individual contributions.

Lotus Notes is not a replacement for a conventional database; it lacks some of the advanced features these offer. Its great strength is that it is not limited to text. Any kind of information, including spreadsheets, graphics, sounds, images, fax messages and voicemail messages can be maintained. Notes has proved successful and so far remains the only product of its kind.

Network hardware

Fax machines and answering machines are a common sight in small offices. Both of these can be replaced by their computerised versions, saving space and sometimes paper. In fact, by offering these services on a network it is possible to serve the needs of an office with much less equipment than might otherwise be required.

There are two ways to create a network. LANs use network cards combined with suitable software to connect computers together physically. Once a connection is made, information can be copied between machines very conveniently, perhaps using some version of the public/shared system described on pages 83–5.

For connections to the Internet or a bulletin board, a special extra known as a **modem** is required. Modems connect your computer to the telephone line and allow it to send information to any other modem-equipped computer in the world. Most modern modems also include a fax facility. With the right software – which is often, but not always, included when you buy the modem – you can send a fax directly from your computer without having to print it out on paper first. The computer can easily maintain a 'fax address book' for common destinations and can also send copies of the same fax to many different addresses automatically. Your computer can also receive faxes. These can be viewed on screen, or printed out if you have a printer attached. Stand-alone modems, which continue to record messages even when the computer they are linked to is switched off, offer the best all-round solution for this kind of work.

Some modems also offer voice recording. With the right software, these can be used as an electronic **voice mailbox** service: outsiders can dial in and leave voice messages. At the lower end of the market, voice-recording technology can be quite crude, and the software may not be up to professional standards. But a fully working professional system – which may cost only slightly more – can boost the image of a small business. For companies that do not have their own switchboards, voice mail can be used as a kind of automatic receptionist. The computer can store callers' messages and even maintain separate password-protected 'mailboxes' for each employee. Voicemail prevents interruptions to meetings and prevents the build-up of stress caused by calls interfering with important work. It can also save money, as one computer can do the work of a number of answering machines. The voicemail system can also be used with pagers. Users can dial in and send a pager message via the computer. The computer can pass the message on to the appropriate pager number.

One problem with fax modems is that they can only transmit information generated by your computer. If you are a designer or artist and need to fax hand-drawn work on a regular basis, or you work with cuttings or other kinds of printed material, you will need to invest in a **scanner**.

A scanner takes an image, be it a sketch or a photograph, and converts it into a form that the computer can use. Once the image has been scanned in, it can be sent as a fax. Some scanners include software for **optical character recognition** (**OCR**). This enables the scanner to read printed text and to convert it into text that can be read and edited using a word processor, sent as an email and so on. This can save retyping. Budget scanners tend not to be very reliable, so OCR – even when it comes as a free package – should be treated only as an interesting optional extra. More expensive OCR packages do a much better job, and some are used professionally in the publishing trade to scan in copy supplied as faxes and manuscripts for later editing. It is not yet possible to scan in handwritten text, so do not expect to get good results from anything other than high-quality printed text, and always proofread the text afterwards. Some fax software includes OCR facilities, so that a fax can be instantly converted into text.

The Internet

The networks discussed so far have been Local Area Networks (LANs), limited to a single site. Wide Area Networks (WANs) offer the same kinds of facilities but across a much wider distance. Many WANs are owned and operated by companies, but one – the Internet – is open to anyone.

The Internet is a public-access network with some unusual features. No one owns the Internet, and there is no overall organising or administrative body. Instead, it works more as a loose affiliation of users, computer system managers, governments and commercial interests. It can be used to exchange information, software and mail between computer users worldwide. Current estimates suggest the Internet is used by over 500 million users worldwide.

The Internet has a very definite culture of its own, with its own vocabulary, ideas and social conventions. It also offers public discussion areas, where users debate issues, gossip and exchange information, often in quite a rough-and-ready manner. In other, more professionally oriented areas the tone is more restrained. The latter areas can be most useful to you as a computer user, since it is here that advice and computer support are exchanged.

To access the Internet you need a telephone or cable TV connection and a modem. You can then open an account with an Internet Service Provider (see Appendix VIII for more details); accounts are either free, or paid for. In return for signing up you are given access to the Internet. Usually this access is via your modem over a telephone link – your computer dials the provider's computer, and a connection between the two is made. What happens next depends on the kind of service your provider offers. Some act as an electronic *poste restante*, collecting mail and other information for you, holding it until you dial in and then forwarding it to you along the telephone lines. Others act as a gateway that connects your computer directly to the Internet. The latter kind of connection is much more useful, but it can also be harder to set up and use. However, it is not necessarily any more expensive, and, once it is up and running, can give you many more options and much better access to the services that the Internet offers.

Some service providers also charge you by the minute for any time spent using their services. A few, such as CompuServe, have a complicated pricing scheme where some services (such as access to certain stock-market prices) cost more per minute than others. There may also be extra charges for email on a per-message basis.

Access to the Internet offers a number of useful services:

Email Messages can be passed from computer to computer directly. Unlike network email, however, the two computers can be anywhere in the world. If you are doing business abroad you can send a couple of pages of text overseas for far less than the cost of a telephone call or fax. You also have the benefit of knowing that your email goes directly to your intended recipient. The transfer of mail is almost instantaneous. In extreme cases it may take an hour or two, but usually it arrives at its destination in moments. At the moment email suffers from two drawbacks. It is best suited to plain-text communications. It is possible to transfer sounds, pictures and even video clips electronically, but this can be an awkward, time-consuming and sometimes expensive process. As the technology of the Internet improves, these restrictions will lift.

The second disadvantage − and for business purposes the greater − is that email is not a secure way to communicate. There have been instances where email messages were intercepted without the permission of either sender or recipient and used as evidence in court cases. To get around this, email can be **encrypted**. This turns the text into gibberish which makes no sense to anyone except the recipient who has a software key to unlock the original message. The best encryption system − PGP (Pretty Good Privacy) − is available as shareware (a try-before-you-buy system discussed further in Chapter 9). It can be slightly confusing to use, but once installed properly it offers near-total security.

Free access to software and other information A large number of software archives around the world offer unlimited free access to thousands of shareware and freeware (see Chapter 9) software packages. Other kinds of information, such as current weather satellite images, recipes, travel information and hints and tips for almost every sport and hobby, are also widely available.

Free access to services which can help you find this information Knowing that the information is available is only part of the story. With the total number of computers on the Internet in the millions, it can be impossible to track down what you want without help. 'Search engines', such as AltaVista and Google, make this easier. These are fast, 'intelligent' search tools that scan the Internet looking for information on a key-word basis. A search based on the word 'mail', for example, would find a list of email-related software and information, and supply you with details of the computers you would need to access to retrieve this data. There are also services which can help you find someone's email address if you know the name and approximate location.

News groups These are the public discussion areas mentioned earlier. There are over 40,000 groups available, and the numbers are increasing every day. They are arranged according to subject matter, which includes everything from computer topics to poodle-breeding and music fan clubs. Most service providers only supply a selection of the more popular and useful English language groups. The computer-oriented groups – and there are many – are a good place to find free support.

Mailing lists Although the news group system remains active, it is slowly being superseded by mailing list services such as Yahoogroups, which offer similar facilities by email. Mailing lists can be used by friends and families for news and gossip, by hobbyist and special interest groups to exchange chat and helpful information, and by businesses to keep in touch with clients and partners. Because mailing lists use email they are marginally more cumbersome (and less widely used for very technical discussions) than the news group network. But for more general chat and discussion they are both easier to use and more popular.

The World Wide Web Part magazine, part art form, part encyclopedia, the Web is a global hypertext system. (For more information on hypertext, see pages 52–3.) Pages of text and pictures contain highlighted words that link to relevant information stored elsewhere, either as part of the same document or as part of a different document on another computer in a different country. Although the Web is visually appealing and easy to use, it is also slow (some pages can take minutes to appear on screen), and therefore less convenient than it might be,

Apart from the search facilities mentioned above, the most useful thing the Web can offer the user is international advertising space. Many organisations and individuals now have their own web pages, and it is an excellent way to reach millions of potential customers.

News wire services These offer direct access to Reuters, Associated Press and other news agencies. A number of electronic news services

AltaVista is a free on-line indexing service that helps Internet users find information on the Web

(such as ClariNet) are also available. For the most part, the cost of these services is in addition to the normal Internet connection. The advantage of subscribing is that you get the news as soon as it happens. Several news-filtering services, the equivalent of press-cutting agencies, are starting to become available.

Do I need the Internet?

You should seriously consider an Internet connection if:

- you deal regularly with overseas businesses with email contact addresses
- you need access to the latest news and stock-market prices
- you already have a basic level of computer literacy and would like easy access to expert help on a wide range of subjects.

As a means of obtaining computer support, however, the Internet is not a reliable option. If you ask for computer advice in one of the public discussion areas, your query may well be read by thousands, perhaps even tens of thousands of users, but it is always possible that none of them will reply or even know the answer. While the World Wide Web has pages that contain questions and answers on many common computer topics, finding this information can be a challenge for beginners.

However, if you are considering an Internet connection for other reasons, such as email, this can be an excellent way to get help. On the whole users do reply to genuine questions. Many manufacturers now have their own help facilities on the Internet, and some provide direct email answers to questions from professional support staff.

The Internet, children and the home

The Internet is ideal for school research, for keeping in touch with others who share similar interests and for both teenage and adult socialising. However, the unrestricted nature of information on the Internet means that some of it is frank and explicit, and therefore unsuitable for children. Furthermore, while in reality it can be really quite hard for children to find themselves on the receiving end of attention from paedophiles and other undesirables, the threat is – unfortunately – not a negligible one.

CompuServe was one of the first on-line services and is still available today

POPULAR INTERNET SOFTWARE

For the Web, the choice is between Microsoft's Internet Explorer (IE) and Netscape's Communicator. Internet Explorer has been built into every version of Windows since Win 98, which has made it the *de facto* standard for home and business users. A less widely used, but worthwhile, alternative is the Opera web browser, which has a reputation for speed. Unlike IE and Communicator, Opera is not free. Both IE and Communicator include simple email and newsgroup facilities, although these are not as powerful or easy to use as good news and email specific packages.

For news Forte's Agent remains a popular and powerful choice. For email, Qualcomm's Eudora was once a reliable option, but recent changes in both the software and the way that Qualcomm does business have made it less appealing (a once-free version now bombards users with advertising). This has left something of a gap in this part of the market, which smaller products such as Poco have tried to fill, albeit without the same success. In practice this means that most people continue to use Microsoft's Outlook Express, although, as already mentioned (see page 75), this has an appalling security record.

Some on-line services, such as AOL, include parental control options which mark certain areas 'out of bounds'. For those with more direct access, a number of products have become available that attempt to restrict what children can and cannot find on the Internet, filter out offensive language and optionally keep a list of Internet accesses, so that parents have a record to refer to. None of these products is totally foolproof. Although they will deter and protect younger Internet users, many computer-literate teenagers will be able to work around them in short order.

This is one of the most politically difficult areas surrounding Internet access, and a workable solution is still some years away. In the meantime, parents should be aware of the dangers and should look out for reviews of the relevant products in the more home- and family-oriented computer press. This is discussed further on pages 94–8.

Bulletin boards and on-line mail order

Bulletin boards were the Internet's immediate predecessors. They offered local rather than global access, and were popular with both hobbyists and some businesses, who were able to use their own Bulletin Board System (BBS) to provide a space where customers and clients could find useful information, communicate with staff and perhaps even place orders.

Although a small hard core of hobbyist BBS users remains in the UK, for the most part the BBS network has been replaced by the more comprehensive and easily accessible facilities provided by the Internet. A very small number of businesses still run BBSs, because they tend to be more secure than the freely accessible Internet. For most applications, though, the Internet offers everything a BBS can, and quite a bit more.

Ironically perhaps, the best place to find details of BBS software and UK access numbers in the UK is to use an Internet search engine such as AltaVista (see page 91).

Chapter 7

Computers and the family

Computers are now well on their way to becoming everyday household objects. As a result, the market in computer applications intended for home rather than business users is burgeoning. As with buying a machine for business use, a computer for home use can easily turn into an expensive source of aggravation rather than delight. Software and support make all the difference. This chapter introduces the more popular domestic uses of computers, and examines the pros and cons of home computer ownership.

Education and childcare

Aside from games, two of the most popular uses of a home computer are in education and childcare. Computers can be used as electronic babysitters, as substitute teachers, as creative play areas (where any messes made remain virtual and harmless), and as exam revision tutors.

CASE HISTORY: John

John Alsop, an editor for a computer magazine, uses the computer to entertain his two children.

'We have an Apple Mac at home, which so far has had mixed reactions from the kids. Gemma, who is four, was playing with the mouse almost as soon as she could walk, and she'd spend hours playing with some basic toy art and sound software. We've moved on to more complicated packages now – some stories and simple games – and she's happy to work her own way through them. She's quite content to play with the same software over and over again as long as it involves plenty of input from her.

'Simon is a year younger, and just beginning to show signs of more serious interest. One problem is that his sister gets first go most of the time, so we may have to start rationing their time on the computer, or making more of an effort to find software they can use together.

'If we want some peace and quiet we set up the software and leave either or both of them to get on with it. As a distraction it's just fantastic.

'I often get asked whether or not it helps their education prospects or whether it teaches them computer literacy. I think the answer is yes to first question, and no to the second. To other parents I'd say – treat it like a toy, not an educational work-out. It can keep your kids busy, creative and curious, which will count for far more in the long term than knowing how to use a spreadsheet. The best thing about computers is their endless flexibility. I think putting kids in that kind of environment is going to be worth more in tomorrow's job market than a more rigid idea of computer literacy.'

While computers may not turn children into computer geniuses, they can help with teaching the basic concepts of English and maths. There is now a wide range of primary-school-level software available which teaches these basic concepts by presenting them as games. The range of titles is quite large, and no one series stands out above the others, but companies to watch out for include Dorling Kindersley, Ablac Learning Works and The Learning Company. For a current list of available software it's best to refer to one of the leisure-oriented computer magazines listed in Appendix XIII.

Later on in their schooling, children can find computers helpful in other ways. Many schools now accept word-processed essays, and – neatness aside – these obviously require keyboard and computer skills. Beyond these basic uses, there are three other sources of academic help.

Educational software is specifically designed to support some parts of the National Curriculum. The standard of this software varies. Some examples are dull computer 'slide-shows' which collect together a few photographs and other graphics on a CD-ROM and link them together with a simple commentary. At the other extreme are the creative, interactive packages that give pupils hands-on experience of a subject. For example, chemistry software may work with complex animations of how various atoms link together to produce compounds, or mathematical software may draw graphs to show how different mathematical principles work. These more colourful and lively packages can be very valuable.

High-quality educational software can be hard to find. However, it is reviewed regularly – although not usually comprehensively – in the more family-oriented computer magazines (see Appendix XIII). Depending on the resources of the school, teachers may also be able to help with recommendations.

'**Edutainment**' software aims to be entertaining as well as informative. It is much more widely available and more popular. The distinguishing features are impressive graphics, animations, interesting sound effects, clever use of humour and relatively basic content – while interesting, it isn't usually matched to the National Curriculum and is less academically rigorous.

These packages can be very useful because they sustain interest by appearing to be more like games than 'serious' educational items. In fact, many packages include games of one sort or another. These almost always have an educational slant – for example, revision of the facts summarised, or animated exercises in various kinds of problem-solving.

Edutainment's main drawback is its expense. Although some packages are available for around £10, most titles cost between £30 and £40 – as much as two or three good educational books.

The Internet is an almost infinite resource for research and study. While it would be an exaggeration to say that the answer to any possible homework question is available on line, an astonishing amount of information (as well as pre-written essays – available at a price) can be found with relatively little effort. Mastering the searching and index system used on the Web is no mean feat, but anyone who has surfed can find information on almost any subject – or access to experts who may be able to help. Until children can do this – and they will need to be taught, as there are few, if any, on-line tutorials designed specifically for them – they are likely to need help finding material. Otherwise they are likely to get distracted by its endless possibilities.

The Internet can cause something of a dilemma for parents. On the one hand, it can be an extremely effective way to inspire enthusiasm for learning and making contact with others; but, on the other, some of the information on the Net is most definitely not suitable for children. At the time of writing, the problem of restricting access to unsuitable material has yet to be solved. Although systems are available that attempt to censor what children can see, none is perfect, and all have the unfortunate side-effect of accidentally barring wanted as well as unwanted information.

The most obvious way to tackle the problem is to use 'Net babysitter' software, which attempts to check web sites for inappropriate content, including sexually-explicit material, graphic violence, racism and so on. The software can look for certain words in the text at the site or can use one of the Net's own classification systems, which work very much like film ratings.

The problem with keyword searches is that they are rather unintelligent. While it is easy to get rid of most 'four-letter words', a ban on the word 'sex' for example, may make it impossible to read completely innocent sites that refer to certain English counties. Meanwhile, Net ratings are still in their early stages. There is no single standard rating system, and only a minority of sites – ironically often the ones with the most explicit content – bother to give themselves ratings. Many sites aimed at children do not do this, and unfortunately some software bars sites that are not rated. As a result, the sites that might most interest children 'disappear'. The latest web browsers are starting to take notice of ratings but, until a system is agreed upon and everyone begins to use it, ratings will remain a patchy and unreliable way to restrict access.

The situation is slightly better on the on-line services, which have a more family-oriented approach. Some services – AOL and CompuServe – offer separate account names for each family member, and these can be set up from the 'master account' so that certain features of the service are unavailable. Access to the Internet can also be controlled from the master account.

One problem is that these controls are set up using a password system, and enterprising youngsters can look over their parents' shoulders so they can 'borrow' their password later. For some children, being left in a special children's web site is not enough, and it is usually very easy to escape and follow links that lead to more adult content.

In practice, the best way to avoid inappropriate information is to rely on active forms of parenting. Finding a balance between effective concern and intrusive paranoia can be difficult here, and the whole subject needs to be handled with tact. A very useful option is moving the PC to a living room, where you can watch what children are doing with it.

One problem that is particularly severe on the Web is the prevalence of manipulative advertising aimed specifically at children. Some 'kids' sites' are really thinly disguised corporate attempts to 'sell' to youngsters. It is useful to review these sites in the same way that you would check for information of a more explicitly inappropriate nature. Parents who would like more advice should try the NCH Action for Children web site at *www.nchafc.org.uk*

Other sources of help and support

A useful resource for parents is the Parents Information Network (*www.pin.org.uk*). This offers a range of services, including a basic introductory guide to PC buying and a selection of educational web sites.

For home schooling, BT and Anglia Media run an Internet-based service called AngliaCampus (*http://home.angliacampus.com*). For an annual subscription of about £50 children can get expert on-line help with homework, remedial lessons in reading and writing and information on languages, sport and study skills. The service currently covers ages 5 to 18.

Adult learning and entertainment

Adults too can benefit from continuing study. The Open University remains the most effective way to study to degree level at home, and now offers both computer- and Internet-based training materials. While a small number of other Internet-based 'distance learning' programmes are available, these are experimental and most often based in the US.

For adults the most useful tools for home learning are still educational multimedia packages. Most of these fall firmly into the 'edutainment' category, and cover subjects as diverse as history, science, the great works of art and literature, astrology, and so on. The wider range of titles and the fact that some are available at 'budget' prices (typically around £10) makes this a much more fertile source of software than edutainment for children.

In the mid-1990s slick design, high prices and relatively shallow content gave early edutainment titles a less than glowing reputation. The market has now matured, though, and titles are more likely to be informative as well as entertaining. As with all software, the quality is variable, so where possible it can be worth asking to see a CD-ROM before buying it.

Entertainment

In many homes the computer is beginning to compete with the TV as a tool for relaxing. By 2005 it's likely that current TV systems will have begun to merge with the Internet – which will be offering wire-less satellite delivery of information. When this happens computers, TVs and hi-fis may begin to amalgamate into a single all-purpose home entertainment system. For now, though, there remain applications for which a computer is essential.

The Internet

Increasing numbers of people are using the Internet – and especially the more popular on-line services that offer live chat – as an alternative to television and nights out. The Internet's great strength from a social point of view is that it makes it very easy to find and communicate with people with similar interests. It can also simplify social arrangements. Sending out a party invitation to 50 people using email is much quicker, cheaper and more convenient than using the post or the telephone (assuming all your guests have email).

In terms of hobbies, information on the Web and the various Internet newsgroups and mailing lists provides an enviably comprehensive collection of useful information and knowledgeable people – although the latter can sometimes seem more argumentative in groups than 'real-life' friends are.

CASE HISTORY: Sian

Sian started using America OnLine with a free introductory offer.

'The software is very easy to use and mostly fun. It is a great way to meet new people. I found that a chap in my area had started up a sports club. The local sports centre wasn't being used much on Friday nights, so they let people use the facilities for a pound. He collects the money, and we all meet up for a laugh and a good time, and some swimming, tennis or badminton.

'There's also a website called Yell that lists all the films in all the cinemas up and down the country. If you want to know what's on in the West End, or elsewhere for that matter, it's no trouble at all to find out. Railtrack has a full timetable on the Web and some of the bus and coach companies have lists of services. You can even order wine. It can take you a while to find these things, but once you do they can make life a lot easier.

'The downsides? I have to say that being female I get a lot of unwelcome attention, some of it of a sleazy nature. And yes, it can be an expensive way to waste time if I'm bored. I've known people who've had bills of more than £400 a quarter! So, even though you start by thinking that the £10 a month you pay AOL doesn't sound like much, you have to watch those phone bills or you'll be in trouble.

'I think these on-line services are probably better for people who don't use the Internet seriously. It's for the fun of it really. I suppose it's just that much more social than flopping down in front of the TV in the evening – at least you're talking to people, even if it is only through a keyboard.'

Games

Games are an extremely popular reason for buying a home computer. While not many people have the resources to spend more than £1,000 on something that is only used for entertainment, those that do seem to be unusually keen. They are not only happy to invest £30 to £40 for each new game when it appears, but also to add the latest game-specific hardware to their PC when it becomes available.

Computer games fall into five main groups.

Shoot-em-ups place a player into an electronic virtual world where he or she (usually he – these games are most popular with adolescent boys) is expected to explore the surroundings and dispatch the 'baddies' in any number of graphically violent ways. The effect is very similar to that of an animated cartoon, and relies on a combination of quick thinking, fast reflexes and occasional strategic planning on the part of the player.

Games such as *Quake* and *Doom* are the best-known examples of the tasteless end of the genre, although much milder and relatively innocuous examples such as *Descent* are also popular. Some are tied in to popular films. Lucas Arts, a division of the media empire run by George Lucas, maker of the *Star Wars* films, has done well with a range of *Star Wars*-related games. *Star Trek* has also spawned its own collection of tie-in games.

In general, shoot-em-ups are ideal for anyone who wants a quick adrenaline rush without having to think too hard. While the graphics used in games improve every year, and the strategic challenges become more complex, the basic premise never changes. Some gamers revel in the familiarity this offers, while others find it dull.

Adventures work at a much slower pace. These build atmosphere with more carefully crafted computer-designed artwork than the relatively crude graphics of shoot-em-ups. The premise of a virtual world is the same, but players are expected to pick up and use a much wider range of items, and typically have much longer to think about their moves. Many adventures are a very elaborate setting for some logic puzzles of varying degrees of difficulty, and it is fair to say that some are much better designed than others.

Adventures can be divided into rough sub-genres. Among the most highly rated adventures are *Myst* and *Riven*, its much more complex and visually impressive sequel, and the *Zork* series of games. *Riven,* in particular, offers astounding graphics and a fascinating imaginary world to explore, although some of the puzzles are ferociously difficult and may leave many people stumped.

Sims (short for simulations), also known as god-games, offer a more complicated gaming experience. In these the player is in charge of developing a virtual environment – which can be anything from a theme park, to a hospital, to a whole civilisation – and is expected to make decisions about how to make the environment prosper. Bad decisions lead to failure, and, to make the games more interesting, some also offer a number of disaster scenarios.

The end result is somewhere between a war game (where the enemy can be fate, or relentless economic forces, or neighbouring civilisations) and a management simulation. (Some academic management courses use sims to prepare their students for the challenges of running a real business.) The original ground-breaking sim was called *SimCity*, which is still available in a number of updated and modified forms, and is perennially popular with players. Examples of this kind of game are always available, and always near the top of the best-seller lists.

In a **flight sim** the player is behind the controls of an aeroplane with a simulated landscape which he or she can fly over – or crash into. The player learns to take off, fly, perform aerobatics and land, often at simulations of real airports. In many flight sims there are no enemies to kill and no weapons to experiment with. However, some flight sims offer a more military-minded slant, and include accurate simulations of real military aircraft, complete with navigation and weapon-control systems, in a variety of battle settings.

Flight sims can be frustrating for beginners because keeping a plane from colliding with the ground can often be more difficult than it seems. However, this is a specialist genre, and more lackadaisical gamers may find that the persistence required to master it demands more commitment than they are prepared to give.

The most popular flight sim is Microsoft's *Flight Simulator*. This offers a range of aircraft simulations, from an old biplane to a business jet, and is upgraded regularly. The game comes with information about the navigation techniques used by real aircraft, as well as very detailed scenery. Recently Microsoft has begun adding combat-based extras to its basic line of flight-sim products.

Related to flight sims are **driving sims**. These are similar, except that they take place behind the steering-wheel of a car that (usually) stays on the ground. Typically these include some element of racing, based either on a realistic simulation of a Formula One track or in a completely imaginary fantasy world.

Other simulations cover a range of games. Pool, snooker, various card games, and Monopoly and Scrabble are all now available in computer-ready form. Perennially popular examples include football games, where players can manage teams and/or play the game directly on the screen, car racing and rallying.

Networks and tournaments

Enthusiastic gamers, particularly those interested in shoot-em-ups, can expand their experience by playing games 'live' with other players. Many shoot-em-ups offer a multiplayer option, which either pits players in teams against various computer-generated enemies or against each other. These add a whole new dimension to the experience – so much so that many of these games are now banned on the networks used by large businesses, because employees find the experience addictive.

Multiplayer options can work over a simple link or a local area network if the computers are physically close to each other, over a direct modem-to-modem connection via a telephone line in the case of two-player games, or over the Internet. (The latter can be slow. However, some Internet service providers even go so far as to offer dedicated 'servers' – large computers dedicated to one particular task – for certain very popular games, so that their customers can play against each other.) Games that offer this option invariably include instructions on how to set it up. BT offers a service called Wireplay which is aimed specifically at gamers and is now completely free, except for local-rate call charges. Gamers can play others in the UK using a special fast network, or over the Internet via a Wireplay connection (an existing Internet connection is not required). More details are available from the web site at *www.gameplay.com/wireplay*. A related feature of the gamer's world are tournaments where players can compete with each other directly – often face to face, or at least in the same room. These are advertised in gaming magazines, on the Internet, and on bulletin boards. Note that on-line gaming can be expensive, even with local call charges.

Finding and choosing games

Full-price computer games are not cheap. Fortunately, there are a number of low-cost options for the aspiring gamer on a budget. The shelf-life of a modern game is rarely more than six months to a year, after which time the game is either forgotten or reappears on a budget compilation – a CD with a collection of popular games – or as a 'white label'. The latter is a repackaged game in a less impressive box sold at a much more reasonable price – usually comparable to or even less than a music CD.

The other option for gamers is to investigate a local exchange store that buys games second-hand for a fraction of their original price and sells them on. Even with the mark-up, this can be a good way to get more recent games at a more realistic price.

As for completely new games, the endless torrent of new releases makes it impossible to keep up with the latest and best without reading any of the monthly gaming titles. These usually have the word 'Gamer' in the title to distinguish them from other computer magazines, and are devoted to in-depth previews, reviews and retrospectives about the various current games.

Game consoles

Why buy a PC when a game console is a cheaper option? Consoles, such as Sony's Playstation series, and Microsoft's Xbox can sometimes (but not always) provide better animation and graphics than a computer, and can also be much easier to use.

The advantage of computers, however, is that they can be used for other things. And computer games can be cheaper than console titles. In the end, though, this is very much a matter of personal choice. For anyone who uses a computer solely for games, the question is largely one of cost and convenience. For those who wish to have a more general-purpose tool in the home, the computer is usually the more sensible, if also the more expensive, option.

Other options

Computers are now regularly used to listen to music and even to watch TV. The speakers available with most computers are hardly true hi-fi, but they can compete favourably with the cheaper mini and micro systems sold in the high-street hi-fi stores. As a result, computers are now often used to play music where previously a small portable CD-player or other system would have done the same job.

When it comes to images the situation is more complex. Some people are quite happy to watch TV and video on their computer's monitor. This is unlikely to become more than a minority interest. TV tuner cards that allow live TV signals from a conventional aerial to appear on a computer screen are improving rapidly, and a number of systems are widely advertised for less than £100. In fact, it is now possible to buy a system that can 'capture' live video to hard disk for less than £300. The size of hard disk required makes this an unlikely replacement for the home video system, but it does allow anyone with a moderate disposable income to set up a small video editing facility for use with a portable camcorder.

The computer world has settled on DVD (Digital Video Disk, also known as Digital Versatile Disk) as the current video format of choice. Disks are now widely available. The fact that DVDs are difficult to copy means that manufacturers are content with the format. Note, however, that disks are copyrighted by 'region'. Only some DVD players ignore region information. Those that do not will be unable to play disks bought outside Europe.

Creativity tools

Perhaps the most entertaining other uses of computers are the creative ones. For the first time beginners can experiment with art, animation and music without spending a fortune on specialist tools. The software available in all these fields ranges from basic tools for dabblers to advanced packages that can also be used professionally. What makes the technology so interesting is that astounding results can often be achieved with very little effort.

In terms of sound and music, software is available to teach basic piano keyboard skills and sight-reading, or to make it easy for anyone to put together very professional-sounding examples of modern dance music. While this 'music-by-numbers' approach may worry purists, it can be an excellent way to get beginners started and provides plenty of continuing satisfaction where more challenging traditional methods can appear too difficult to master.

For art, it is possible to buy a graphics tablet and some software for not much more than the cost of a collection of high-quality acrylic paints, an easel and a pad of artist's paper. While this approach is rather more expensive than starting with a 6B pencil and a rubber, it can help beginners overcome their fears about making mistakes. Some beginner's software also includes features that make it easy to create very impressive results with some simple experimentation. For example, Corel's Dabbler has a range of 'filters' that can modify an existing image in various ways. While not art in the conventional sense, this can still lead someone with a good eye for shapes, colours and textures to create results that are very satisfying and impossible to do any other way. Similarly, 'world creation packages', such as Metacreations' Bryce, can produce images of realistic virtual landscapes with an astonishing degree of detail that would previously have required years of traditional art training.

All of these options can make it easier for beginners to investigate their potential creative talents. In a handful of cases this has even led to people developing interesting new career opportunities for themselves.

A music collection?

The arrival of a number of new, efficient ways of storing music inside a computer (for example, the MP3 system) and the relatively huge disk capacities available in modern machines mean that some people are now storing complete music collections inside their computer – often inside a laptop, which can then replace a number of tapes and CDs when on the move.

While it's possible to convert tracks from existing CDs to the MP3 format, it's also easy to copy completely new music from the Internet. A number of web sites, such as MP3.COM (*www.mp3.com*) offer music created by amateurs and available for free. The owners of the site make no editorial choices, and so the quality is variable. However, the best music compares well with commercial recordings, and the system as a whole offers a creative outlet to anyone who makes music that is unlikely to be released in the usual way.

Currently, it takes a long time to copy an MP3-format song to a computer. However, as Internet speeds improve and hard-disk capacities increase, it's likely that separate hardware players will eventually become much less common than they are now. Instead, computers and laptops will be used to store complete music collections.

Home video

An increasingly popular option is home video recording and editing. Affordable camcorders and editing software have made it possible for anyone with a talent for story-telling to produce their own films. At the very least it is now relatively easy to use a computer to put together a visual record of important family moments.

Video editing remains one of the few areas where computer speed and power really makes a difference. If you are interested in this area, bear in mind that you have a choice between spending perhaps another £500 to £1,000 over and above the price of a general-purpose machine, or waiting frequently while the computer works on an editing task for you. For more details see Appendix II. Reliability is another issue here. In theory software and hardware are capable of all manner of impressive creative feats. In practice, beginners often find that the technology doesn't quite work as advertised (or sometimes doesn't work at all), and it's fair to say that this is an area of computer use that requires even more patience and persistence than most.

However, for those who find a safe path through the pitfalls, the rewards can be great, and some people who have mastered computer video have even found themselves with new jobs, or at least a new source of income.

Let the buyer beware!

There are many good reasons to be wary of buying a home computer. The most obvious is cost. At more than £1,000 for a full system, a computer is a major investment. It is useful to look realistically at the benefits this outlay will bring, and also to be aware of 'hidden' costs such as upgrades and support.

The question of upgrades is a particularly difficult one. Business computers are most often bought as a package that fulfils a specific need. The need is unlikely to change over the life of the machine, and – unless the business expands or changes significantly – the package as a whole can be expected to offer more than five years of sterling service before becoming obsolete.

The situation is different in the home. To give of its best a home computer needs a steady diet of new software titles. This is not only expensive – far more expensive than creating a videotape or CD collection – but much more demanding of the hardware. Where a video recorder or CD player can be expected to last perhaps five years, it may be as little as six to twelve months before a particular computer is heading towards obsolescence, as the latest software titles demand more and more from its performance. The only options then are either to forgo the more interesting software releases, or to spend even more money on an expensive upgrade.

Manufacturers seem indifferent to the chaos that this can cause in the home market. One notorious example occurred in January 1997. With minimal warning Intel released a completely new kind of processor chip – the MMX range – which compromised the value and usefulness of Pentium-based computers bought in the run-up to the preceding Christmas. While it took some time for MMX-ready software to appear in the shops, the confidence of many new computer owners was dented.

If you are thinking of buying a computer for home use remember that a computer is not so much a one-off purchase as an ongoing investment. Like cars, computers cost a lot to run. Taking out a long-term loan or a hire-purchase scheme can be particularly foolhardy in this context, as you will need to find further money for upgrades long before you have paid off the original amount.

Learning the lessons

When buying a computer for use at home you could save yourself some grief by following these four steps:

1. **Learn the basics** At the very least it's useful to be able to compare different processor chips and memory sizes, to know what Windows is, and to understand what a hard disk does.
2. **Always get a package price** Multimedia is now standard on all home PCs, and it is reasonable to expect a computer system to include a printer as well. If any free software is included, check it carefully to see how useful it really is.
3. **Shop around** Some high-street stores sell systems at an astonishing mark-up – as much as 100 per cent in some cases, compared to certain smaller retailers. A thorough survey of comparable machines in the various computer magazines should make it clear what the average price of a given system is. Cheaper is not necessarily better, but in the computer trade more expensive is not necessarily better either. To facilitate your choice it can help to consider technical after-sales support and location as well as price.
4. **Support, support, support** This is critical. As with business purchases, customers looking to buy a computer for home use can learn a lot about a retailer's approach to support from the helpfulness of the sales staff. Helpfulness should not be confused with professional charm, but should combine a thorough knowledge of the options available, a willingness to demonstrate their differences, and an awareness of new developments. Ideally support should be local. Telephone support is perhaps better suited to those who are no longer complete beginners.

Retail vs mail order

While there are no hard-and-fast rules about the difference between buying over the counter or by mail order, retail sales can often be a better choice for first-time buyers. The advantages are purely practical – the computer can be taken home immediately, and if there are any problems it can also be returned to the shop. Stores that don't offer this kind of over-the-counter support should be thought of as having more in common with the mail-order suppliers.

Mail order is perhaps better for more experienced computer users who already know something about what they are getting for their money. It is **very** important to compare prices and specifications thoroughly when buying by mail order, and to talk to sales staff – again to get an idea of the company's approach to sales. Trained salespeople will always try to 'close' a sale by asking 'So would you like to place an order?' as soon as they can. It can be useful to time how long each sales person takes to get to this phrase, as a rough guide to how much more concerned they are with selling you something than with deciding what is best for you.

The biggest advantage of mail order is that there is no pressure involved. Buyers can pick and choose between different companies and different specifications in their own time, without any feeling of obligation. This can be harder to do in a retail setting, where sales staff can use the time they spend demonstrating a system to pressure a buyer into a purchase. The main disadvantage is a lack of hands-on experience with the computer. Sometimes the extras – mouse, keyboard and especially the monitor – can say a lot about the internal build and general quality of a machine. Many of these questions are commented on routinely in magazine comparative reviews. As with all computer buying, a little research can go a long way. For more details about mail-order buying (including shopping for computers on the Internet) see pages 166–70.

Chapter 8

Job-specific software and computer utilities

All the software we have discussed so far has been aimed at home or general-purpose business use, but your computer can also help you with your work itself. Job-specific software is not as widely available as the common business-related packages. It is usually written by professional users for other professional users in the same trade. They tend to work independently of the large software manufacturers and often sell their products as **shareware** – a 'try-before-you-buy' system discussed in Chapter 9. Many of these programs are advertised in specific trade journals.

CASE HISTORY: Ted

Ted Smith runs a small electronic design consultancy.

'Computerising some aspects of my trade has freed up a lot of my time. First, we can model circuitry mathematically without having to build it. There are a lot of calculations involved in design, and now the computer does them. So we have time to experiment with different ideas and approaches when attacking a problem. We can also answer "what-if?" questions, such as checking for the effect of component tolerances.

'Second, the computer helps with circuit board layouts. This used to be very time-consuming. You have to lay the components out within a certain area and then work out where to make the connections. It's a tough job to do by hand, and there used to be a lot of trial and error involved. There was no guarantee we'd got it right either. The computer does it all for us automatically. It also prints out the track pattern, and we can use that as the master artwork for the circuit boards. On some projects we've cut development times by 75 per cent.

'I found the software in a shareware catalogue. Off-the-shelf products tend to be expensive. The shareware was much cheaper, and I've been in touch with the author with suggestions that he's included in new versions. If there are any problems I can call him up and ask him about them. Of course not all shareware authors live in the UK, so I've been lucky there. There is also a level of personal contact you wouldn't get with a larger company.'

Software can also be used for non-technical jobs, and more and more trades of every kind are taking advantage of the possibilities that computers offer. Whatever kind of work you do, there is a good chance you will be able to find software to help you do it more effectively.

CASE HISTORY: Delia

Delia Shepherd breeds toy dogs known as affenpinschers. She uses a computer to keep track of pedigrees and also to watch out for possible genetic defects.

'I used to draw the dogs' family trees by hand, but now I get the computer to do it. They're not just for fun. A very small number of dogs are believed to suffer from a rare recessive gene that can cause them problems. The computer helps me keep track of which dogs are likely to have the defect, and I keep that in mind when arranging matings.

'The software isn't particularly hard to use. It's advertised in the popular dog-breeding magazines and is fairly affordable. I don't know much about computers and I'm not really interested in learning. In fact I don't know how any of it works at all. A friend set it up for me and showed me how to use it.'

Computer-aided design

Some work-specific products are popular and widely available. Although they started out as tools for particular trades, they are now almost as common as the ubiquitous business office suites.

Computer-aided design (CAD) is one of the largest of these practical applications. At its simplest, CAD offers an electronic replacement for the drawing board. Plans can be created and printed out without the tedious and time-consuming business of drawing them by hand, and changes can be made on screen without leaving a trail of untidy and distracting correction marks.

Using a CAD system, an architect, for example, can create perspective drawings from any position and can shade materials (the technical word is *render*) in different ways, so that images can seem almost real.

CASE HISTORY: William and Martha

William and Martha Philips, who design and install kitchens, use a CAD program to help with floor layouts and three-dimensional visualisations.

'We started off with a simple package designed for architects that gave us a top-down or side-on view of the working area. It was like a drawing board, but on the screen. We could draw in different units, experiment with positioning, and then show a client the various possibilities. The greatest advantage was the speed with which we could move things around. If someone said, "No, I want the washing machine there", we could pick it up, move it and shuffle everything around to suit. That's what makes CAD so much better than a drawing board. Once we'd got the layout settled, we'd use that and the side elevations as the basis for the final plans. The computer did these too.

'At the moment we're experimenting with a system that enables us to do three-dimensional visualisations of a finished kitchen. The pictures are in colour, and have the right textures – wooden areas appear woody and so on. We can show night and day views by changing how the scene is lit. We can even move around inside a view to try all the different perspectives – including impossible ones, such as looking down from the ceiling!

'It's very impressive, but it's also very time-consuming; it takes ages to create a new design. We have a library of units – or rather, pictures of units – inside the computer and we can slot these into a view without having to redesign them from scratch. Even then, telling the computer exactly where every last thing has to go can take ages.

'CAD is very demanding: we have a powerful machine – fast processor, lots of memory, a big screen – and you couldn't do what we do with less. The 2-D stuff is fine on just about any machine, but if you start working in three dimensions you need something that can really move. What we've found though is that speeds have really improved over the last few years. Our latest computer does in a matter of hours what used to take a day or so – which has made our lives a lot easier!'

Early CAD software was geared very much towards the professional user. This meant it was powerful but also difficult to master. A variety of much simpler CAD packages are now available which are designed for specific tasks, for example, garden design. These can vary in quality, but at their best they make the CAD process much more straightforward and accessible than the older CAD packages did.

Image manipulation

While CAD is used for plans and diagrams, image-manipulation software works with photographs, illustrations and other images. This is a rapidly growing field, which is now encompassing some of the work previously reserved for professional photographic studios, and can be used to help with advertising and promotion.

CASE HISTORY: Lyle

Lyle Kennet used a combination of image manipulation and desktop publishing to produce a brochure and price list for his software sales company.

'We used to use a photographer for the photos, and I'd hire a design shop to do the layout. This year I thought I'd have a go myself. I took the photos at home on the dining-room table – I used a sheet for a backdrop – using a digital camera. This let me copy the images straight into my computer without using any film at all.

'I'm no expert, and the photos weren't actually that great, but I ran them through the Adobe Photoshop package to sharpen them up and bring out the colours. I also added some interesting background effects.

'I used a standard DTP package to lay out the photos and text. It took about two days to do the double-page spread. I sent it to the printer on a data cartridge, and we got the price lists back soon after.

'I based the design on what we'd used in the past. The logo was already in the computer, and the rest just slotted in around it. It's not quite as slick as a designer could do, but it does the job. It took me about four days, doing it in my spare time. I think I saved myself something like £2,000. It will be even quicker next time, and I can reuse some parts when I do it again.'

Route planners

Route planners are automated maps. You specify a start point and a destination, and the computer works out the best way between the two. The possible criteria for 'best' include the fastest, cheapest or shortest route, and the computer can combine all of these to create a route based on your personal preferences, for example avoiding motorway routes. Typical speed and fuel consumption figures are used to give an estimate of journey time and fuel cost.

CASE HISTORY: Melanie

Melanie Scott is a sales rep with a major cosmetics company, and she uses a route planner to help her manage her time efficiently.

'When I started I used to sit there with a map trying to work out the best way to visit all our customers. Now I get the computer to do it for me. On average I think it's saved me between half an hour and an hour a day when I'm on the road, and I can work out my expenses in advance.'

Route planners have proved invaluable for haulage firms, courier companies and sales forces, as they make it possible to estimate costs and delivery times accurately and to work out the most time- and cost-efficient ways to move people and products around from place to place. Some of the latest products include a GPS option which can link them with a GPS location device, to produce a map that always shows the user's current position.

Project management tools

These are used to keep track of large projects. Project management (PM) consists of planning, communicating and managing, and PM tools help with the first two of these.

CASE HISTORY: John

John Adams runs an architect's practice and has been using a project-management software package for three years.

'The architect's job is not just to design the building so it fits the setting and doesn't fall down. We're also responsible for overseeing construction as a whole. This involves keeping track of information, resources, raw materials and people to make sure the project is finished on time and within budget.

'The most useful PM tool is the Gantt chart, which shows a breakdown of the project in terms of what is due to happen when. With the software we use we can track resource usage as part of each Gantt line, so that we keep abreast of costs. It also shows where we are, as opposed to where we should be. If the project starts to slip, the software warns us, and we can take action.

'We use critical path calculations to work out which parts of the project matter the most. This helps us identify key tasks that we can't afford to have running late. The next stage is to assign the tasks to people, and that's when the different charts come in useful. It's a good way to give everyone an overview and to show where they fit in. They can then take the information away and use it with their own teams. Since using the software we've been a lot more organised about the work that we do, and it's been a great help to the practice.'

Computer utilities

As well as tools to help you with specific jobs, there are also more general computer utilities which make your computer work better, faster and more efficiently. They are available to help with most aspects of computer use. If you are a beginner you can usually get by without them, but more confident users find them useful.

Screensavers

These are entertaining, if largely useless, decorative programs which blank out the screen if you stop working on your computer for longer than a set time. On older machines there was the possibility that, if left for too long, a picture on the screen could burn into the phosphor on the inside surface of the monitor; screensavers were developed to prevent this. After a period of inactivity the picture on the screen changes to something with some movement. As soon as the user presses a key or moves the mouse, the old screen is restored, and work can continue.

Over the years screensavers have developed into something of an art form. A screensaver called 'After Dark' started the trend with a famously surreal scene of flying toasters, complete with wings, and included options such as a fish tank with convincingly animated fish and ferns. This led to increasingly ornate animated cartoon sequences, some with full musical backing, and various film and TV tie-ins. Meanwhile on the Internet screensavers are being used as part of huge collaborative computing projects. For example the SETI@home screensaver uses the relatively slow processing power of home computers to check for radio messages from alien civilisations. Users copy information to their PC, process it while their PC would otherwise be idle, and then send the results back when complete.

Unless you enjoy the sheer whimsy of these products and have no objection to spending money on random entertainment, you can ignore most screensavers. Modern monitors are much less prone to burn-in, and newer software such as Windows comes with simple but effective screensavers of its own. The only good practical reason for using a screensaver is that some offer a measure of security if you need to leave your machine unattended for a time.

Disk doublers

When computers had much less storage space, a popular accessory was the disk doubler. By compacting the information, this could give you up to twice as much free disk space using your existing hardware. However, disk doublers have several disadvantages: very occasionally information would simply be lost; compatibility problems with certain kinds of software were also reported; and speed was another problem, because compacting and restoring information every time the disk is accessed slows work down considerably.

In general, disk-doubler software is not necessary any more for desktop work. Storage hardware is now so cheap that there is no reason to settle for a small disk and augment it artificially, when for a few tens of pounds more you can buy all the storage space you need.

For users of portable computers, however, disk doublers can be a useful option. Storage areas on portables are much smaller, and it is much more expensive to buy larger sizes for a portable than for a desktop. If you have a lot of software installed you could easily find yourself running out of space, and a disk doubler can solve this problem.

Some computers come with free disk-doubling software. For example all recent versions of Windows (see page 241) include a disk doubler called DriveSpace. If you need this option you should ask your dealer to set it up for you before you buy the machine.

Disk managers

A more useful tool is the disk manager. Disk drives are sometimes organised into smaller sub-units called partitions. Doing this carefully can make the whole machine appear to work slightly more quickly. It can also be useful to copy the contents of one hard disk to another in its entirety. This can be an excellent way to keep a backup of the information inside a computer. It is also essential when upgrading a hard disk to a larger one.

Disk managers such as PowerQuest's Partition Magic can perform all these tasks in a fairly simple and accessible way. For example, when installing a larger hard disk Partition Magic can copy all the old information, including all the computer's settings, to the new disk. The information can then be rearranged so that the extra free space on the new disk becomes fully available. For more advanced work, the program is also useful when working with alternative systems such as Linux (see page 247.)

Memory managers

These are now a historical curiosity rather than a practical tool, although you may still come across them when buying a second-hand machine or trying to install or reinstall Microsoft Windows (see page 309). Originally IBM-compatible PCs used memory in a notoriously inefficient way. The original design for the PC set an upper limit of 640 Kb on how much memory could be used. At the time it was felt that this would be enough for any user. A few years later, however, it was clear that this was in fact a major limitation of the design.

As a result two different schemes – extended memory and expanded memory – were devised to break through the limit. Neither of these works particularly efficiently and both slowed down the whole computer.

PCs and software that use Windows 95 or Windows 98 system are much less prone to these kinds of complications. Windows 95 can – in theory – be set up to make the best possible use of all the available memory whatever the application, and can also run older games with full control over how the memory should be set up for each one. In practice, Windows 95/98 isn't perfect, but it is a huge improvement on the convoluted and confused system that earlier PC users had to contend with.

Speed enhancers

Speed enhancers take off where memory managers left off. It is possible to speed up certain operations quite noticeably, and speed enhancers such as Hurricane will attempt to work out where this can be done. The practical benefits are perhaps not as dramatic as one might hope, but some retailers supply these products for free, and it can be worth experimenting with them.

Uninstallers

Another useful utility is the uninstaller. When you install new software, new information is copied to various parts of your machine.

Removing this information later can be very time-consuming if done manually. Windows 95/98 seems to be particularly clumsy in this respect – often the process used to remove software simply appears not to work correctly, and a manual clean-up is required to finish the job properly.

The best uninstallers keep a list of the type and location of new information added by a software package. You can then uninstall the software with a single command. A less useful type tries to guess where information is kept. These will often ask you first before they delete anything. Unfortunately, even experts can be confused about what is and is not relevant to a given piece of software.

In general, if your set-up is fairly fixed and you do not spend a lot of time trying out new software, then you will not need to worry about using an uninstaller. If you plan to add to your computer throughout its life, however, then it can be well worth investing in one of these simple and useful tools.

System checkers

Some products claim to offer PC support 'out of the box'. They look at your computer and your applications, check out the whole system, warn you of any problems and sort them out for you automatically.

These can be very appealing to beginners. Unfortunately, in practice few of the current crop work as well as advertised, and many are useless. Although they offer help for popular software, this often applies to versions of software that are no longer current. The troubleshooting features are also limited. If you want support you will need to learn how to do it yourself or pay an expert to do it for you.

Compression and decompression software

When archiving or transferring information from one computer to another it can be useful to compact software and data so they take up less space. This is a two-way process. First, compression software is used to perform the compaction. This squeezes the information into a smaller space, but also renders it temporarily unreadable. To restore it to its original form decompression software reverses the process. Shareware (discussed more fully in the next chapter) is often supplied in compressed form, as this is the only way that a complete package can be made to fit on to a single floppy disk. WinZip is the market leader, and creates files in the popular ZIP format. Aladdin's StuffIt is a worthwhile alternative; it includes tools that work with a number of other compression systems, including those that are popular with users of the Apple Mac.

General-purpose 'tool kits'

These include a collection of useful tools, such as Norton's Utilities, to help you manage your computer more efficiently. Many of these have been rendered redundant by the newer operating systems (Windows for the PC, and Mac O/S for Apple machines). If you use an older operating system, however, they can make your machine easier to use – rather like the computer equivalent of a Swiss army knife. A good example of a typical tool they include is the undelete utility, which recovers information if you accidentally delete it. Another useful option is a graphic display of the way that information is arranged on your computer's hard disk. This makes it easier to find what you are looking for and also to copy and move information from one place to another.

Backup software

The backup process (described on pages 151–5) can be simplified with suitable backup software. Examples are sometimes supplied for free with backup hardware, but even these can often be improved upon. The best backup software keeps track of changed information for you automatically, works around a proven and reliable backup scheme, and can handle a number of different backup hardware options.

Chapter 9

Choosing the right software

For business and serious home use, it is important to avoid buying software without trying it out first, unless you have absolutely no alternative. A 'try before you buy' approach can save time, temper and money in the long run. To a large extent, the software you choose determines whether you will be happy with your computer.

Training courses can be a good way to try out software before buying it (these are discussed in more detail in Chapter 13). Another alternative is to visit a dealer. This can present some problems, however, as many dealers and high-street stores will have neither the time nor the inclination to demonstrate a software package in detail. In itself, this is useful, as it can show you which dealers are prepared to be helpful. A dealer who is interested enough to discuss and demonstrate your software options is preferable to someone who resorts to high-pressure sales talk.

Magazine reviews can be another useful guide. Many magazines run multiple tests that compare different products with each other. Even if you do not understand them fully, you will get some idea of how well one piece of software rates against another. The best reviews include usability and productivity ratings, and use independent testers in work-related situations. These give an excellent indication of how easy it is to use a piece of software, and also how easy it is to get useful work done with it (the two are not always related).

Free offers

Free copies of trial software are often given away with computer magazines. Sometimes the software is fully functional, but not the latest version: a special offer inside the magazine lets you buy the current version at a reduced price. Alternatively, the software is a trial version which is limited in some way; it may be designed to work for a certain number of days, or a set number of times.

Older, trial versions are an excellent way to try out software. As software dates far more slowly than hardware, you may find that an old version does everything you want it to. Unfortunately, manuals are not usually supplied with such trial versions, although they may be available for a small charge from the manufacturer. Paying the extra also renders you eligible for free help from the manufacturer.

Limited-use trial versions allow you to try software for nothing. There are no notable drawbacks to this approach, and if you buy the full version it may be possible to keep the work you created using the limited one.

A variation of the trial version is the **encrypted** demonstration. This contains both a demonstration copy of the software that you can try out in the normal way, and a full working version which can be used only with a special access code. To obtain this code you telephone the manufacturers with your credit card details and make a payment; they then give you the code over the telephone and agree to send any manuals and other extras you need.

Be wary of the encrypted demonstration. You may be tempted to make an impulse purchase. Test the software *thoroughly* before buying to be sure it really does meet your needs. You will pay the full recommended price for software bought this way, whereas by shopping around you can often get a sizeable discount on software.

Demonstration versions and money-back guarantees

Some business software vendors offer a 'no-quibble, money-back guarantee'. You can try their software for a limited period (usually 30 days), and if you return it you get a full refund. This kind of approach gives you a relaxed opportunity to try out competing products. Always ask if this kind of deal is on offer before you buy software.

Shareware

Shareware (often known, slightly inaccurately, as **public domain** software) is explicitly provided on a try-before-you-buy basis. The software is available for a nominal amount and comes with a legal agreement which states that it may be used for an evaluation period – typically 30 days – without payment. Once this time has elapsed the software must be either **registered** – you do this by sending a cheque to the author – or removed from your computer.

Most shareware is produced by independent software writers who work from home and do not have access to the development resources of a large company. The quality of such software can vary. The best shareware packages can compete with professional products costing many times the price, and for those on a very tight budget can be a cost-effective alternative to mainstream products. The worst examples are badly designed, hard to use and unreliable. Some professional products are also badly designed, hard to use and unreliable, but they are, as a rule, at least partially usable. Unfortunately this is not always the case with shareware.

Many shareware authors add incentives when users pay for their work. These include copies of a 'full' version of the software with useful extra features, or perhaps a properly printed and bound manual. (Most shareware documentation is supplied as text on a floppy disk.) There may be some kind of irritating regular message or warning that you are using an unregistered copy. Registered versions will not have this.

Some authors take a more extreme approach and release shareware which is all but crippled. For example, an accounts package may allow a maximum of 100 entries, or word-processing software will only work with very small documents. Limitations like these can be irritating, but even a hamstrung version of a package will still give users an idea of whether the package suits their needs.

Many shareware authors are in the US, and payment is often specified in US dollars. It is rare for an author to accept foreign currency or credit card payments directly. Registration can be made difficult if the address given in the documentation is no longer the author's current address. Some authors have tackled this problem by setting up national dealerships which collect registration fees.

As a convenient alternative, many authors are now able to collect payment by credit over the Internet via a payment service. This collects money on behalf of a number of authors, tallies who has been paid what, and passes on individual payments. Often these services are combined with registration. Typically you will be asked to supply your card number, and a registration code – which may also unlock some of the software's features – will be emailed to you. Some full-price software from larger software developers is available using a similar system.

In spite of all the bad publicity, these payment services are usually at least as safe as using a credit card to make a telephone payment. As with more conventional payments, it's impossible to guarantee that your card details will remain absolutely safe. It's worth noting, though, that any fraudulent activity is paid for by the payment service rather than the card company, and so these services have a strong incentive to make sure that payments remain secure.

There are three main sources of shareware: bulletin boards, the Internet (see Appendix VIII) and public shareware libraries. The Internet is now the most popular source, simply because the range of available shareware is huge – almost every shareware product that has ever been available can be found there. Collections such as Shareware.com (*www.shareware.com*) include search facilities, so that shareware for a specific task and specific kind of computer system can easily be found. Many magazines now include a small selection of popular shareware copied from the Internet on their monthly free cover disks.

Bulletin boards and shareware libraries have been eclipsed by the rise of the Net as a medium for shareware distribution, but still offer a valuable resource for anyone who wants to investigate what kinds of shareware are available, but does not want or need a full Internet connection. Shareware libraries act as clearing houses, cataloguing and supplying shareware for the cost of a small copying fee. Apart from shareware, they now also provide a range of information copied from the Internet and supplied as CD-ROMs. One example is the *Libris Brittaniae* series sold by most libraries, which offers summaries of information and shareware relevant to electronics, maths, scientific developments, and so on. The same information is available on the Net, but buying it on CD-ROM is often more convenient than having to find it oneself. Note that the content of these CD-ROMs is rather less rigorous and more patchy than that available from textbooks and more formal sources. In spite of this, some of these products offer a fascinating, if perhaps slightly eccentric, overview of a field, and can be of interest to serious students and dabblers alike.

Freeware

A handful of software titles are freeware. As the name suggests they can be used for free. The author maintains the copyright, but the software can be legally copied and used by anyone. (Strictly speaking, only freeware should be called public domain software, as only freeware is genuinely free of copyright charges, and hence truly in the public domain. However, the words are traditionally applied to shareware as well.)

Freeware tends to be written by hobbyists or enthusiasts and is unlikely to offer much to the less experienced user. For example, the POVRAY2 computer graphics package can produce very impressive photo-realistic images and animations, but demands a high degree of technical knowledge.

Related to the freeware idea is the open-source software concept. Here, not only is the software free, but the details used to create it – known as the source code – are also freely available. From the average user's point of view, this is of only passing interest. But small businesses may find that combining an open-source product with some customisation work by a paid programmer offers a cheaper and more reliable alternative than a bespoke software project.

To date, the most significant open-source product is the Linux operating system, which is attempting to create an alternative to the Windows system installed as standard on most home and business computers (see page 247).

Custom software

Unless your needs are very unusual, you should be able to find a software package off the shelf or a standard package that can be adapted to suit your requirements.

If you cannot find one, you have the option of commissioning a programmer to create some custom software. However, this is not to be undertaken lightly. It is an expensive option: a good programmer can charge in excess of £1,000 a week. It can also be a lengthy option. You may be lucky and come across a programmer who gets the job done in time, but this often proves impossible, for any number of reasons, and so it is wise to allow yourself a generous schedule and an equally generous budget.

Software writing is still as much an art as a science, and for many reasons a project can go over time and over budget. It is advisable to negotiate a fixed-rate contract, with an initial payment, a stage payment when the first version is completed and a final payment when everything has been tested thoroughly. The final stage – known as 'bug fixing' – will take the longest. Getting a piece of software 90 per cent right is comparatively easy; getting it 99.9 per cent right sorts out the professionals from the cowboys.

To find a programmer, look in *Yellow Pages* and the classified ads of computer magazines. Your local training and enterprise council (TEC) or business centre may also be able to make suggestions. Follow the same criteria you would use to find a consultant (see Chapter 2). Previous experience is particularly important here. The most appropriate programmer for a project will have done one or more very similar jobs in the recent past and will be able to offer references.

Deciding what you want

Choose your software first and then find the hardware. This rule of thumb bears repetition. It is far more important to choose the right software than the right hardware, as most reasonably priced hardware today can handle anything needed to run an office. If you work on this principle you are almost certain to get a smooth-running, efficient system that does what you want it to.

When buying a software package, watch for the following:

Ease of use Does the package do what you want in a simple and straightforward way, or do you have to work around its quirks before you get results?

Features Be wary of packages that claim to do everything. Some office-oriented software packages now come with so many options that a number of the features remain unused. Sometimes a cheap and basic package can be much better value – and prove more useful in everyday terms – than a more upmarket product.

A spreadsheet, for example, is a good general-purpose tool for financial analysis, but if you want something to help with your accounts it may not be the ideal purchase.

Productivity How much more easily and quickly will the software help you get your work done? (This is not quite the same as ease of use.) Some packages are tricky and slow to set up, but once up and running are speedy and efficient. Others are easy to understand, but can seem laboured once you have mastered the basics and are feeling more confident.

The best software includes shortcuts and automation features for commonly repeated tasks. It also has on-line help – a brief summary of the manual within the program itself.

Hardware requirements How much hard disk space does the package take up? How much memory does it need? How fast is it? Here again, modern software packages can be very demanding. A full installation of Microsoft's Office 2000 system – a popular package which includes a word processor, spreadsheet, business presentation generator and database – can take up at least 400Mb of storage space. Competing packages from other major software companies make comparable demands. If you plan to install a number of applications, you will need to be sure that you can afford the hardware to cope with this.

Operating system requirements Within the hardware specification you will find a reference to an operating system. Operating systems are a special kind of software that run your computer. (For further details on operating systems see Appendix III.)

The last two points are particularly important, as they will dictate what kind of hardware you should buy. Together they give you a detailed hardware specification to shop for.

Software buying tips

When buying software you should be very careful to make sure that it does what you want it to – in practice, as well as in theory. The most widely advertised business packages are **office suites**, which include a word processor, a spreadsheet, a database, a business presentation package and also extras such as a personal information manager, or a home accounts program. These may seem appealing at first sight, especially as they are often sold at a discount, but they may not do exactly what you want. If all you want is some simple accounting tools to help with income tax and VAT, and a way of keeping track of your business contacts, you may well get better value from simpler and more specialised software.

CASE HISTORY: Richard

Richard Kent discovered that office suites are not always as useful as they can appear to be.

'I work as a computer and music journalist, and it was becoming obvious that I was losing work because I didn't have a PC. It took me six months of research to find the system I wanted at an affordable price. By then prices had come down as well, which helped.

'I found an office suite package advertised for £175, excluding VAT. This seemed like a very good price, so I phoned the dealer and got him to confirm. He told me it was a "competitive upgrade". I said I didn't even have a PC, never mind any competitive PC software. He told me not to worry – that was all sorted. I gave him my credit card details and ordered the software.

'It arrived a couple of days later. I installed it, and for a long time was very happy. The word processor was much better than anything I was used to, the computer was very fast, and the organiser was – and still is – a godsend.

'But nine months on, I'm beginning to wonder if I got over-excited. The package also included a business presentation creator, a spreadsheet and a database. I deleted all three of these a couple of weeks after I got the package, and I still haven't used them yet. I may reinstall the spreadsheet to do my tax – but then again, I may not.

'I think these packages are designed for medium-sized businesses and corporate users. They are good packages – there's no doubt about that – but for a single person working at home they're not really necessary. I could have done with more help organising my tax returns and my invoices, neither of which I'm very good at, but they didn't help at all there. I'm sure they could, but I can't be bothered to set them up. And it would be easier to buy a proper package for exactly those jobs from somewhere else.

'In general I'd warn people to be cautious of software advertising – especially "free" software. You may be lucky and get exactly what you need, but also you may not. I was lucky in that I got a good deal and didn't really waste any money. If you need a word processor, buy a word processor – and don't get a whole suite unless it's only slightly more expensive, or you know what you are getting, and it really is what you want.'

Upgrade deals

Richard's story illustrates another useful buying tip – the 'upgrade' deal. Some software is quoted with three prices. The first is the official retail price. The second is the 'competitive upgrade' price, which applies if you have a competing software product from another manufacturer. Often the new software checks to see if the competing software is installed, so this approach only works if you can find, or already have, copies of a competing product. Some dealers will supply you with free software that qualifies for the upgrade deal, so you can buy from them at the reduced rate. You may even find a suitable competing product given away free with a magazine.

The third price is the 'version upgrade': if you already own an older copy of the software, you can get a new copy – with improved

---

OFFICE SUITES

Many computers are supplied with an 'office suite', either as part of the package or as an optional extra offered at a discount compared to the prices usually charged in computer stores. As shown in Chapter 1, these suites include a complete set of business tools – a word processor, spreadsheet, address book and, typically, extras such as a presentation manager and a database.

Microsoft Office has become the standard for office suites. Many documents are now prepared using the Word word processor; for formatted text Word has become a *de facto* standard. The latest version of Office, known as Office 2000, makes it possible to exchange documents using the HTML Internet standard, as well as using Microsoft's own proprietary system. This helps to make Office documents easier to share with people who don't use Office. (At the time of writing, a newer product called Office XP is about to be released, which integrates HTML and other Internet-ready tools even more tightly. However further details are not yet available.)

The most sophisticated version of Office is aimed at businesses which need a system where employees can make sales and track contacts on different computers that have been networked together. As well as providing all the usual appointment-management, email and other groupware facilities, it enables sales to be made and tracked automatically on the Internet, and managers can see summaries of

---

features – by paying this price. The numbers and letters after the name of the software are important if you decide on this price level. For example, Word Pro v2.0 means you are buying version 2.0 of the Word Pro program (sometimes the 'v' is left out). The higher the number, the newer the software (thus WordPerfect 6.0 is newer than WordPerfect 5.1). Version numbers are usually included in advertisements. Unfortunately the millennium led to a spate of products with less obvious version names, such as 'Millennium Edition', '2000' and 'XP' To some extent making sense of these is a matter of common sense. If confusion sets in, any dealer should be able to help you.

By shopping around you can pick up one of these older versions at a bargain price and use it as the basis for an upgrade deal. Often you will pay less for the old version plus an upgrade than for the new

business activity at any time. A budget version called 'Works' is sometimes offered as an alternative. This is a simplified version of Office that lacks the more sophisticated features, but is powerful enough for casual home and small business use.

Lotus Corporation (now part of IBM) offers its Smartsuite series in competition. The latest 'Millennium' edition of Smartsuite includes the same general set of tools as Office 2000, but without the most recent Internet-oriented sophistication. Older versions of Smartsuite are sometimes given away free by magazines, and these can be worth looking out for by anyone on a tight budget, or who simply wants a free high-quality word processor. The Millennium edition comes with IBM's ViaVoice speech-recognition system built in.

Corel Corporation's WordPerfect Suite is not as widely available. A completely free version is available for users of the Linux system (see Appendix III). Otherwise, WordPerfect Suite is perhaps most notable for its inclusion of the WordPerfect word processor, which many users find preferable to Microsoft's Word.

Even when supplied 'free', a full office suite may not be a good all-round business solution. For typical home users even the simplest version of Office is likely to be overkill in terms of both price and facilities. Suites use a lot of computer power and storage space, and offer many features which are often left unused, or even undiscovered. When they are bought commercially, prices are relatively high.

package. But you may find that the older version does the job you want and you will not need to upgrade.

Vouchers

With some upgrade deals, however, you may not get the software immediately. Instead, you will be given or sent a voucher that you then pass on to the manufacturer, sometimes with proof of ownership of relevant older or competing software. The software will arrive through the post. This can be irksome if you need to get on with some work quickly.

Before ordering an upgrade of any kind, check to see if there are any vouchers involved, and if so, what the time scale will be. If you are going to have to wait for three weeks, you may want to reconsider your purchase or factor this delay into your schedule.

Academic prices

Software is sometimes sold to students (in practice this means anyone in full-time education, from secondary school age upwards) at a heavily discounted price. Proof of study from a teacher, lecturer, headmaster or other authority is often required. However the very loose criteria used to assess whether or not someone is a student mean that parents can sometimes use this method to obtain low-cost software. In any case, students can find it very worthwhile to inquire whether perhaps academic pricing is available.

Bundles

Another way to get cheap software is to accept a bundle that comes with your computer when you buy it. Many larger hardware dealers include an office suite as a bundle. If you do not want it, you can delete it or choose not to install it, but unless the software is what you want anyway you should be wary of allowing a bundle deal to sway your decision about where to buy.

In practice, some bundles are not quite as good value as they appear.

CASE HISTORY: Ralph

Ralph Harris, a wine and spirits wholesaler, discovered this for himself – but managed not to waste his money.

'I'd been thinking of computerising my operation for a while, and I was asking advice from a friend. After months of checking I'd found a likely-looking deal in a magazine and I wanted to know what he thought. The deal included accounts software for free and a good price for the hardware. There were some other bits and pieces thrown in – a route planner, a couple of games, that kind of thing.

'I was surprised how dismissive he was when I told him about the deal. He told me that most of the software would be pretty useless and that offer deals were put together to shift the software by giving it away.

'All the same, I decided to buy the whole lot. The price was so good that I could add some good software later.

'In fact he was right. The accounts package was terrible, and the games wouldn't even work on my machine. It turned out to have something to do with the way the memory was set up. I phoned the dealer, and he told me I needed something called a memory manager. As I'm not much bothered about games, I decided to leave it.

'But I must say the route planner has been a great toy and very helpful with deliveries. So it wasn't all completely wasted.'

Disks and manuals

If you do decide that a bundle is right for you, check that the disks and manuals are included.

Having a copy of the software on your hard disk is not enough. If something goes wrong and your hard disk loses the programs you have lost your software. You can of course make safety copies of your own, but this can be extremely time-consuming. With manufacturer-supplied master disks this problem can be avoided. The software can be reinstalled, and work can continue as before (assuming that your information has also been backed up regularly). The same applies to the manuals. Although modern software often includes a help feature, this can be sketchy. Access to printed manuals is essential for beginners and for reference.

Most dealers are willing to supply disks and manuals for an extra charge – a typical price might be around £80 for a full set of manuals and disks. Even with this extra cost you may find a bundle can save you money.

Buying over the Internet

It is now possible to buy directly over the Internet. Software can be ordered online and delivered by post. Or it can be can be 'downloaded' (copied) to your computer's hard disk. From there it can be installed in much the same way that software is installed from a CD. Sometimes an access code is sent by email as an additional security feature. Alternatively, the software may be downloaded in a 'demo' (trial) form, and the access code unlocks the full program, as with some shareware.

There are advantages and disadvantages to buying software in this way. The biggest advantage is speed. You can start to use the software as soon as it arrives, and do not have to wait for it to be delivered by post or courier. The biggest disadvantage is the time it takes for the software to be copied over the Internet to your computer. For large programs this can take a few hours. If the connection fails at any point you may find that you need to start again.

Paper manuals are obviously not practical with this approach. Many companies are now supplying manuals (even for some boxed software) in Adobe's PDF format (see page 52), which is designed to be read electronically rather than printed out. This limits you to reading the manuals at your computer, or spending time and money printing them out at your own expense.

Perhaps the biggest issue with direct Internet sales is the cost. On the one hand, you will not be able to haggle or ask for a discount, as the prices are always fixed electronically. However, downloading software from the US means that you do not usually have to pay VAT or customs charges – factors that typically make software sold in the UK more expensive than it would otherwise be. But if you buy boxed software from the US and have it delivered by post, you will be liable for both VAT and import duties. These can add significantly to the price, so this approach is not recommended except for those few situations where software is compellingly cheaper in the US, or cannot be obtained here at all.

Even if buying full packages this way does not appeal to you, Internet buying can be the best, and sometimes the only, way to get newer versions of old software. Many manufacturers provide an 'upgrade version' which adds the latest features to an older piece of software. This is usually much smaller than the full version, and always much cheaper. For some of the less widely used software, upgrade versions are often hard to find in the shops. This makes some experience of Internet buying very useful.

Chapter 10

Choosing the right hardware

From the outside one computer looks very much like another. So why are some computers so much more expensive than others? How can you find the one that best meets your needs?

Several factors influence the selling price of a computer. Some, such as performance, can be measured objectively. Others, such as brand image, offer more elusive (some would say illusory) benefits. But to a beginner or a professional user support stands out as being particularly important.

Features to look out for

The following factors will affect the cost of a computer:

Speed A computer's price is directly related to how quickly it can perform a task. Most office work does not require the fastest machines available; an 'average' machine will be sufficient and the best value for money.

Space for your information There is a limit to the amount of information a computer can store. As a rough guide the more your computer costs, the greater the limit. The limit depends on what you want the computer to do. The whole of this book, for example, takes up less than 1/400th of the total storage space available on the computer on which it was originally written and would take up less than 1/40000th of the space available on a modern machine. Unless you need to keep track of huge amounts of information, have to deal with thousands of clients' records or want to use your computer to work directly with sound or video, then the space available on almost any modern machine will fit your needs.

Room to grow Most computers can be upgraded to offer new facilities and better performance. This is easier to do on some machines than on others. Computer technology is improving all the time, and extras designed for the latest machines may not work with older ones.

Deciding whether or not you will need to upgrade can be difficult. Many new features are bought for fun rather than for good business reasons. Fortunately, you should be able to upgrade any modern machine with ease. Older computers are more problematic, and you should assume that you will not be able to upgrade them. (This is something of a simplification, as often you will be able to add extras — but not as cheaply or easily as you could with a modern machine. In some cases you may end up spending more than a new machine would cost.)

Build quality Some computers are built more solidly than others. Variations — which include better ventilation, more robust and perhaps aesthetically appealing case designs, and internal differences in the electronics — can affect long-term reliability and also the ease with which you can upgrade. Buying from a good dealer should ensure that a machine is solid enough for your needs.

Brand image In theory you should get a better-quality product and better support from a large and established manufacturer than a smaller one. But a computer made by a large company with a famous name will cost more than one made by a small-scale start-up business. The reasons for this are partly historical. Larger computer manufacturers traditionally sold to big businesses, which could afford to pay higher prices. Over the last few years this has changed, but some of the big-name brands — such as Compaq, Dell and IBM — still carry a price premium. Brand image can be a red herring for the unwary buyer. Unless you are impressed by the products and support service of a big-name manufacturer, there is no good reason to go for the extra expense. A big name does not automatically guarantee you a better computer and may sometimes mean you are paying a lot for some fancy lettering on the case. However, it is more likely that a larger manufacturer will remain in business for the lifetime of the computer. And some of the larger companies, notably Dell, do make an effort to provide high-quality support (although effective support remains an area where improvement is possible across the entire industry).

Support The important question to ask here is 'What happens if my computer goes wrong?' You might expect the quality of after-sales service to be reflected in the price. This is not always true. Many buyers have found that they get better service from a small, locally based retailer who also sells hardware at a reasonable price. Small companies are sometimes run by enthusiasts who take the time to build up a good working relationship with their customers. A large company will often treat its customers more impersonally.

It is advisable to find out about a dealer's support service *before* a problem occurs rather than after. Although there are no guarantees of support, you can check a dealer's attitude to support by asking a few questions. Someone who is enthusiastic and helpful will give you much better support and in the long term could prove a much better supplier. Good support is vital, and it is well worth paying a little extra to be sure of it. Some dealers will take the long-term view and provide you with help and advice in the hope that you will buy from them in the future. Others will take your money and send out the goods, but will not offer any more service. However, if you have access to expert help from elsewhere and therefore do not have to rely fully on the dealer, then you can sometimes get bargains from these latter dealers.

What's inside the box?

By choosing your software first and making a note of the specifications required by that software, you are on the way to ensuring that you get a system that will fit your needs.

However, some basic computer knowledge can also be useful. Here is a short introduction to the inside of a computer (more detailed explanations are included in the Appendices, especially Appendix IX).

A computer consists of a main system unit with attached extras such as the keyboard, screen and printer. Inside the main system unit are the parts of the computer that do the actual work. They include:

A motherboard This is the heart of the computer. It holds the processor chip that does the calculations, and also the **RAM** (random access memory) that the processor uses. The processor does all the work, rather like the engine in a car, and the memory works rather like a desk in an office – it is used as a work area, where information can be held temporarily while being worked on.

Hard disk drive (often shortened to **hard drive**, or **hard disk**) This provides fast-access, longer-term storage and is equivalent to a filing cabinet. Information held in the computer's memory is lost when it is turned off, so it has to be saved to the hard disk beforehand. It is loaded from the hard disk when it needs to be used again.

Floppy disk drive This is used to get information into and out of the computer. Software is often supplied as one or more **floppy disks** – small plastic wafers with a metal catch that protects a thin disk of magnetised plastic inside. The plastic holds the information, and the rigid case protects it from finger prints and other hazards.

Memory, hard disk and floppy disk capacities are all measured in **megabytes** (Mb). One megabyte is roughly equivalent to one million letters – including spaces and punctuation marks. You will also come across **kilobyte** (Kb – one-thousandth of a megabyte) and **gigabyte** (Gb – one thousand megabytes, occasionally shortened to 'gig') as units of information capacity. The text of this book – which is approximately 70,000 words – takes up roughly 700Kb. A long letter might take up 3Kb. A large piece of software will need around 40Mb. Typical capacities are between 64Mb and 256Mb for a computer's main memory, 1.44Mb for a floppy disk drive, and 9Gb and upwards for a hard disk drive. Floppy disk drive capacities are more or less standard across all machines but the other figures can vary. Hard disk drive capacities are increasing rapidly.

At the time of writing (Spring 2001) hard disk capacities have begun to fluctuate wildly, with sizes between 10Gb and 40Gb offered as 'standard'. The former is ample for light office use; 10–20Gb should be enough for serious gamers; any more will only be required by those who wish to use their PCs for sound or video editing.

Meanwhile, floppy disks are now technically obsolete, but seem to have retained their grip on the hardware market. None of the available alternatives (see page 225) has become a new standard, although there are signs that CD burners (see below) are now being used for the same kinds of work as floppy disk drives once were.

Extras are either internal and plug straight into **expansion slots** on the motherboard, or external, plugging into **serial parallel, or USB ports** on the back of the machine. Expansion slots provide a direct connection to the computer's internals and allow you to add extra features, such as sound and graphics, by plugging them straight in. Most computers include blanking plates at the back to hide the slots when not in use.

Serial and parallel ports are connectors on the back of the computer and are used to get information into and out of the machine in a less direct way. The printer is usually connected to the parallel port, and the mouse (a small palm-shaped pointing device that is rolled around the desk) is connected to the serial port, a connector called a PS/2 port, or one of the USB ports. (Parallel and serial refer to the way the information flows – either in big chunks or spread out along a single wire.) Modern computers are also supplied with **USB ports** which are designed as a replacement for both serial and parallel ports, and work much more quickly. Some machines also include **IEEE 1394/Firewire** connections, which are currently used to connect video cameras, but in future will be used for a wide range of other extras as well.

Common extras today include:

Soundcard, which allows your computer to record and play back sounds and music. Often a small pair of loudspeakers will come with a soundcard. Less often you will also be supplied with a microphone.

CD-ROM or DVD drive, with which, in combination with a soundcard, the computer can play ordinary music CDs (and videos in the case of DVD drives). More importantly, it can also access information and software that is now also being supplied on a special kind of CD known as a CD-ROM. Examples include the *Oxford English Dictionary*, some encyclopaedias, games and even some business software. CD-ROMs have become popular with manufacturers because they are a good way to supply a lot of information (over 650Mb for CD or 5Gb for DVD) on a single small piece of plastic. They are also ideal for the new breed of multimedia applications which combine text, sound and video.

Since the end of 2000, CD-RW drives (also known as CD burners) have become almost as cheap and widely used as CD-ROM drives. A CD-RW drive can create CDs as well as reading pre-recorded ones. DVD drives have also become ubiquitous, to the extent that modern machines typically have either a CD-RW or a DVD drive, and some more expensive models offer both.

DVD-R drives are also becoming available. These can create a DVD, and can be used to store huge amounts of computer information, or to record home video. Currently these drives are still extremely expensive, and there is some confusion over competing standards. As prices come down, however, they will become standard items, replacing CD technology completely.

Modem, which is used to transfer information along the telephone line to another computer and to connect to the Internet. Most modems can also send and receive faxes and work as an auto-dialler.

IBM or Apple?

There are two kinds of computer that are widely available and they are sold in slightly different ways. Your choice will depend on the software you want to use. Businesses tend to use the common **IBM-compatible standard** (also known as a **PC**). Such machines are designed and built by a huge range of manufacturers and are available from all kinds of outlets, ranging from high-street stores to specialist dealers. The word 'compatible' ('clone' is sometimes used for the same thing) means that all these machines are designed to work to the same specification. Hardware and software that work on one modern machine will work on all of them. (Note that this applies only to new designs. Old software will usually work in new machines, but the reverse is not true.) It is easy to exchange information between different brand names and models.

Users with creative or artistic interests tend to favour computers made by Apple. Apple controls the production and distribution of its machines very strictly. Apart from a brief period in the mid-1990s when it licensed its technology to other manufacturers, Apple's machines are made by Apple itself and sold through a strictly controlled network of dealerships.

In general, Apple machines are much more popular with their users and inspire an almost religious devotion unmatched by other systems. Perhaps this is because Apple-compatible systems – both hardware and software – seem much more colourful and 'human' than their IBM counterparts. Apple hardware also tends to be more appealing aesthetically. However, the IBM market has the advantage of scale. Competition is very fierce within the PC market, and prices can and do fall spectacularly.

For home or light business use there is very little to choose between the two lines. The same kinds of software are widely available on both machines, and it is a case of trying out each brand to see which feels the most comfortable and easy to use.

For more serious and professional use, the markets diverge significantly. Apple machines are used more for applications such as design, and book and magazine publishing. Both the hardware and the software tend to be geared towards these areas of use. IBM machines are used for everything else. Equivalent 'creative' software is available, but powerful IBM machines tend to be used more for business-oriented applications. Prices diverge at this level too, with Apple machines becoming approximately half as expensive again as equivalently powerful IBM models – although this does not become a factor until the very top-line models in each range are compared. Apple machines tend to hold their resale value slightly better.

How much can you expect to pay?

Even with the pace of technological development, computer prices have stabilised into price bands, from second-hand 'antique' to showroom-new. (Note that these are prices for the main hardware only: the main system unit, the keyboard, the screen and an operating system. You will need to allow for software, support, maintenance and other extras such as a printer before you can estimate the total system price.)

Vintage – between £50 and £100

These machines are more or less obsolete and are only available second-hand. They cannot be upgraded to offer new features, they work very slowly and many cannot work with modern software at all. For tasks such as basic word processing, however, they can fit the bill perfectly. Many are still being used successfully ten years after they were purchased.

Dated – between £100 and £250

Although almost obsolete, these machines are still viable for light-duty work such as letter-writing and basic accounts. They are significantly more powerful than vintage machines, but not powerful enough to work with the very latest software. There are severe restrictions on how easily they can be upgraded, so they should be bought on a 'what you see is what you get' basis, rather than with an eye to future possibilities. Many of these machines are still used in offices today, although they are now available only on the second-hand market.

Recent – between £250 and £500

These machines are at the trailing edge of recent developments and are still available new. They can be upgraded but there will be limits to what they can do. They will work with the latest software, albeit very slowly. They offer a good deal for medium-duty work such as simple spreadsheets and payroll calculations for a small company.

Because Apple has such a tight grip on its market, Apple computers do not appear in this price bracket. When older models become obsolete Apple simply replaces them with newer and more powerful designs; only very rarely are these older machines sold off as 'bargains'.

Entry level – between £500 and £750

These are the cheapest of the modern machines. They will work with all the latest software. It is possible, but not certain, that you will be able to upgrade them to work with the very latest extras.

Although much faster and more powerful than older machines, they may appear slow when compared to more expensive models. However, this speed difference will only become apparent when you attempt more demanding work. More modest applications will hardly show any difference at all.

Established – between £750 and £1,000

These offer the best price/performance ratio of any computer design. They provide enough speed and power to cope with recent software and can easily be upgraded. If you expect your needs to increase over the next couple of years, you should consider an established machine.

Advanced – between £1,000 and £2,000

These offer more performance than the established designs and are intended for users who require speed. Typical applications include professional-quality DTP, video editing, financial analysis, graphic design and the latest games. Other kinds of work will leave them idling most of the time, and the extra power they can offer will be wasted.

Professional – between £1,500 and £10,000

These models are aimed at business and scientific users and are suitable for supplying the computing needs of an entire office or company. They are not designed for individual users, and hence are beyond the scope of this book. It is sometimes possible to buy a cheaper machine for the same kind of work that these models are used for, although whether or not to go down this path is perhaps best decided in conjunction with a consultant's professional advice.

Desktop vs laptop

You have one more choice to make when deciding on a specification, and that is whether or not to buy a laptop (i.e. portable) computer. The advantages of a laptop are obvious – you can use it anywhere, you can keep your important information with you all the time, and you can even use it to keep in touch with a larger computer at home or at the office. Laptops also tend to be more visually appealing. Some, such as Apple's Powerbook and Sony's Vaio range, have attempted to turn this factor into a major selling point.

There are disadvantages too: cost and security. Laptops tend to be much more expensive than a desktop machine with a similar specification; you can pay £5,000 for a top-of-the-range model, although prices for reasonably powerful machines start at around £1,000. As for ensuring the security of your information, you can install password protection on your portable as an attempt to keep your information safe if it is stolen. But anyone who is computer-literate can work around most password systems fairly quickly. As a number of high-profile news stories have shown, laptops and portables need extra security measures if used to work on very sensitive or valuable information.

Battery life, weight and repair costs are three further considerations. Only the very best laptops offer more than a few hours of useful working time before their batteries need recharging, so their usability in the field is limited. Also, some laptops are quite heavy (the shirt-pocket computer that can replace a desktop machine has not quite arrived yet). Repair costs, once the guarantee has expired, can be crippling, since laptops rarely use the same standardised off-the-shelf parts that desktop machines do. Repairs have to be carried out by a specialist with laptop experience, and spare parts can be expensive and very hard to get hold of.

Some people like the freedom and glamour of a laptop, and if you can see yourself writing letters in bed before breakfast, then a portable will be perfect for you. But for most ordinary office tasks a desktop machine will be cheaper, safer and easier to maintain and to use. (See Appendix VII for more details on portables.)

Upgrades

All recent computers can be upgraded to take advantage of new technology as it becomes more widely available. If you buy a reasonably priced computer – costing around £1,000 or so – you will almost certainly find you have a range of upgrade options to choose from.

When starting out, however, it is prudent to ignore these until you are familiar with your machine and have got the most you can out of it. If you have an older machine you may find yourself under pressure from trade magazines (perhaps even from friends) to bring it up to more modern standards. Think long and hard before you do. If your computer serves all your current needs, there is no reason for you to upgrade. You should only start to think about this seriously if you feel that your machine is annoyingly sluggish at times, or if some new software arrives which could be useful to you but will not work on your machine.

Deciding whether to buy a high-specification model or a low-specification one that can be upgraded later can be a bit like playing the futures market on the Stock Exchange. In general, it can be worth buying a slightly more powerful machine than you need. For office work, however, it is unlikely that a working system will need to be updated more than once every few years at most. This corresponds to the time it takes a generation of computers to move down from the leading edge to obsolescence. It is not usually advantageous to get a cheap machine with a view to upgrading later.

The situation is slightly different for home computers that are used for playing games as well as for work. Surprisingly, perhaps, games are much more demanding of computer power than most office applications. You will find that a computer used for games has a much shorter active life and will also need to be upgraded regularly. If games are a serious interest then consider buying the very best computer you can afford.

Buying step by step

By choosing your software first, you have already decided on the hardware needed to make it work. Most software comes with a minimum, or a typical, hardware specification that is mentioned somewhere on the packaging or in the manual. You can quote this directly to a dealer, even if you do not understand what the words mean. Where possible, choose a 'typical' or 'recommended', rather than a 'minimum', specification, as these will give you the extra power to work comfortably. By following the specifications you will get a computer that does what you want, rather than one the industry wants to sell you. What you choose depends on your requirements. If you foresee your needs expanding, choose a better and more powerful machine than the software specification suggests. If you are looking for a system for basic office work that you can install and forget, ignore the high-pressure sales techniques and follow the specifications.

Once you have a rough specification, you can start contacting a few dealers. The best place to look first is in your local *Yellow Pages*. Quote the specification you need, explain which software you will be using, mention that you are a beginner and will need good support, and see what kind of response you get. If you find someone sympathetic and helpful, ask if they can do a package deal which includes all the software you want.

In any conversation with a dealer, note down the time and date, the name of the person to whom you spoke, and any prices you are quoted. You can leave any further details, such as warranties and extras, for a later call. Make a list of the dealers who seem knowledgeable and approachable, together with their best quoted prices. If you find a dealer who responds positively on the telephone, it is worth making a visit to see how you are treated in person. Do not be surprised if you find yourself in a shoddy-looking shop instead of a stylish showroom; it is the level of enthusiasm, interest and professionalism which is important.

Your next step is to repeat the exercise with dealers from further afield. You will find these advertised in any computer magazine. Buying long-distance has its drawbacks, but finding out the going rate for hardware on a nationwide basis can sometimes give you a good negotiating position with your local dealer.

The advantage of buying from a larger company – such as Dell or Gateway – is that they are more likely to be financially stable and less likely to disappear overnight. The disadvantage is that they will often charge you more for their services.

Smaller dealers will usually offer slightly better prices. Some machines are assembled in garages and bedrooms, advertised in the low-cost trade weeklies and sold by mail order. Others are built by huge companies with multi-million-pound turnovers. Both kinds of dealer use the same sets of parts, which are bought in bulk from wholesale electronic design companies in south-east Asia. The only thing that distinguishes these wares is the level of support the dealers can offer you, and the care and attention the manufacturers give to assembling their machines.

Advertising ploys

Smaller dealers sometimes quote rock-bottom prices, and it is not until you read the small print that you discover that the system is incomplete – a keyboard, screen and mouse are extra. Another tactic is to sell the operating system (Windows) as an 'optional' extra. This can add around £70 to the quoted price. To get around this you should ask if the price you have been quoted includes everything you need to run your software right away. Then, just to be sure, check if there are any 'extras' you need. As usual you should make a note of the replies.

Another marketing tactic is to pepper a specification with emotive words such as 'fast', 'powerful' and 'huge'. Often such words are used to confuse the unwary and hide the fact that the system is no better – and sometimes significantly worse – than average. The more of these words you find in a specification list, the less likely it is that you are dealing with someone you can trust.

Your short list

By now you should have a short list of dealers. You still need to sort out support, maintenance and (perhaps) insurance for your purchase, and you will also need to think about security and protecting your information. These will be discussed in the following chapters.

Chapter 11

Insuring and protecting your computer

Before you buy your computer, you need to be sure that you are protected from the various things that can go wrong. Computers can and do break down. They can also be stolen or damaged. Sometimes the problems are easy to fix, and no harm is done apart from a few hours' delay. At other times the results can be catastrophic, with months or even years of work obliterated in seconds. How can you protect yourself? And what other dangers do you need to take into account?

Warranties

As a first step, it is essential to make sure you get a warranty with your computer. The simplest is the **back-to-base warranty**. Under this scheme your computer will be repaired and defective parts will be replaced if, and only if, you send the computer back to the retailer. You pay the cost of this initial delivery, although the retailer usually pays for the return of your machine.

This is the standard minimum warranty you will be offered. It has very serious limitations if you are planning to rely on your machine for business purposes. First, the warranty is worth nothing unless you can return the machine to where you bought it. If your retailer is not local you can expect to pay between £10 and £15 for a next-day delivery using a courier service.

Second and far more important, this kind of warranty does not usually guarantee how quickly your machine will be repaired. If it needs to be sent back to the manufacturer it may take weeks. If you rely on your computer on a daily basis, this kind of delay can be extremely inconvenient.

Reputable dealers may be willing to provide you with a temporary machine while the repairs are being done. This is a useful option to have, but bear in mind that when your computer goes back to the manufacturer, so does all the information – including the software – you keep on it. Even if you keep safety copies of your work, recreating your working environment on a new machine can take anything from an evening to a few days.

A variation on the back-to-base warranty is known as **collect and return**. Although popular once, it is now becoming increasingly rare. With this warranty you do not have to pay carriage costs. This is a slightly better option, but all the same caveats apply.

Far more useful is the **on-site warranty**. Under this scheme your supplier contracts to send an engineer to you when something goes wrong. Unfortunately, it is still no guarantee that your computer will be repaired immediately.

On-site warranties vary greatly. Sometimes they are available as an optional extra when you buy a machine. You may even get one year's free on-site service as part of the initial purchase deal, and another year or two for an extra fee. However the deal is arranged, check the small print of the service contract. Watch out for the following:

Call-out time and repair time A warranty that guarantees that your computer will be looked at within eight hours of your call is worth much more to you than one that states that it will be looked at within five working days. Very few companies will guarantee a repair time, but this is obviously a highly desirable feature if you come across one.

Charges What exactly does the warranty cover – parts, labour, both or neither? Is there an excess charge for the first part of any costs?

Company reputation Many dealers subcontract their warranties to independent support firms; some of these are reliable and professional, others are cowboys. Try to get the telephone number of the support company from your dealer. Then telephone the support company and ask about their charges, call-out times and references from customers. The quality, tone and efficiency of the answers will indicate the kind of support you can expect. If you like the way the company works, take the opportunity to ask about their services. You may even want to think about taking out a longer-term contract.

Company stability The worst possible situation to find yourself in is with a warranty contract from a company that has gone out of business. This does happen, and the results vary from the inconvenient to the disastrous. You could ask the company directly about its financial stability. Someone in a professional and stable company will understand the need for your question and should be able to reassure you immediately.

Experience and references Does the company know what it is doing? Some firms have been known to claim to maintain certain types of computer, when in fact they have no experience of them at all. If in doubt, ask for references. Experienced and professional companies will be able to provide you with references.

Resources Ask about the company's 'back-room' technical resources and repair facilities. Does it subcontract the work?

Contract Is it possible to see a standard contract in advance? If not – be very wary.

Location The company should be within easy travelling distance or have a local office.

Quality control Is the company certified as complying with the ISO 9000 or older BS5750 quality-control standards? Or is it applying for certification? These impressive-sounding titles guarantee the existence of quality-control procedures, but offer no further assurance that work really is done to high standards. In practice, the certification system seems to be open to potential abuse, and some quality-control professionals are unhappy with the loopholes that exist. It is likely that these standards will be changed soon. In the meantime it is wiser to judge a company's reliability on the other criteria mentioned here.

Service contracts

In many cases now, PCs are being sold with additional service contracts which extend the existing warranty for an additional period, typically an extra year or two. The value of these is problematic, and depends on the reliability of the hardware in question – something that is obviously unknown to most buyers.

Factors to consider when deciding whether or not to pay for an extended warranty include:

Disruption caused by failure If a non-working PC will cause major problems for your business, then the value of the peace of mind offered by a service contract increases. Conversely, a machine occasionally used at home is unlikely to need such a high level of service.

Contract details As with standard warranties, it is important to check exactly what you are paying for. For a business, the only extra warranty worth considering seriously is an on-site one. As before, it is essential to check the call-out time and turn-around time you can expect if something does go wrong.

Repair vs replacement For a business using a number of PCs, it may actually be cheaper to buy a spare machine than to take out a service contract for all of them. It is relatively straightforward to transfer information and settings to an identical machine. (Usually all that needs to be done is to take the hard disk from the dead machine and fit it into the new one – something that should take an experienced technician two hours at the very most.)

Contract repair vs one-off repairs It can be worth checking alternative local sources of repair and comparing prices for piecework with a full formal service contract. A good way to do this is to get a list of prices for standard operations, such as replacing a hard disk, a motherboard, a processor chip, and so on. Very serious faults can usually be fixed quickly by simply replacing a dead part with a new one, and this makes the potential costs easy to estimate. Sporadic faults are more problematic, harder to guesstimate, and much less predictable.

Insurance

An increasingly popular option for some businesses is to take out insurance. This pays for the cost of any repairs and may also help indemnify your business against problems caused by the loss of your computer.

Your existing household insurance may cover your equipment and public liability if you work from home in a small way. But you must tell your insurer that you work from home, or you could find that your cover is invalid. Your insurer is also likely to insist on a special policy once your business equipment rises above a certain value, if your work involves people visiting your home, or if the risk of fire or theft is increased (because you store flammable materials, for example).

Several companies now offer policies specially for people who work at home. Some of these provide you with the equivalent of a maintenance contract – some insurance policies compare favourably with maintenance arrangements, and you should investigate both to give yourself the widest range of options. Others are fully comprehensive policies that cover you against damage by water, fire, theft, and may even include extra funds to allow you to hire a machine while your original computer is being repaired. A number of policies also include options that cover the costs of 'reinstating' data, which can mean recompiling it from the original sources, or paying someone else to do this for you.

Some will even cover you for 'consequential loss', although this is usually an expensive option. This means that if you lose work because your computer is out of action, you will be reimbursed for some or all of your financial losses.

As with any insurance policy, it is a good idea to read the small print to see what conditions you have to fulfil for the policy to be valid. You will normally be charged an excess – typically £50 – if you make any claim. Some policies also stipulate certain security arrangements you need to take to minimise your risks. These vary from making sure that data is safe, by keeping safety copies and checking for viruses, to making your premises as theft-proof as possible – perhaps bolting your computer to your desk. If you work in an 'unsafe' environment, expect to pay extra. Most British policies cover the use of notebook computers in the UK, but if you travel abroad a lot you will usually be asked to pay a higher premium. A useful source of more detailed information about insurance is the free booklet *Insurance Advice for Small Businesses*, available from the Association of British Insurers (see Addresses).

Backups

Even without insurance, you can take steps to make sure that your information is as safe as possible. This is *vital*, especially for business use.

Your first step is to *save your work regularly* on the computer's hard disk. If something happens it will still be there when you turn on the machine again. Some software has an **auto-save feature** which does this automatically.

Once your information is on disk, you need to make copies and keep them somewhere safe. These are known as backups, and are a time-consuming but essential chore.

CASE HISTORY: Simon

Simon Jones is a computer consultant.

'Half of the phone calls I get are from people who have accidentally lost some work on their computer and want me to try to get it back for them. I try, sometimes I succeed, but often I don't. The users may have deleted what they want by mistake, had a faulty hard disk or had their machine stolen. In all these cases their most urgent need is for the data which is now unavailable for whatever reason. If they had taken regular backups this problem would simply not exist.

'I try to drum into them the value of taking regular backups of work. It may seem time-consuming and silly at the time but it will save heartache and bad temper in the long run.'

Floppy disks are ideal for low-volume work. You can simply copy the information from the computer to a floppy disk: 50Mb is about the maximum you can comfortably archive on floppy disks. (This is how the backup copies of this book were maintained – the text fits on to a single 1.44Mb high-density disk.) Most computers come with a free backup utility that packs the information more tightly on to each disk and also automates the process across multiple disks. As a rough guide, you can expect to spend about 20 minutes archiving 50Mb of information. Newer LS120 drives (see page 228) can fit nearly ten times as much information on a single disk, but are also relatively slow.

For higher-volume work, the cheapest options are the various **tape cassette** systems now available. These can store varying amounts of information – 1Gb, 3.2Gb and 4Gb are typical sizes. The units are fairly cheap – around about £200 for a 4Gb system. They are slow but, unlike a floppy-disk-based system, you can leave them running overnight unattended. The cassettes themselves are also cheap – around £20 for a 4Gb cassette.

Tape cassettes do not have a reputation for reliability. Where possible you should verify information after you have backed it up to confirm that it has been recorded accurately. Backup software is usually supplied with the tape streamer. You should make sure that it includes a 'verify' option.

Many cassette systems offer a 'compressed' option which attempts to squeeze even more information on to a tape: for example, a 4Gb tape can hold around 8Gb of compressed information. Where possible use the uncompressed option – again because it is more reliable.

DAT (digital audio tape) systems are more reliable, but also much more expensive. DAT is suitable for serious professional and business use. At the time of writing DAT systems cost around £800, and offer 24Gb of storage – ample for most situations. The system also uses tape cartridges, but these are much smaller – around half the size of an audio cassette – and much more robust. A DAT system is recommended if you need a 'bulletproof' backup system. DAT backups are also very much faster than other tape systems. An 8Gb backup can be done in as little as 20 minutes, as opposed to an hour or more.

Tape-based systems suffer from the disadvantage of being linear – the information is arranged in order along the tape. If you want to restore some information that is at the end of the tape, you have to wait for the tape to wind to the right position. A tape system is recommended if you do full backups of everything on a regular basis, which you should do at least once a month, ideally once a week. It is also possible to do incremental backups. These only backup the information that has changed since the last full backup. This should be done daily.

Tape backup systems also suffer from more subtle drawbacks. Tape wear can be a problem if you use the system regularly, and this can lead to wasted time if you regularly have to back up the backups to prevent information loss. Another problem is print-through – information tends to leach to adjacent loops of tape when the tape is tightly wound. In large organisations which maintain huge tape archives, these are regularly unwound and retensioned to minimise this problem.

153

One final backup option is **CD-R** – you create a CD with your own information written on it. These special writable CDs are as reliable and robust as any other CD and offer a high capacity – around 650Mb. Disk blanks cost around 50p – much less in bulk. At between £100 and £200 this is now a very affordable option, and also offers the additional advantage of allowing users to create their own music CDs for use in the car or on the hi-fi. CD-RWs (see page 139) can also be used for short-term back-ups. These are more fragile, less long-lived and more expensive than CD-Rs but can be used for a temporary backup while working on a project; the information can then be archived permanently to CD-R when the work is completed.

Other systems

A number of other products are very affordable and work very much like floppy disks, but have greater storage capacities. The most popular are the Iomega **Zip** and **Jaz** drives. These are discussed in more detail in Appendix II.

Software backups

As well as keeping your information safe, it is a very good idea to make safety copies of the software you use. If it was supplied on floppy disks, you should make copies and never use the originals. You will need between 50 and 100 floppy disks to make a backup of a typical full set of business software. Although it is a tedious chore, the advantages of this single task outweigh the disadvantages. If your hard disk loses its information and your software originals have become defective, you will have to buy the software again – even if it is one disk out of ten that is at fault. Making safety copies can save you time and temper later.

Storing backups

All backup copies should be stored somewhere safe and secure. The ideal is a fireproof safe, or perhaps – if the information is sensitive as well as valuable – a bank safety-deposit box. A cheaper option is simply to keep safety copies somewhere off the premises – perhaps at home, or at a friend's or relative's house. If your business is burgled or burns down, your safety copies are intact.

As a further aid to security you may want to encrypt your work before you back it up. This will make your information look like gibberish – even to the trained eye – and can give you near-perfect security. The most secure encryption software available today is a shareware package called PGP (see page 89). PGP is available from most shareware libraries. It is slightly awkward to use, but provides near-perfect security.

Uninterruptible power supplies

While the UK National Grid is usually solid and reliable, under extreme conditions, or in remote rural areas, the power supply to your computer can become erratic, and this can cause problems. In extreme cases a lightning strike or other power surge can actually damage your hardware.

A **UPS (Uninterruptible Power Supply)** solves these problems. It smoothes out fluctuations in the mains power level so that your computer always receives clean, steady power. UPS units also offer a short-term backup power source. In the event of a power cut your computer will remain on for a few minutes; this will allow you to shut down the system in a controlled way without losing any work. More expensive models will perform a controlled shutdown automatically.

Although UPSs are not cheap – prices range from a hundred pounds or so to thousands for 'industrial-strength' models – they are recommended if you use your computer for 'mission critical' applications. UPS systems are available from all the larger computer mail-order companies.

If you use a modem, another useful extra is the **line surge protector**. Every year a handful of computers are frazzled by lightning strikes coming in directly over a telephone line. (The risk may seem negligible, but one insurance company reported over 20 lightning-based claims a year.) BT wall sockets include basic surge protection but are not designed to cope with a direct strike. Fitting a surge protector can ensure that your computer stands a good chance of surviving a strike. While stand-alone protectors are usually only available from electronics specialists, many high-street stores and mail-order companies sell computer-ready mains extension blocks that include a built-in phone-line surge protector, and perhaps also protection for a TV aerial connection (a name to watch for here is Belkin). These blocks also include simple mains protection which can filter out power spikes and short surges, and are well worth considering as a relatively cheap but effective piece of computer protection.

Chip coolers

A very useful – and recommended – hardware protection device is the **chip cooler**. This is a small metal radiator (known as a **heat sink**) that clips on to the computer's main processor chip and conducts heat away before it can do any damage. More recent examples include a built-in fan to cool the chip even further. Chip coolers come as standard on Pentium II, Pentium III, Celeron, AMD K6-II, AMD Duron and AMD Athlon computers.

Viruses

Computer viruses come in two types. Most are simple, small programs that hide among useful information and copy themselves into your computer. They can then copy themselves onto any floppy disks or even home-recorded CDs that you make. If you swap information with a colleague or friend, his or her computer will also be 'infected'. Software copied from the Internet can also include this kind of virus.

A different kind of virus is the *macro virus*. This takes advantage of the automation features in an office suite – most often Microsoft's Office, as this is the most widely used suite. A good example is the Melissa virus, which infected many Internet users in 1999. This copied itself by searching through a user's address book in Outlook Express and then creating a new set of email messages, which it then sent out automatically. Recipients found an official-looking email in their inbox. When they read it, the process started again.

Many viruses are harmless. Some are little more than elaborate practical jokes. However many can be very destructive. The worst a macro virus is capable of is wiping all the information on a hard disk, or bringing a company's mail system to a standstill until it is eliminated. Non-macro viruses can be even more destructive. The CIH/Chernobyl virus, which activates itself on 26 April every year (the anniversary of Chernobyl – some variants activate on the 26th of every month) not only wipes all the information on the hard disk but also attempts to wipe the computer's BIOS as well (see page 194). If it succeeds, the only way to restart the computer is to have a new motherboard fitted. Without virus-checking tools it is impossible to tell whether or not your computer is infected or to do anything about it. Fortunately these tools are readily available, easy to use and affordable.

It used to be the case that software sent over the Internet could contain a virus, while text, graphics and other kinds of messages were safe. Various games and novelty software were typically used to spread viruses, and the problems caused by these could easily be avoided by using a virus checker on the software before it was started. As a rule of thumb, if a message contains an 'attachment' – i.e. isn't simple, straightforward text – then it may harbour a virus. All attachments sent from strangers should be treated with suspicion, and – if possible – deleted without being read. This will prevent infection by viruses such as 'I love you' and 'Melissa', both of which caused literally millions of pounds worth of damage to businesses because this simple precaution wasn't followed.

However, it is also possible to create viruses which exploit a loophole within the Windows system. These can be spread through any email message that is sent as formatted text (for example, prepared using Microsoft's Word, or created using a web page editor.) Fortunately a virus that uses this approach hasn't caused any major damage yet – though, realistically, it is only a matter of time before someone creates one that does.

Of course it is impossible to check whether text is formatted before reading a message. The best defence against these viruses is again to treat messages from strangers with suspicion, and to keep track of the latest developments in virus-checking software. An alternative is to use email software that doesn't include the 'Microsoft viewer', or is set up to treat formatted messages as ordinary text. The disadvantage of this approach is that it will render many messages hard to read; unfortunately, though, better security is very difficult to achieve.

If you need to work with other people's floppy disks, **anti-virus software** is recommended. This removes existing viruses and keeps new viruses out of your machine. Anti-virus packages respond only to viruses that have already been isolated and analysed. New viruses are being created all the time, although most infections are caused by a small number of well-established viruses. Many packages now include a subscription option that will keep you safe from the latest examples.

McAfee and Norton are two names to watch for in magazines. Free virus-checkers are available for download from the Internet. These are unlikely to be completely up to date, but will be able to protect you from the most common virus attacks. Trend Micro also offers a completely free Internet-based scanning service. For more details see *http://housecall.antivirus.com/housecall/start_corp.asp*.

Computer security systems

If you work with other people, you may need to make sure that your private information remains private. Short of encrypting information (for example, using the PGP system mentioned earlier), there is very little you can do to prevent a computer expert from gaining access to your computer. Desktop computers simply are not secure, and most security systems have loopholes.

On PCs, the most secure option you have is to use a **BIOS password**, which you type in when the machine is starting up. This can only be changed by opening the case and short-circuiting or removing the battery on the main computer board. There is no easier way to change it if you forget it. Unfortunately not all PCs have this option. Check with your dealer if security is important to you.

For less secure applications, you can use a **screensaver password**. Most screensavers include a password feature that locks your machine so it cannot be accessed if you leave your desk. (A BIOS password offers protection only while the machine is starting up. Once it is running there is nothing to prevent anyone getting access to your records.) Password protection is perhaps the most useful feature of a screensaver. The protection can easily be 'hacked' by an expert, but it will deter casual users from trying to access your machine.

Many networks include reliable security features, most of which are password-based. If you forget your password, your network supervisor will be able to create a new one for you.

All password systems can be fallible if the password is obvious, or obviously visible. Never use a password that can be guessed easily – such as the names of friends, children or spouses, or words associated with your hobbies. PIN numbers are another bad choice. The best passwords are nonsense combinations of words and letters which are all but unguessable.

Avoid typing in your password if anyone is standing close by. Never write a password down, but if you have to, don't keep it anywhere near the computer itself. It is traditional in some businesses to keep passwords on sticky notes under the desk or in a drawer or as a note in an address book. Avoid all of these options. Finally, make sure you change your password regularly – at least once a month, preferably once a week, perhaps even once a day if security is very important to you.

Some security systems are hardware-based. The most common of these is the **floppy disk lock,** a disk-sized square of plastic that can be locked into the floppy disk slot with a key. Disk locks are a good way to avoid viruses and unauthorised copying of software, but they will not protect you against unauthorised access to your computer.

Many insurance companies will ask you to improve security before they will agree to give you a policy. They will consider loss-of-earnings policies for home and business users, but may start to insist you secure your premises. The theft losses have been quite staggering. Some insurers used to do a flat rate, but now are including location-based payments. Premiums can vary by as much as 400 per cent between safe and high-risk areas.

Personal firewalls

It is shockingly easy for outsiders to connect to a computer that uses the Windows system and is linked to the Internet. Although it's rare for ordinary individuals to specifically attract the attention of nefarious electronic outsiders, would-be hackers can use Internet scanning software to find vulnerable computers. (According to a presentation given at a computer crime convention in 2001, it takes about 8 hours for a new and vulnerable computer to be spotted by hackers) Once a computer has been targeted, a hacker can easily read all the information inside it. On a business network, a hacker can do far more damage, perhaps using computers on the network as a base for further criminal activity.

A firewall is a piece of software that attempts to minimise this risk. It acts as a filter between a computer and the rest of the Internet, only allowing authorised accesses. Good firewall software is relatively cheap – between £30 and £90 – but current offerings typically require some technical knowledge to set up correctly. And a business network may need to hire outside help to make sure that the firewall is installed and working properly.

Names to watch for include Norton's Personal Firewall, Black ICE Defender, and Zone Alarm (the last being a popular and highly rated free program available on the Internet). This is a fast-moving field, and the best way to keep track of current developments is to use the Internet. A search for 'intrusion detection' or any of the names listed above will produce a long list of relevant information, product suggestions and locations from which software can be copied or bought.

Computer theft

Preventive measures

A senior crime prevention officer with first-hand experience of computer crime advises on how to prevent it.

'I'd look for a good standard of security generally. The first step is to keep the burglars out. That means curtains and blinds to hide the equipment so it can't be seen from outside, as well as good locks.

'Internal security is important. Who's doing the cleaning, for example. If it's contracted out, who are the contractors using? Are they secure, or are they likely to leave the key with someone? Laptops are another problem. Some thieves just walk in in broad daylight and help themselves to anything that isn't watched or secured.

'Once the burglar is in the building the alarm system means he needs to work fast. We [the police] can get to an alarm in under ten minutes, but it's important that the keyholder is on hand to let us in – sometimes this can take an hour or more, by which time it's too late to do anything. If the criminals can get in without an alarm, they'll spend all night taking things apart. Now that lock-down plates are common, some gangs are taking computers apart and just stealing the chips.

'Property marking is another useful deterrent. It makes it harder to resell things. Big organisations such as health and education authorities are going down the route of overtly marking everything very clearly. It's easy to change the case on a PC so it's not so important there, but with Macs it's harder and marking is more of a deterrent.

'For software and work, backups are essential. I've known some businesses that folded when they lost everything because they didn't protect their work. Boxed sets with the original packaging are very appealing to thieves. They can be sold at car boot sales, so I'd suggest people take the software out of the nice boxes and throw them away.

'If you take serial and model numbers, get rid of attractive packaging, anchor the hardware, reinforce the doors, put in an alarm and make regular backups, you're as safe as you can be. But we still like to go to individual premises, so I'd suggest people call in their crime prevention officer – the advice is free – preferably before it happens.'

CASE HISTORY: Josh

Josh Brown is director of a desktop publishing bureau. He has been a victim of computer crime several times.

'It started in 1993. We got in one morning and all our Macs had gone – over £75,000 worth of equipment vanished overnight. It was a complete and utter disaster. The thieves took all our backup systems as well as the main machines. Most people had left backup cartridges in their drives, so we lost the lot.

'That almost killed the business. We lost a lot of work, a lot of goodwill, and it took a long time before our insurers came up with a cheque. Fortunately, we were covered for consequential losses. Otherwise that would have been it.

'We took advice from our insurers when we replaced the machines. As a result we put stronger locks on the doors and fitted an alarm system. But these gangs are professional, and three months later we were hit again. They broke in through the first-floor windows, ignored the alarm and took everything again. However, by then we were keeping backups and had taken to leaving them somewhere safe each night.

'Now we have bars on the windows, all the locks and the doors have been specially strengthened, and our Macs have been bolted to the desks with lock-down plates. I looked at having the desks reinforced as well, but it turned out to be too expensive.

'We've had no problems since, but it's been a complete pain to live with. Maintenance takes forever now, as we have to pull the machines apart on the spot before we can take them anywhere. And, of course, you can't just pick up a computer and move it now. You have to unbolt it first. Everyone hates it, and I don't blame them. But it's either that or the risk of losing everything all over again.'

Chapter 12

Buying a computer – the small print

The bulk of the cost of your computer system will come from your initial investment in hardware and software. By telephoning around and asking for quotes you should already have an idea of what these are likely to be, but there are other costs you also need to consider. The most important ones are:

Electricity How much power will your computer draw? Exact figures depend on the make and model involved, but typically you can expect the following:

Computer unit	200W
Monitor	80W
Laser printer	70W
Total	350W

This is roughly equivalent to keeping six 60W light bulbs lit. A rough calculation shows that this adds between £10 and £15 a quarter to your bill, assuming an average use of around six hours a day.

Consumables If you are considering a laser printer, make sure you find out how many pages it prints before it needs new supplies. Then estimate how many pages you are likely to print. To get a realistic idea of how many you will print, double this number – at least. This allows for mistakes and misprints. Also check consumable costs. Although ink-jet printers are cheaper, if you are printing in bulk the laser is typically one-third the cost of the ink-jet (comparing ink with toner). (See Appendix II for more details on printers.)

You will also need to budget for consumables for backups. Prices vary from around 50p for CD-R blanks bought in bulk to around £20 for multi-gigabyte tape cartridges. If you know in advance roughly what your backup needs are, buying in bulk is usually cheaper. Computer stores and mail-order houses typically offer better deals than office-supply companies.

Maintenance, training and support costs How much is your maintenance cover going to cost? How much do you expect to pay for support? At the very least, you should allow for the purchase of books and magazines to help you get the best from your investment. At the other end of the scale you may opt for access to a full technical support line and a few training courses. These costs should be included in your budget before you buy.

Insurance Are you going to insure your machine? Will your policy cover you for a replacement if it is damaged or stolen, and will you also insure yourself against loss of business if your computer becomes unavailable for any reason? You need to decide on just how vital your computer will be to your business, and how much you can afford to be without it – as well as how much you can afford to pay to cover yourself against this.

VAT and delivery charges The prices of most computer equipment are quoted without VAT, so allow for this in your cash flow if you are VAT-registered, or simply write off the extra if you are not. You will probably also have to pay for the delivery of your system. This can add another £20–£50 to the quoted price.

Telephone charges If you are buying any of the pay-as-you-go rather than fixed-rate on-line services, allow for their charges, and also for increased telephone-line use. Bills of over £100 a month are not unheard of, but can usually be reduced with careful planning.

First, since 1997 there has been a price war between BT, NTL and a small number of other telecommunications companies, so it is worth investigating their special offers.

Second, try to use the service during off-peak hours. It is possible to set up a system so that the computer sends and receives mail and picks up news automatically during the early hours of the morning. Unless you need access to mail immediately, it's worth waiting till after the 6pm watershed.

And, third, if you are expecting to spend a lot of time on-line, make sure you get the fastest modem you can. This can halve your costs and is well worth the small extra initial outlay.

Do not underestimate the cost of consumables and other extras.

CASE HISTORY: Colin

Colin Taylor runs a poster and card shop. He tried to expand his business to offer desktop publishing and design services.

'Doing the work was the easy part. We were getting plenty of casual trade from local businesses. The problem was, it was costing much more to run than I thought. After about six months it became obvious just how expensive our laser printer was. For starters we were getting through reams and reams of paper. What you get on the screen always looks slightly different when printed out. Some clients were very fussy, and it was taking ten or twelve printouts before they were happy.

'But it was the other costs that really surprised me. We were getting through a toner cartridge – at £100 a time – every few months. And after a year the drum needed replacing. I worked out that after two years we'd paid out more for the extras than the printer itself. Another big expense was backups. Desktop publishing needs lots of space, and a cheap backup system wasn't enough. We invested in an external tape drive and started to run a proper backup and archiving system. It's worth it for the business, because customers can come back to us for minor changes. We can put a new date on a poster without starting from scratch.

'And then there's security. We're insured against theft, and that's not cheap. We can't afford a loss-of-business policy – they're just too expensive – so we're only insured on the basis of like-for-like. If we lose the machines, we get new ones.

'By the time you add it all up, we're spending well over £1,000 a year on extras. If I was starting again I'd look more closely at the price of extras before committing myself. With printers in particular, it's worth finding out how much the consumables cost and how many pages they're good for.'

Renting or buying?

You have three options:

- an outright purchase
- purchasing with a loan or other finance
- renting.

Each of these options will affect your cash flow and tax position.

Buying a computer can represent a sizeable investment for a small business, and buying one outright can jeopardise cash flow. However, you can claim this money back against tax as a 'writing-down allowance'. Originally writing-down allowances were spread over four years, but following the 2000 budget small businesses that invest in information and communication technology equipment (computers, software and Internet-enabled mobile phones) over the three years from 1 April 2000 will be able to claim 100 per cent first-year capital allowances, thereby getting immediate relief on the whole cost of their investment.

Computers can also be classified as 'short-life goods' with a separate writing-down allowance. If you sell your computer, you are allowed to offset the loss against tax, instead of being taxed on the income from the sale. Because computer equipment depreciates so quickly, this can make a significant difference to your tax liability, to the extent that the sale of an obsolete computer at nominal cost can sometimes be very worthwhile indeed.

Purchasing with finance can be a better deal, at least as far as short-term cash flow goes. You will usually need to put up some of the money yourself – banks and loan companies are not keen on 100 per cent loans, unless you are borrowing a lot less than you can afford – but you will be able to spread the cost over a much longer period. If the computer brings in extra work and improved profits, this can be an excellent investment.

Interest payments are also tax-deductible, so in effect you have the loan partly 'for free'. The capital value of the computer is depreciated in the usual way, and on top of this you simply add the interest from any payments you are making.

Renting is similar, with one important difference. *All* payments are immediately deductible as a direct business expense. Many renting schemes provide the option of buying the machine outright at the end of a set period – usually three or four years. The sums charged are nominal, and at the end of the rental period it is highly possible that the computer is still adequate for your needs. An outright purchase can be a sensible option at this point. Rental payments have been written off against tax, so with a single modest payment you can purchase the computer. This final payment can also be claimed as a capital allowance.

One disadvantage of renting is that it can be much more expensive. It is advisable to avoid short-term rentals unless you need the equipment desperately. Most business rental schemes work out significantly more expensive than an equivalent loan repayment system. However, the rental scheme covers you against equipment failure and other problems, and when you include these extra factors in the equation a renting deal can become more appealing.

As ever, you should read the small print in the rental contract to check the nature of the support that is offered. If it meets your needs and is still cheaper than an equivalent outright purchase, then renting is more advantageous for you than buying.

Renting seems to have become a fairly rare option. Computer magazines occasionally carry advertisements for rental computers, and a small number of high-street stores currently operate rental schemes.

While renting hardware may be a good idea, renting software usually is not. Over the course of a few years you may end up paying two or three times more to rent software than to buy it outright. Some package deals include software at a good price, and some companies ask for extra payment for software. In the latter case, it is worth shopping around to compare the price of buying the software.

Painless buying in detail

Now is the time to talk to each retailer in turn and check the other services they offer, particularly technical support, warranties, money-back guarantees, delivery charges and delivery times. Confirm the quoted price. Make sure you get a price that includes VAT.

If you are buying everything, including the software and a printer, from one supplier it can be worth trying to negotiate a lower price for the package. If the retailer is local, and you can collect the goods in person, it can also be worth negotiating a price for cash. Some retailers, especially the smaller ones, prefer to take cash, as it avoids cheque charges.

Don't be afraid to haggle! If your retailer refuses to reduce the price, try asking for essential extras (such as a couple of packets of floppy disks or a printer cable) to be thrown in for free. These are often low-margin items for retailers, and they can comfortably afford to give them away in small quantities. At worst you will get a refusal. At best you can save yourself some money.

Smaller retailers may well ask you what the best price you heard elsewhere was. Some would rather have your business, even with wafer-thin margins, than lose your custom to a competitor. It is important to be honest here, because if you quote an unrealistic price the next question will often be '...And did they say they had them in stock and ready to go?'

Be wary of high-pressure 'special offer' deals. Some larger retailers will attempt to use sale techniques to close a sale, by implying that the offer will only be available for a limited period. Although very, very occasionally you may miss a genuine bargain, the general trend in the computer trade is for more power at a lower price – even six months can make a big difference. Unless you really want to order right away and have already decided on a particular retailer, then it is prudent to deflect the salesmanship and say that you will think about it.

If you are a complete beginner, ask whether you will be sent any instructions on how to connect up your system before you place an order. A typical PC comes with five or six different items that need to be linked together, and it is not always obvious how this should be done. More thoughtful dealers include an instruction sheet or will be happy to talk you through the process over the phone. Remember to ask about this before you commit yourself to buying, as this kind of small extra can save you a lot of time later.

Confirm your order in writing, either through the post or by faxing it. For those buying by mail order, many magazines offer pre-printed order forms that you can cut out and fill in, and then send or fax to your retailer as appropriate. *It is important to keep a copy of this document*, which is your proof that you purchased an item via the magazine. If your supplier goes out of business before your order is fulfilled and the magazine subscribes to the MOPS (Mail Order Protection Scheme) the magazine is then liable under MOPS to make up your losses (see box).

If you need to have your order fulfilled quickly and have already discussed this with the retailer, make a note to that effect across the order – the suggested wording is 'to be delivered on (insert date here) as discussed with (insert salesperson's name here). Time is of the essence in this contract'. If there are any problems, and delivery is delayed, this wording gives you the option of cancelling the contract.

The preferred method of payment is by credit card. If the retailer goes out of business the credit card company is liable for your loss, as

JUST WHAT CAN YOU EXPECT FROM MOPS?

In theory, MOPS should protect you if a retailer ceases trading. In practice, however, most magazines limit themselves to a fairly low ceiling on compensation payments: £30,000 for any given retailer, and up to £100,000 in any given year.

Realistically, therefore, MOPS is best thought of as a last resort. Your first line of attack should always be to take up the claim with the company's receiver, and then with your credit card company. If you are paying for your purchase with a loan or with extended credit, you may also find that you are insured against non-delivery of the goods. The details will be in the small print of your agreement. If this is the case you will also need to register a claim with your loan or credit supplier.

MOPS awards are *discretionary*, which means that there is no legal and binding obligation on the part of the magazine to pay you more than it thinks is reasonable. A large computer retailer may receive hundreds of orders a day, and may be trading on the verge of bankruptcy for weeks, or even months. A payout of a few tens of thousands of pounds will not amount to much if it has to be split between thousands of buyers. Although you may be lucky, especially if you are dealing with a small retailer, the harsh truth is that it is unwise to expect more from MOPS than a token compensation payment.

long as the cash price of the individual item you are buying is more than £100. (There are exceptions to this rule: corporate credit cards and purchases made by anyone other than the named card-holder will not be covered by the credit card company.) Transactions with companies registered overseas should also be covered. In general, this method of payment should give you effective protection against a supplier going out of business or not fulfilling your order for any other reason.

If paying by credit card, make sure that you will not be charged until the goods are despatched. It is not unheard of for companies to take an order for goods that are out of stock, take the money immediately and then fulfil the order a month or two later when the goods arrive in their warehouse.

Also check whether a credit-card surcharge will be added to your bill. Many smaller suppliers (and even a few larger ones) do this to offset the commission they have to pay the card company for each card-based transaction. Make sure you know where your supplier stands on this before telling it your card number.

Most retailers also now accept debit cards (for example Switch, Delta). These give you *no protection at all*. Beware – some retailers will try to surcharge on these as well. Debit cards are not liable to the same surcharges as credit cards, they do not offer you the same degree of protection, and they cost the retailer a fixed transaction fee, exactly like a normal cheque. If you have to pay by debit card (and this is not recommended unless you have no other option), make sure that you get an assurance that a credit surcharge will not be added to the bill. You may need to argue this point strongly. If your retailer insists on applying the surcharge, go elsewhere.

If your retailer is local, you may prefer to pay by cash and pick up the goods yourself. This could save you the delivery charge (usually not more than £20 or so) and may give you the option of negotiating a better price. Not all retailers accept personal calls, and not all prefer cash sales.

If you decide to collect the goods yourself, ask if you can see your system working before you take it away. Apart from peace of mind, this also gives you a chance to see for yourself how to connect up the different parts of your computer – for a beginner this can be a major confidence booster. It is also a chance to ask the support staff any simple technical questions.

Unfortunately only smaller retailers are able to provide this level of personal service. Some, although not all, larger companies tend to keep their sales and delivery teams well apart from their engineering and support staff. If you are dealing with one of these it is far more likely that you will be presented with a stack of boxes.

If you run a medium-sized business it can be worth trying to pay on account – 30-day terms are often possible if you can supply trading references. This offers all the usual advantages of improved cash flow, but these have to be offset against the amount of work you need to do to set up an account in the first place. If you are likely to be using a single retailer for most of your computer equipment purchases it can be advantageous to arrange an account facility.

When the goods are delivered write 'Goods not yet inspected' on the consignment note. This improves your legal standing if you need to return the goods for any reason. Inspect your order as soon as possible and, if you have any queries, contact the salesperson responsible for your order immediately. Follow this up with written confirmation of any defects or missing items as soon as you can.

Buying on line?

It is now possible to order and pay for a complete computer system over the Internet. Dell and Apple pioneered this approach, but a number of other companies now offer a similar service. The relevant web site shows all the different options that are available, and potential customers can design a computer to their own specification by choosing from these, obtain a final quote, and then pay for the system by entering their credit card details.

As with buying by mail order, on-line buying typically assumes a higher level of technical knowledge than buying in a high-street store. It can be hard (if not impossible) to ask questions, and of course this approach leaves no room for haggling. The advantage is that the process is relatively quick, and knowledgeable buyers can create a machine that suits their exact needs.

In practice, credit card security issues seem to be only a minor problem. 'Secure' sites – which are usually labelled as such – include technology which makes it impossible for casual snoopers to steal credit card details. However, a record of any order, with relevant order numbers and confirmations, should still be kept scrupulously.

Teething troubles

Not all costs are financial. You will also have to spend some time setting your system up once it has arrived and dealing with any teething troubles that arise.

Even for a small, single-user computer system, you should allow at least a day after the machine arrives for checking and general setting-up. This should give you enough time to become familiar with the system and work out how all the parts link together. If you are a relative newcomer, allow at least a week before you think about using the system professionally. This gives you time to make mistakes without worrying about the consequences. It also gives you a chance to get to grips with the software.

The best way to avoid problems is to choose your dealer wisely. A good dealer will be more likely to sell you a machine that has been fully set up and is less likely to misbehave. *Skimping on good support is a false economy, especially in a business setting.* By the time you have allowed for your time, a cheap system can prove to be far more expensive than one with excellent support that costs that bit extra.

Even the best dealer will sometimes make a mistake, and you may be left with a system that does not function properly. At this point the time you have put into looking for good support will pay off. If your computer does not work, double-check all the connections. If everything is as it should be, call the technical support number and explain what the problem is. The Sale of Goods Act 1979 (as amended) covers your contract with the supplier. It is the supplier's responsibility to provide a product that is of satisfactory quality and fit for the purpose for which it is purchased. If the product does not work properly, you may reject the product and claim your money back (but only if you reject it within a few weeks of purchase) or at least claim that the supplier should put the problems right at his or her cost. Always confirm any complaint in writing and keep a copy.

When telephoning, make a note of the name and position of the person to whom you spoke. This gives you a chance to establish a personal contact inside the company. Explain the problem, make a careful note of any solutions the person suggests and then try them out. You will have a much better case if you do this as soon as you can. If, after a week or so of trying, your computer is not functioning properly, consider taking the matter up with the company director(s) and – if necessary – ask for a full refund.

Chapter 13

Finding effective support

The majority of computer problems are minor and easy to put right: for example, you lose your last few minutes' work. Every once in a while, however, something serious goes wrong.

Problems fall into three categories: user errors, software problems and hardware problems.

User errors

These happen when you try to do something your software was not designed to do. Often the software simply does not work the way you think it should. (This is a very common problem.) Most user errors are caused by insufficient training or bad software design. There is very little you can do about bad software design, other than choosing your software carefully. Good training and support can prepare you to deal with further problems. If you are a complete beginner, training and support are *essential*. Very little software is clear and simple enough for a novice to pick up on the spot. Training can help you find and use all the features your software can offer you (according to one estimate, most users are familiar with around 20 per cent of the features in a typical office word processing package).

Software problems

Unfortunately, software is not infallible. In fact, by the reliability standards of any other trade, some software is really rather poor. Even the best programs are about as reliable as an old car on a frosty morning. Most of the time they work well, but occasionally they will do something unexpected or refuse to work at all.

Software problems – known colourfully as **bugs** – take various forms from the obvious (your computer stops responding – this is known as a crash, and the computer is said to have hung), to the extremely subtle (information starts to disappear for no good reason). There is very little you can do to protect yourself from bugs.

To date, the software industry has managed to survive without proper consumer resistance to its bad reliability record. If washing machines, cars and video recorders were sold with the same reliability problems the public outcry would be deafening. The unprofessional attitude to quality control of some of the major companies stems from the industry's roots in the hobbyist movement of the 1970s. Hobbyists – and this includes many computer professionals, who started out as hobbyists – are happy to work around problems, but consumers should not have to. A number of individuals and companies have taken legal action against software providers, but these are usually settled out of court in great secrecy. If the details were made more widely available, it is likely that more actions would follow.

If you have software that does not work properly or causes serious problems, you should complain in the same way you would with any other product. If more consumers take action, the industry will be forced to sit up and take notice, and the quality of its products will improve. Companies do respond to direct action. In late 1994 the Intel Corporation, which makes computer chips for most IBM-compatible computers, climbed down from what many felt was the high-handed position it had taken over a defect in one of its chips. Intel denied there were problems, but then, after a month of vociferous complaints and threats of legal action from angry consumers, apologised and went on to offer a free lifetime replacement to anyone who bought a computer with a defective chip. Similar action by software users could revolutionise the industry.

In the meantime, you can expect regular problems with many common software packages. Some features will not work as advertised, others will cause error messages to appear on the screen, and very occasionally you will find software that crashes your computer. Increasing familiarity with the software will confirm that these kinds of problems are not a result of user error. But until consumers start to demand an acceptable standard of performance from the software manufacturers, problems such as these will remain a fact of life.

In general it is a good idea to register your software. This necessitates filling in a short questionnaire and sending it by post to the manufacturer, or going to the manufacturer's web site on the Internet – some software is set up so it finds this for you automatically – and entering your details there. However, electronic registration in particular can lead to unwelcome advertising messages or other information of dubious interest. Watch out for 'no advertising' options or tick-boxes, and make sure you choose this option if you find this kind of advertising and promotion annoying.

Setup and installation problems

Before you can use your computer both the hardware and the software have to be fully installed. This is one area which can cause problems for beginners, and if not done correctly it can affect the performance of the whole system. If you have bought the system from a dealer, the dealer should do this for you. A scrupulous dealer will make sure that everything has been installed correctly. However, not all dealers bother, and as a result you may get a computer that appears to work but which may not have the full range of options available. You can avoid these kinds of problems by choosing your dealer carefully. Also, if you are a complete beginner check that you will receive some kind of documentation that illustrates how to connect up the various parts of your computer system before you use it.

Hardware problems

Hardware problems are rare. Most computer hardware works reliably most of the time, and you are unlikely to come across hardware problems if your system has been set up properly. When they do occur, however, they are serious and can render your computer useless.

Typical hardware problems include:

No power You turn on the power switch, and nothing happens.

No hard disk The power comes on, but the hard disk does not work – or it appears to work, but all the information has disappeared.

No picture The computer whirrs and beeps, but nothing appears on the screen.

No keyboard and/or mouse The computer does not respond when you type or when you move the mouse. This can often be a software problem, but if you turn your computer off and on again and the symptoms remain, it is a hardware problem. Also check all cables and plugs. Is everything plugged in properly? Are any of the connecting cables loose? Is there anything lying on the mouse?

Computer doesn't start properly This can have a variety of causes. Sometimes it means a hard disk has 'crashed' and all the information on it has disappeared. A less heart-stopping possibility is that the computer has a flat battery. Both PCs and Macs have small batteries inside that maintain important settings. If the battery goes flat these settings disappear, and the computer does not function. Changing the battery and resetting the machine are jobs for a professional.

A surprising number of hardware problems can be solved by making sure that cables are connected firmly, so always check all the cables, including power, monitor, keyboard and mouse connections, before calling for help. More complex hardware problems require expert attention, and it is at this point that support is most needed and any warranties, insurance policies and maintenance contracts you have taken out will prove their worth.

CASE HISTORY: Andrew

Andrew Thomas, an independent computer consultant, is familiar with computer crises of all kinds.

'The most common problem I deal with is rogue software. I train all my clients to use the tools effectively, but I still have to field complaints from them when the software bombs or misbehaves. I warn clients in advance about the problems they'll meet. Each package has its own quirks, and I've started avoiding some of the less reliable ones because it's not worth my time trying to explain to clients what the problems are. Some of the bigger packages can do a hell of a lot, but if they're not totally reliable, they can be more trouble than they're worth.

'Occasionally I'll have to deal with a big hardware failure. It's not something I can guarantee against, so I make sure that there's always a proper warranty or support policy involved. But I'm often called in to pick up the pieces afterwards. In one case a newsagent lost all his information when his hard disk failed. It literally disintegrated. I opened the case up at home and all that was left was some fine dust and a few small pieces. He was covered by a warranty and had a replacement fitted the next day. But he couldn't get the safety copies of his work back on to it.

'In his case it was easy to sort out, and everyone got their papers as usual the next day. Sometimes it's not quite so easy. But if you keep backups of your information and have a good support or insurance policy then you're pretty much bomb-proof no matter what happens.'

Training

Good training minimises your software support requirements, helps you to make effective use of your software and builds your confidence. It will also help you avoid bad habits. Many packages allow you to get the same result in different ways, and training can help you find the way that works best for you. It can also show you useful tricks, such as how to undo your last action if you make a mistake.

There are two kinds of computer training. The first relates to specific software. This will teach you how to do specific tasks – lay out a page in a word processor, check the spelling of the text, and so on – with a certain product.

The second and perhaps more useful option is one that offers general computer literacy. This teaches you the skills you need to use any commonly available piece of software. It is a much broader level of training, and one that can help you become more self-reliant in the way that you use computers.

Sources of training include:

- manufacturers' training programmes
- independent training programmes
- dealers
- college or night school
- books and videos.

Training programmes run by software manufacturers tend to be expensive. You get extra support and a guarantee that the training will get the best out of the software you have. But this level of support tends to be corporate in both approach and cost and is not suitable unless you run a medium–sized business and have cash to spare.

Manufacturers usually use external training companies. Sometimes these companies go through a certification process which guarantees a certain level of competence, both in the subject and in training ability in general. This should – in theory – improve your chances of being taught properly. In practice, training can be a personal thing, and you need to find a training environment in which you feel comfortable. A beginner's first steps in computer literacy can be nerve-wracking, and it is important to find training that can support you through this phase.

Independent trainers vary considerably. At one end of the scale there are the smaller consultancy and training services which offer affordable and friendly help for anyone starting out. At the other end there are larger training companies who are geared more towards corporate accounts and charge accordingly. There is no lack of training options available (as always the *Yellow Pages* is a good place to start), and after some initial enquiries you should be able to find someone who is offering their services at the level you require.

Getting training and help from a **dealer** can be much more problematic. Only the larger, explicitly business-oriented dealers offer this level of service, and even then they may simply recommend a local training service with which they have good links. Unless you are getting a package as an all-inclusive service from a consultant, you will often be better off doing the research yourself and finding a source of training that suits you, rather than your dealer.

Training at **college or evening classes** has its advantages. You will get a chance to practise in a relatively unpressured environment and may be given access to computer equipment outside class hours. This can be an excellent place to start if you know nothing at all about computers and want to learn the basics. Many colleges run classes in business-related computing which can give you practical experience of business software. Attending one of these before you buy your system can give you some insight and knowledge to enable you to make a wiser purchase. You may even be able to ask your tutor for help or free buying advice.

The only disadvantage of college courses is that the content is often determined by the software the college supports. Larger training organisations cover most of the software options that are available, but college courses can sometimes, although not always, be more limited in their scope. You may find that you learn to use software that turns out not to be right for you. Fortunately the basic skills you gain can usually be transferred to another package.

A recent development is an EU-wide attempt to produce a standardised definition of computer literacy, covering basic computer use and business skills, and leading to a recognised qualification. The program is known as the European Computer Driving Licence (ECDL), and relevant tuition is now available from many colleges. ECDL training is more suitable for business rather than home use, and does not include information about general computer skills, such as buying a computer, adding new hardware or software and dealing with common problems. It is worth considering for anyone who works in an office environment.

Some office-skills teaching organisations offer basic courses in various word-processing programs. These tend to teach very much by rote, rather than giving you the wider background you need to be truly computer-literate. But if you are not worried about using your computer to do anything other than certain kinds of work you may find them a good choice.

(A list of educational resources is given in the Addresses section at the back of the book.)

Finally, some people find **the do-it-yourself approach** appealing. There is no lack of books, magazine features and videos offering help and guidance in computer techniques. Working from the printed page or television screen enables you to go at your own pace and to make mistakes without feeling self-conscious, but the usefulness of these training materials varies hugely, and if you get stuck you have no one to ask for help.

Your best approach to choosing training materials is to browse as thoroughly as you can. You may find that some styles are distracting. Many computer books are written with a humorous edge, which suits some people; others prefer a no-nonsense style. (Books for the computer user are discussed in more detail under Further Reading.)

CASE HISTORY: Beth

Beth Waites ran through most of the available training options when she was starting her carpet-cleaning and house-valeting business. Her experience shows that expensive training is not always the best.

'We'd budgeted for a good computer for the bookkeeping and promotional work, and I knew I needed help to get started. We bought a budget machine on the advice of a friend, so we didn't expect much in the way of help from the dealer. It was obvious I was going to have look elsewhere.

'I started with a magazine feature on business training. But that looked too heavy for me. And the prices were outrageous. There was no way that I was going to pay £1,000 for a week away, even if it was in a plush venue. The subject matter didn't suit either. I wanted to know how to design flyers and leaflets and make our correspondence look professional, and wasn't fussed about pivot points in spreadsheets or graphical trend analysis. I leave that kind of thing to our accountant.

'I tried the local college, and that looked promising. The courses looked right, but I had missed the start of the next one and didn't have a year to spare waiting for the one after. But I talked to the course tutor, and he let me on anyway. By then I'd missed the basics, so after the first couple of classes I felt like giving up. But the tutor suggested a couple of books, so I went out and got those and started working through them at home.

'Now, this worked. They were done as tutorials, so I could start at the beginning and work my way through. Every so often I'd get stuck and I'd ask the tutor to help me out at the next class. Between us we managed to cover everything I wanted to know, and I definitely feel I've mastered the basics now.

'I didn't try videos. I've always preferred to talk to a real human being. Books are cheaper and tell you just as much, but without the pictures. If I was doing it again I'd follow the same route – books and maybe magazines, together with evening classes. It worked for me and I'm not exactly Einstein when it comes to these things, so I think anyone should be able to do it.'

Note that Microsoft, Novell and a range of other companies offer 'formal qualifications' in the use and maintenance of their products. Proficiency is tested by examination and based on an established curriculum. The full range of qualifications available is covered in detail in *The Which? Guide to Computers for Small Businesses*. For anyone who wants to become proficient in these products such qualifications are worth considering. Apart from computer basics, the curriculum includes practical network installation and maintenance skills.

Unfortunately, suitable courses teaching the information required to attain certification are very expensive. This puts them out of reach of most small businesses and home users. Cheaper home study courses are also available, although even these rarely cost less than £600. Larger businesses, or those that are very profitable, may find that training a member of staff as an 'on-site consultant' can be a good investment.

When it comes to videos, your choices are more limited. If at all possible you should ask for a demonstration or sample video to get some idea of each company's approach to the subject. Ideally you should also be able to look at videos on approval, although for obvious reasons most video sources are unwilling to allow this. Avoid gimmicky videos. It is all very well having famous names on a training video, but you are paying for information and educational content and should assess it on that basis. Video training is advertised in most of the computer magazines.

Software support

Unlike training, software support is more of a continuing investment. Ideally, if you have sorted out your training needs properly, then you will be left needing minimal support. This is the best possible – and often cheapest – position to be in. In practice, of course, you may come across situations that you haven't been prepared for, and this is where support becomes essential.

Like training, software support is available from a number of sources, including:

- manufacturers' support lines
- independent telephone support services
- consultants and friends and colleagues
- dealers
- computer clubs
- on-line services.

Manufacturers' support schemes

If you buy software from one of the big names (Microsoft, Lotus, Novell and so on) then you will be eligible for access to their help lines. Unfortunately, this is not always as useful as it sounds.

Some manufacturers now charge for technical support, so you will not be able to get help and advice unless you pay in advance. Others offer free support for a 'running-in' period – usually 90 days – and charge after that. Check the details when you buy software. Free initial support is definitely worth taking up, but a paid-up scheme that ties you to any one manufacturer is *not* a good deal. Manufacturers' own-brand support schemes tend to be expensive and will not always offer you the service you need. Sometimes one manufacturer will blame another for the problems you are experiencing. If you contact the other manufacturer it may point the finger back. From a support point of view you are left floundering.

It is worth remembering, too, that technical support lines of major software manufacturers can get very busy, and you could be kept on hold.

Independent support services

A much better solution is to use one of the independent technical support lines. These cover all the standard packages. They can help with problems that you may have getting different software packages to work with each other.

There are two kinds of support schemes. The first gives you a premium-rate telephone number. When you need support, you call the number. You can call as often as you like, for as long as you like, but remember that you pay by the minute for this kind of help. In general, such support schemes are recommended if you simply need occasional help with occasional problems and are confident with your computer. If you have sorted out your training, you may find that this is all the help you need, and it will also provide you with a cost-effective way to get access to professional help when you are unable to work out what to do on your own.

The other option is the flat-rate scheme. This can be expensive – perhaps £100 for a year's support – but you will be able to ask all the questions you need and will also have the benefit of support for a wide range of industry-standard software. This circumvents the 'It's not us – it's some other software' problem that besets some manufacturers' support facilities. These schemes are advertised in computer magazines and may also become available from other sources in the future: for example, BT now offers a computer support line.

Some schemes offer a sliding scale, whereby you get access to better support by paying more per year. Training is a better way to spend your money than on this kind of open-ended support. A recent development is combined support and insurance services. These can

181

be very good value, although it is prudent to check in the usual way that both the insurance and the support facilities are up to par.

The managing director of a large company that provides a variety of PC support services, including support lines for a number of monthly computer magazine titles, explains what the services include. 'We find that 80 per cent of problems are manual-related. People simply haven't read the manual or had the training they need. But we're not here to train people, just to solve specific problems.

'We work according to very definite guidelines. We're open 24 hours a day, 365 days a year. Our busiest day last year was Boxing Day − it's when everyone is trying their new kit out − and we were ready for that. We guarantee to answer the phone within six rings, which means we always keep an adequate level of cover.

'When people phone us they're usually irate and frustrated, so the first thing our staff are trained to do is to calm them down. If you've got a problem you don't want to be messed around with tone phones, you want a real person to talk to right away. Our staff are taught to identify the problem. This isn't always what the caller thinks it is. If a printer isn't working it may just be that it's not switched on, so our staff will check all the options.

'If we can't solve it right away, we guarantee to call people back within ten minutes. We have a database of problems that we can refer to which has all the common problems and their solutions. If that doesn't help we keep copies of all the software we support, so we can call up the real live version and try things for ourselves.

'I'd suggest to anyone looking for phone support that they check response time, the number of packages that are supported and whether support is available all the time.'

Note that in the 2000 budget it was announced that the government planned to spend £60m to help small firms get on to the Internet. This included £20m for a new call centre and web-based advice and information services, £10m for a major boost to advice and training for small firms on using IT, and £30m to build a secure infrastructure for electronic communications between government, business and citizens. It is probably fair to say that previous government schemes, such as the 'bug-busters' scheme (which was supposed to create an army of trained programmers to tackle the Year 2000 problem) have had disappointing results. But small business owners may wish to find out exactly what is available from their local TECs nonetheless.

Consultants and other help

If you have arranged for an all-in-one deal with a consultant, then your consultant should be your first port of call when you need support. You may also be able to call up a consultant and ask for help with a specific problem. Some consultants are unwilling to do this unless the problem is major and is likely to require a large amount of time to put right.

As with buying, a good source of help is from friends and colleagues. It is very rare to come across problems that have never occurred before, and you will often find other people have encountered and perhaps dealt with your difficulty already.

Informal support from dealers

You may, if you are lucky, be able to find a dealer who can answer your questions for free. Some dealers see this as part of the service they offer, others as an unwarranted intrusion on their time. If you have chosen your dealer prudently you should be able to get a basic level of help. It is unrealistic to assume that your dealer should know everything about every possible piece of software, although for hardware-related problems a call to your dealer should be your first choice.

Computer clubs

Local computer clubs tend to be the domain of hobbyists, and this does not suit everyone who is in need of support. However, they can be a good source of useful advice and information.

There is also a national support group: the PC Users' Group (PC-UG). It offers support on a more or less non-profit basis and takes a keen interest in keeping users happy. It also offers buying support (although it does not advise on hardware) as well as a range of other services. The PC-UG also prints a monthly newsletter, *Connectivity*, and runs regular training courses and conferences in London. It can also supply information about training organisations. Membership fees are very reasonable.

On-line services

Some on-line services, such as AOL and CompuServe, include areas which list common problems and solutions, and where you can ask for

The Web includes many helpful sources of free information, some of which are just as comprehensive and useful as any book. This page shows a collection of hints and tips about how to get more from Windows 98.

computer advice. Similar facilities are available on the Internet The advice is free, as it comes from other users. (Parts of this book were written with the help of complete strangers on the Internet who were able to provide detailed technical information.) If you already have an on-line connection, or are considering one, then you should investigate this kind of support. However, you need a certain basic level of technical literacy to start to make use of the system (or at least access to someone who can set up a connection for you), and there are no guarantees that you will get an answer to your problem. In practice you usually do, especially for the more commonly asked questions.

Another on-line resource is the FAQ (Frequently Asked Questions) document (see the example illustrated). This is exactly what it claims to be – a list of common questions, with useful answers. FAQs are maintained on an informal, volunteer basis, and there is no guarantee that the information is correct, although technical FAQs are usually maintained by experts, and mistakes are soon corrected. FAQs are regularly posted to newsgroups on the Internet. (For more about on-line resources see Chapter 6 and Appendix VIII.)

Friends and family

Computers are now so widely used that expertise is no longer the sole preserve of professionals. Many people know a computer enthusiast or hobbyist, who can perhaps be gently persuaded to offer practical help, buying advice and even repairs and upgrades. The advantages of this arrangement are obvious, although it can be worth checking discreetly on the hobbyist's true level of competence before arrangements are made for any work that requires money to change hands.

Appendix I

A beginner's guide to hardware

Many advertisements for computers are little more than a list of technical specifications, which mean less than nothing to many people. What follows is a guide to that will help you understand such advertising and compare like with like. Readers who are not interested in technicalities can skip this section and simply quote the recommended hardware specification of their chosen software. (If you are interested in games or multimedia titles, then use the recommendations for these as your base specification, since these applications will need more powerful hardware than business applications.)

Since 1993 any new Apple or PC computer has been more than powerful enough for basic business use. If this is all you need a computer for, you are spoiled for choice. Like cars, however, computers come in economy and performance versions. Performance computers go faster, and – surprisingly, perhaps – are better suited to play than work. Computer games and leisure products tend to put much higher demands on machines than basic business software.

Most of the information in this Appendix applies to PCs. These are often sold on the basis of a specification, rather than as a brand name. The fact that a computer is made by IBM, Dell, Gateway or any other supplier tells you very little about its performance – although it may offer some hints about build quality and support – and marketing titles such as 'Premier' or 'Executive' are simply window-dressing. What matters is what is inside the box, and it is now traditional to list a certain basic set of specifications so that buyers can see what they are getting.

The situation is slightly different with Apple machines, because these are sold more as commodities, and also rely far more on the visual impact of novel case designs than the relatively utilitarian beige box style of most PCs. The number of Apple suppliers is much smaller, and the market is much less competitive. For the sake of comparison, however, some of the basics – processor type and speed, memory and hard disk size and so on – are often quoted anyway. The two ranges are not strictly comparable, and you should still take the time to sit down and try out each kind of machine for yourself before you buy. However, you can use this section and the one that follows to understand specifications for either kind of machine.

The processor

This is the technical name for the main chip at the heart of your computer. This chip does most of the work, and its speed and power largely determine the capabilities of the machine as a whole. The rest of the hardware exists to get information into and out of this chip.

The chips themselves are sold as square ceramic slabs with hundreds of tiny pins, or as large, long 'modules' that plug into a thin slot. The top surface is printed with the chip model number. The underside contains the pins arranged around a sliver of processed silicon which is visible in the centre through a glass window. This sliver does the work. The chip is in fact a tiny circuit board, with microscopic circuit elements etched into place using a variety of chemical processes.

The most important thing about a processor is its model identifier, which can be a number (e.g. 68040), a name (Pentium), or a cryptic combination of letters and digits (604e). Associated with the code is an optional modifier (e.g. MMX, II, etc.) and a speed rating with the letters 'MHz' after it (e.g. 800MHz). The modifier tells you the sub-class of the chip. Sub-classes differ slightly in efficiency and the features they offer – some older chips were deliberately hobbled for marketing reasons, while others offer extra facilities. For example, Pentium III chips are slightly faster than older Pentium II chips, and also offer extra features that make certain kinds of software work much more quickly and efficiently – especially that which works with sound and video.

The model code, modifier and speed rating tell you everything there is to know about a chip and give you a very good foundation for assessing the power of the computer as a whole.

Processors used in PCs

One company – Intel – has been associated with the PC product line from the beginning. As machines have become more powerful, each development has become synonymous with one particular kind of Intel chip. So a computer built around a Pentium chip is simply known as 'a Pentium'. A complete list of Intel chips is shown in the table on page 190.

All processor chips use the standard speed rating system. This is measured in MHz (MegaHertz – millions of ticks a second) and indicates the 'heart rate' of the machine, also known as the clock speed.

The higher the speed rating, the faster the chip works. Each chip model is available in a range of speeds. For example, 'Pentium III' series chips are available in speeds from 500MHz to 1200MHz (also known as 1.2 GigaHertz, or GHz). Older Pentium II chips covered the range 233MHz to 450MHz. Pentium 4 speeds will eventually go beyond 2GHz.

Chip speed is similar to engine capacity in a car. A two-litre model will be faster than a one-litre design, but never twice as fast. The same applies to computer chips: a computer built around a 200MHz chip will not run twice as fast as one based on a 100MHz chip, but it will run noticeably faster.

Since 1995 Intel has been facing increasingly stiff competition from various other chip manufacturers, notably Cyrix (until 1999) and AMD. These offer chips that work as well as, and in some cases even better than, Intel's own designs, but cost significantly less. While Intel has tried to create a strong brand image for itself with an 'Intel Inside' marketing campaign, this has not worked as well as hoped, and the market is now much more open to computers built around other chips than it was at the start of the 1990s. This is good news for consumers, as prices are being driven down steadily, while performance improves by leaps and bounds.

As a buyer, there is usually no compelling reason to go for an Intel-based PC. For most applications computers built around competing chips are well worth considering, and in some cases can offer a significant cost saving. In fact since around 2000, computers built using AMD's chips have been both more powerful and significantly cheaper than those using equivalent Intel models.

Overdrive processors

On many PC models you can change your processor chip to another one of the same family that goes faster. So, for example, you can change a Pentium II 333 chip to a Pentium II 450 chip simply by taking out the old one, changing a few settings on the motherboard, and plugging in the new one. However, there are limits to how far you can take this process. These depend on the motherboard that the chip plugs into.

An 'overdrive' processor works in the same way, but is designed to work around those limits. These processors are often sold as an easy and convenient upgrade option; in general though, they are not good value. For a relatively small extra investment it is possible to fit a much faster chip and a new updated motherboard. This will improve performance far more dramatically, and, as an added bonus, you may be able to sell your old processor and motherboard to recover some of the extra cost. The disadvantage of taking this route is that it makes the upgrade more complicated.

Apple processors

The processors used in Apple computers are made by Motorola. Motorola has developed its chips in a much more straightforward way than Intel, and the chips used in Apple computers are not available in the same bewildering variety of speed and performance options. A list of Motorola chips is shown below. Motorola and Intel chips are not strictly comparable, but the table does offer a guideline when trying to assess equivalent performance.

And the rest?

Cyrix and AMD have produced their own chips which compete with Intel chips. They have advantages and disadvantages.

Pentium chips are now no longer available. They had competition from the Cyrix 6x86 and the AMD K5, both of which were significantly cheaper and apparently faster overall. However, both the Cyrix and the AMD chips were slightly slower at tasks that required intensive numerical calculations. Because of this they remained a relatively obscure option, ignored by major manufacturers.

Pentium MMX chips are also no longer available. They had competition from the AMD K6 range and the Cyrix M2 (confusingly,

Model designation		Performance rating
Intel	**Motorola**	
8088/8086	68000	Vintage*
80186		(never made available to the public)
80286	68020	Vintage*
386 series	68030LC	Vintage*
486 series	68040 series	Vintage*
Pentium	601	Very dated*
Pentium Pro	n/a	(For specialist applications only)*
Pentium MMX	603e	Dated*
Celeron and Duron	604e & G3	Entry level
Pentium III, Pentium 4 and Athlon	G4	Established
IA-64/Itanium	(n/a)	Next-generation, leading edge available 2001

* Now only available second-hand

also known as the 6x86MX). Both these chips appeared to offer slightly better performance at a lower price, and were used by major manufacturers instead of the Pentium MMX range.

Pentium II chips have been replaced by the slightly slower, but very much cheaper, Celeron range, and also by competition from the AMD K6-II 3D. Both the Pentium II and the AMD K6 were discontinued in 2000. Cyrix withdrew from the market in 1999, so there are no more competing Cyrix chips to consider.

Celeron chips are simplified versions of the Pentium III. They offer better value for money, in return for slightly worse performance. Their main competition comes from the AMD **Duron** chip range, which was announced in 2000 and is a simplified Athlon. Duron chips offer better performance and are slightly cheaper. Systems built with very fast Pentium IIIs and Athlons (i.e. 1GHz and above) offer a small but noticeable performance jump over and above what might reasonably be expected from the faster clock speed.

Pentium III chips have competition from the AMD (**Athlon**), which in some ways is a faster and better processor, although it lacks the Pentium III's enhanced KNI features. Again, the Athlon is significantly cheaper than the Pentium III.

Pentium 4 chips represent a sideways step for Intel, and not the advance it had hoped for. Like the Pentium III, these are outclassed by AMD's Athlon range of processors, which perform comparably but are very significantly cheaper. Except for certain games and video editing tasks, an Athlon computer will reliably offer better value, and better or similar performance, than a Pentium 4 computer.

Xeon Pentium II, Xeon Pentium III and Pentium 4 chips are advanced versions designed for corporate computers. They are very expensive, and so are likely to be out of reach of home users. They are usually only sold as part of a general very-high-performance computer package. Business users should note that they often offer exceptionally poor value for money, and sometimes also surprisingly poor performance. By accepting the slight performance degradation offered by conventional Pentium II and Pentium III models, you could make a huge saving.

One advantage of the Xeon range is that these chips are designed to work together in **multi-processor systems**, which dole out all the work among a number of computer chips – typically between two and eight – instead of making a single chip do it all. This requires a significant technical overhead, which means that a multi-processor system will not usually be as fast as might be hoped. (For example, two processors are likely to be only 1.5 times as fast as one, at best.) This approach is only suitable for situations where money is no object and very high performance is required.

Making sense of the pattern

While the huge number of chip names and numbers can seem bewildering, it is possible to sketch out a simple map which shows how the different options relate to each other. Different chips are aimed at different kinds of users. The names and numbers have changed, but the underlying pattern has remained very similar since the early 1990s.

Undemanding work includes basic word processing, simple office work, email, web browsing and other Internet use. Games will run very slowly. These models use a crippled version of the day's standard technology. This makes only a slight difference while they are being used, but it will significantly depress second-hand prices.

Standard models are the average computers of the day. They can do all the work that an undemanding model can, but slightly faster. They can also be used for games. In general, they offer the best value for money, although shopping around among different dealers will show that there can be a price spread of as much as £500 between similarly specified computers in this category.

Advanced models are for those who want a 'performance' computer. They are ideal for getting the best from the latest games and for anyone who needs to do demanding work, such as computer animation or graphic design. Typically costing some 50 per cent to 100 per cent more than the standard models, they are aimed at people who want the best possible performance and are happy to pay a price premium for this.

Professional These models are aimed at medium to large businesses, and are typically too expensive for the general public. Where domestic computer chips typically cost manufacturers between £50 and £400, these chips can cost thousands. They are most often sold in server computers, which are designed to be used by an entire department or company.

The future

Not only does the industry move fast, but developments are speeding up. At the time of writing, the Pentium III is well established, but is likely to start becoming obsolete during 2001. AMD's Athlon range remains a strong competitor, with some tests showing that for certain kinds of work an Athlon can be up to a third faster at the same MHz rating.

Year	Undemanding	Standard (Intel)	Standard (AMD)	Advanced (intel)	Professional
1992	386 16MHz	386 20MHz	–	386+387 33MHz	–
1995	486SX 25MHz	486DX/2 66MHz	K5 50MHz	486DX/4 120MHz	–
1997	Pentium 12MHz	Pentium 166MHz	K6 200MHz	Pentium MMX 200MHz	Pentium Pro 200MHz
1998	Celeron 266MHz	Pentium II 300MHz	K6-III 300MHz	Pentium II 350MHz	Pentium II Xeon 350MHz
2000	Celeron 600MHz	Pentium III 800MHz	Athlon 800MHz	Pentium III 1GHz	Pentium 4 1.5GHz
					Athlon 1.2GHz
2001	Celeron 800MHZ	Pentium III 1.2GHz	Athlon 1.5GHz	Pentium 4 1.7GHz	Itanium 1.5GHz
2002	Duron 1GHz	Pentium 4 2GHz	Athlon 2GHz	McKinley/IA-64 2GHz	Sledgehammer 2GHz

(Note: McKinley and Sledgehammer are codenames. Commercial products may be named differently.)

In the longer term, the picture is less clear than it once was. Intel has been working on a completely new kind of chip, codenamed Itanium, using a new kind of chip specification called IA-64 (Intel Architecture 64-bit). Initial samples of Itanium have performed so disappointingly that some industry wits have dubbed it 'Itanic.' It now seems likely that Itanium will not be released as a mainstream product, and that Intel will wait until a second improved version of the new chip design, currently codenamed McKinley, becomes available.

AMD meanwhile has been working on an alternative system, and promises to offer two chips, called Clawhammer and Sledgehammer, during 2001 and 2002. These offer a number of technical advantages over Intel's plans, and should in theory also be more affordable.

The situation is complicated further by an apparent split between Intel and software company Microsoft. Until now the combined forces of these two companies have driven the course of PC design. But now Microsoft appears to be looking for other industry partners, especially with regard to its Tablet PC project. The Tablet PC appears to be an attempt to reinvent the familiar, if rather cumbersome, desktop PC as a more portable 'information appliance' that isn't tied to a single location and can be used at home, at work, and on the road. Microsoft intends to make the Tablet available during 2002. It remains to be seen what these developments will mean for the computer buyer, and whether the Tablet will replace today's PC, or provide a useful and complementary range of parallel products.

Apple, meanwhile, is already selling its G4 processor, with a speed upgrade known as the 'velocity engine'. Although some way from the projected performance of the IA-64 series, it offers a significant improvement over earlier Apple models. However, Apple's processors are designed by a three-way coalition of Apple, a company called Motorola and IBM, and there are signs that diplomatic relations between these partners are not as relaxed as they once were. As a result, it is possible that Apple's development programme may slow down relative to the Intel/AMD race.

Unfortunately, it remains difficult to gauge accurately the relative performance of Apple chips against those of Intel and AMD. Apple's own tests, which claim that a 500MHz G4 can match a 1GHz Pentium III, have been criticised for being partisan and unrealistic. It seems reasonable to agree that the Apple chips are more efficient and can match a faster Intel/Athlon chip. However, quantifying the difference is hard, and for most kinds of work raw speed is secondary to Apple's improved ease of use and other advantages.

Motherboard

After the processor chip, the motherboard is the second most important component in a PC computer. (Apple computers use proprietary motherboard designs which means there is less variation, and differences are much less important to purchasers.) For IBM-compatibles, the choice of motherboard determines the following:

- Maximum possible memory
- Maximum possible processor speed (e.g. 1GHz)
- Memory type (SDRAM, DDRAM, RAMBUS, etc.)
- Compatibility with non-Intel processors (not all boards will work with AMD and Cyrix chips)
- Number and type of 'expansion slots' for extras that fit inside the case
- Built-in extras, such as sound cards and graphics cards
- Number and type of connections for external extras
- Hard disk connection system (EIDE, Ultra DMA/33, /66 or /100, occasionally SCSI)
- General operating efficiency (more modern boards are faster and more efficient than older designs)
- The ability to use more than one processor chip at once (known as SMP – Symmetric Multi Processing).

An increasingly bewildering and acronym-laden range of motherboard options is now available. Below are some of the terms you may come across in advertising material in the mainstream computer press:

BIOS – Basic Input Output System. This is a special piece of software burned on to the motherboard that makes it unnecessary for the rest of the computer to know exactly how to go about getting information to and from a hard disk drive, a printer, and so on. BIOSs are made by many different companies. Popular examples include Award, AMI and Phoenix. Apart from minor technical differences, one BIOS is much like another, and usually there is no advantage to having any particular one.

'Form factor' Computer industry jargon for 'shape and mechanical dimensions'. For motherboards, two main types are available – AT and ATX. These specify the physical size of the board and where the screw holes are placed. When upgrading a motherboard you will have to make sure you buy one of the same type, otherwise it will not fit into the existing case.

Speed As with processor chips, motherboards are now being supplied with a speed rating in MHz. This indicates the speed at which the board can move information around. The current standard is 100MHz, although 133MHz boards are sometimes available. AMD's Athlon processor uses a 200MHz to 266MHz system, which makes it work significantly faster than existing designs. It is important not to confuse motherboard speeds with processor chip speeds. Where two numbers are shown, the slower will be the motherboard's specification.

Chipset This is a code that specifies what kind of chips surround the processor on the motherboard. While the main processor chip does most of the useful calculations, these other chips connect the processor to the outside world – for example collecting information from the keyboard and mouse, sending information to and from the hard disk, and so on. Most chipsets are made by Intel, but some, such as the VIA and 'PC Chips' sets, are available from competitors. Unfortunately, chipset designations follow no rhyme or reason, and the only way to keep track of which ones perform better is to attempt to interpret reviewers' comments in the various PC magazines.

Socket type This is the physical socket into which the processor is fitted. 'Socket 7' is the older standard once used for Pentiums but now co-opted by AMD for its K6 range. 'Slot 1' is used for the Pentium II, Pentium III and certain Celeron chips. Slot A is used for pre-2001 Athlon chips. Socket A is used for more recent Athlons. Some Celeron chips also use a 'PGA' (Pin Grid Array) socket. From a buyer's point of view, the technical differences between these different standards are negligible. It is, however, essential to know what kind of socket is used in a PC if you wish to upgrade the processor.

Extra features Points to look for include:
USB (Universal Serial Bus – see page 207)
IEEE1394/Firewire (for connecting to video cameras – see page 207)
AGP (Advanced Graphics Port – see page 209)
Ultra DMA/33/66/100 (see page 199).

Main memory

A computer's memory is rather like desk space in an office. The more you have, the easier it is to have all kinds of documents and other information scattered around without having to look things up in a filing system. If you have too little memory, then applications will either not work at all or will slow down dramatically as the computer continually swaps information between the main memory and the hard disk.

Like hard disk space, memory sizes are measured in Mbs. On modern PCs and Apple computers, a minimum size, adequate for most work, is 64Mb. Because memory is so cheap now, it is more common to find 128Mb or 256Mb as standard. More expensive models offer 512Mb or more. This is possibly overkill for many users, but in practice it makes a minimal difference to the price of a PC, and the extra breathing space it adds is very useful. Web browsing on the Internet can be particularly demanding of memory, so 128Mb should be considered a minimum for anyone who plans to do this regularly; 128Mb will also appear to speed up a computer that is regularly used with lots of different software working at once (for example, a word processor, spreadsheet, web browser, diary, email software, and so on).

On almost all computers, extra memory can be added at a later date. This is a cheap and simple operation that more experienced users can do themselves. At the time of writing, an extra 128Mb costs around £50. When adding memory, it is essential to know which type to buy. EDO (Extended Data Output) RAM is used on older, slower computers. It is supplied as SIMMs (Single In-line Memory Modules). More recent machines uses SDRAM (Synchronous Dynamic RAM), which is sometimes also labelled 'PC100 SDRAM'. This is much faster than EDO RAM and is supplied as DIMMs (Dual In-line Memory Modules).

As we go to press, two new memory technologies are planned. 'Rambus' memory (also known as 'DRDRAM' – Direct Rambus Dynamic Random Access Memory) appears to perform very poorly and is very expensive compared to existing memory types. However, it is being pushed by Intel, which means that it is likely to appear in at least some designs. DDR (Double Data Rate) SDRAM is a 'next-generation' version of SDRAM that – very simply – works twice as fast. It is more affordable, but is currently being marketed by a smaller collection of companies.

Apart from memory type, speed is sometimes quoted. This can appear as a PC number (usually PC100 or PC133) or in MHz. The higher the number, the faster the memory. 'Latency' is also sometimes quoted. This again is related to how fast the memory works. 'CAS 2' memory is faster than 'CAS 3' memory products. In practice these are very fine distinctions, only of interest to 'power users' who need the absolute fastest computer hardware available. Less demanding users are unlikely to notice a significant performance difference.

You will sometimes see memory advertised as 'non-ECC RAM' (ECC is an acronym for Error Correcting Code). Computer memory is not perfect, and occasionally it will mis-remember information; ECC memory includes automatic correction circuitry which makes it more reliable, and 'non-ECC RAM' is standard memory that lacks this feature. ECC RAM can be very much more expensive than standard memory, and is recommended for network servers, where reliability is very important. For typical home and small office use it is overkill.

Cache memory

This is super-fast memory used as a convenient and speedy notepad by the processor chip. On Pentium models this was available as an optional extra, but now it is physically built into all available processor chips. The amount cannot be changed. Cheaper processors such as the Celeron and Duron ranges offer less cache, which is one reason why they perform more slowly.

The hard disk drive

This is the computer's filing space. Although a typical hard disk unit may be roughly the size of a paperback, it will have enough room for more than 4,000 copies of the text of this book.

Hard disk capacities are measured in megabytes (Mbs), where 1Mb is the space needed to store one million letters or other characters. The more Mbs, the more room the computer has for software, records and other information. A gigabyte (Gb) is 1,000Mb, and multi-gigabyte drives (which are large enough to store long snatches of sound and video) are now common. Disk sizes of 20Gb and upwards are now standard. These offer plenty of space for all but the most demanding users. If you are buying a new computer do not buy less than 9Gb. The difference in price between smaller and larger sizes of hard disk is now so small that there is very little reason to settle for less than 9Gb unless your budget is very tight indeed.

Apple computers offer similar-sized hard disks to PCs. Both Apple and PC computers used for multimedia work, such as audio and video editing, need very much higher disk capacities: 20Gb is a reasonable minimum for anyone who does this kind of work professionally, although 40Gb or more is not unreasonable for video projects, and 60Gb and 80Gb disks are now available, although these larger sizes will usually have to be ordered and fitted specially.

Note also that, while a completely new machine should have no problems even with extremely large disks, on older PCs the BIOS cannot handle disk sizes above a certain size. On very old models this size was 9Gb, on more recent ones the limit may be around 30Gb, and, even if you buy and fit a larger disk, you will not be able to use more than this maximum size. And the disk may perhaps not work properly at all. Some disks are sold with special 'disk mapping' software pre-installed on the disk to solve this problem. This approach may slow the disk down, and if a serious problem occurs – for example, if Windows has to be reinstalled – the software may be lost, rendering the disk unusable. A better approach is to make sure the BIOS can handle larger disks directly. If you plan to use larger disks, it can be worth asking whether there is any limit before you buy your PC, or whether a BIOS update (see page 306) that can solve the problem is available.

Hard disk types

Size apart, not all hard disks are the same. Different systems have evolved to connect the disk to the motherboard and transfer information as quickly as possible. These fall into two main families – SCSI (Small Computer Systems Interface – pronounced 'scuzzy') and IDE (Integrated Drive Electronics). Both of these have evolved a number of sub-types.

In general IDE is used for undemanding work, while SCSI is preferred for high-performance applications. SCSI disk drives tend to be slightly faster, and they also transfer information more efficiently; very fast SCSI drives can be very expensive indeed.

Both SCSI and IDE can be used to connect other devices to a computer. IDE is limited to two items on the same cable (although most computers offer two cable connectors, making for a maximum of up to four items) and is never used outside a computer's case. SCSI, on the other hand, can be used with up to 16 different items, some of which may be outside the computer. Compatible options include scanners, CD-ROM drives, CD writers, external hard disks and even music synthesisers. SCSI is available in a dizzying range of variations which differ according to speed, the number of items that can be used, the maximum length of all the connections together, and so on. Full technical details are outside the scope of this book, but an Internet search for the words 'SCSI primer' or 'SCSI basics' should list all the most recent relevant facts.

IDE is a much simpler system. The current standard for IDE disks is known as 'Ultra DMA/100', sometimes shortened to just 'DMA/100'. Older standards, such as Ultra DMA/33 and /66, as well as the original 'IDE' and 'EIDE', will be available on second-hand machines.

A recent trend in hard-disk design is to speed up the rate at which the hard-disk drive rotates. Inside each is a collection of platters, rather like a pile of flat plates. The speed at which this spins has a direct effect on the speed at which the disk can move information as a whole. The original standard speed was 5,400rpm. Some drives now offer 7,200rpm, and a few offer 10,020rpm. The latter tend to become very hot in use, and may need to be cooled with an extra fan.

Another recent trend is to add cache memory to some IDE designs. This works rather like cache memory on the motherboard, and can appear to improve the apparent speed of a disk. A minimum cache size is 512Kb, but some high-performance drives offer as much as 2Mb. Cache memory is well worth having, as it can speed up a disk dramatically. It is also especially useful for sound and video editing work.

Floppy disk drive

This is a slot at the front of the computer that takes plastic wafers known as **floppy disks** (usually shortened to floppies) — which are now rigid, not flexible. The information is stored on a thin disk of magnetically sensitive plastic. The tough outer casing protects the sensitive surface from fingerprints, dust and other damage which might destroy the information.

All modern PCs include one 3.5-inch 1.44Mb floppy disk drive. This means that you can use two kinds of floppy disk with them – high-density 1.44Mb disks, and older, double-density 720Kb disks (now no longer available), which hold half as much information. Either will work in the same slot. (Note that both the iMac and the G3/G4 ranges from Apple lack a floppy disk drive; if one is required, it has to be purchased as an optional extra. Suitable drives use the USB connection system described on page 207.)

The 3.5-inch floppy disk is a venerable old standard but is now technically obsolete. Unfortunately, no single new standard has emerged as a replacement. However, some computers are now sold with LS120 drives instead of floppy disks. These work with existing floppy disks, but can also use new LS120 disks, which can store up to 120Mb of information (see page 228).

Some antique machines use a different kind of floppy disk. These are 5.25 inches across and protect the inner disk with a much thinner floppy plastic sheath. They hold less information (a maximum of 360Kb) and take up more space. Unless you buy a computer with a dual-format disk drive (and these are very rare) or with one of each kind of disk drive (also rare, and now usually available only to order) you will not be able to use either kind of disk in your machine. The two systems are mechanically incompatible.

Very rarely now you may find specialist software sold on 5.25-inch disks, although these are now all but obsolete. If you need this software, make sure you find a source of 5.25-inch disks and drives before buying. Alternatively, check to see if it is available in a more modern format, such as a 3.5-inch disk, or CD-ROM.

Monitor/screen

Monitor is just another word for screen – the part of your computer that displays information while you work.

There are now two sorts of monitor available. **Cathode Ray Tube** (CRT) monitors look rather like small television screens. They are bulky, heavy and comparatively fragile, but relatively cheap. **Liquid**

Crystal Display (LCD) monitors use a flat plastic panel that has display circuitry built into it directly. The latter are much more convenient, use much less power and offer comparable – in some cases better – picture quality than CRTs; they are also considerably more expensive. LCD monitors are sometimes known as **TFT** (Thin Film Transistor) displays. Both kinds of monitor work by displaying a rectangular grid of tiny dots, each of which can be made to light up in various colours. Because the dots are so small, the monitor can easily show text, photographs and even video clips.

The monitor is one of the most important parts of your computer system. It is essential to choose a model that does not cause eyestrain. To some extent specifications are something of a sideline with monitors. *Never buy a monitor without checking display quality first.* This will tell you far more about whether or not you can live with it on a daily basis than any number of facts and figures. However, specifications can be useful. Various factors in the specification to watch for include:

MPRII, TCO-95 and TCO-99 certification ensure that as little stray radiation as possible is released. TCO-95/99 are the most stringent specifications. These two standards are virtually identical, and a monitor certified to either will produce minimal stray radiation.

Power-saving features NUTEK, Energy Star and VESA DPMS (Display Power Management Signalling) are all energy-saving options. They will switch a monitor to low-power 'standby' operation after a period of inactivity. Although they are unlikely to make a huge difference to your electricity bill, these features are worth having and using for environmental reasons.

Dot pitch is the size of each dot on the screen. The smaller the dot size, the sharper and clearer the image. Some monitor manufacturers use a 0.30mm dot pitch. Avoid these. Aim for at most a 0.28mm pitch – the current standard. If you can afford it, a monitor with a 0.26mm pitch will give an even crisper image.

Scan rate tells you how rapidly the screen flickers. Typically one or two numbers are shown. The 'horizontal scan rate', typically shown in kHz (kilohertz) is related to the fineness of the image. The more important measure is vertical scan rate, which is shown in Hz (Hertz) – in this case flickers per second. Anything below 72Hz tends to cause eyestrain. One essential point to check is whether this scan rate is interlaced or not. A non-interlaced monitor gives you a solid picture. Interlacing effectively halves the scan rate, so a 60Hz interlaced monitor will flicker 30 times a second. Most people find this unbearable, even for short periods. Avoid interlaced monitors if you can. It is worth noting that many PCs are sold with the scan rate set to 60Hz, even if the hardware can do better. When buying a PC check if this can be altered, and if so ask the dealer to set it as high as it can go.

Screen size Monitors are available in a range of sizes. Like television screens, they are based on the size of the picture tube measured diagonally from corner to corner. Not all of this may be available. For example, a 21-inch monitor may have a visible diagonal of just under 20 inches. Most PCs are now sold with 17-inch monitors; 15-inch models are now something of a penny-pinching option, while 19-inch and larger models are becoming increasingly popular as prices for these models fall sharply. A high-quality 21-inch monitor now costs around £700, although cheaper models with poorer screen quality and a more limited range of resolutions are available for around £500. Screen size, resolution and scan rate are intimately related. For details see the table opposite.

In April 2001 the Advertising Standards Authority stated that all advertising for both monitors and televisions would have to explicitly state the visible diagonal picture size. Most advertisers responded by recasting their specification listings into a new format – typically '21-in monitor (19.5-in. visible diagonal)'. Please bear this in mind when reading and comparing specifications.

Resolution tells you how much detail the screen can show. The more dots there are available, the finer the image becomes. A good minimum to watch for is the SVGA standard, which is 640 dots across and 480 dots vertically. Each dot can be one of 256 colours. This is enough to reproduce photographs with some semblance of realism. Other standard resolutions are 800×600 and $1,024 \times 768$, $1,280 \times 1,024$ and $1,600 \times 1,200$. You will need a larger monitor to make use of these.

The number of available colours also varies. The minimum is 256 and is best avoided; 64,000 ('16-bit') and 16.7 million ('24-bit') are the other common options, although you will sometimes also see '32-bit' colour. Almost all modern machines are capable of displaying 16.7 million colours at once on the monitor they are sold with. If you need this degree of detail with a larger working area, check to make sure that your computer's graphics card will be able to offer 16.7 million colours at higher resolutions on a larger monitor.

At the time of writing, plasma displays are starting to become available. These are thin, flat panels that can be hung on a wall. Physically they typically offer a 40-inch diagonal and are designed to be viewed from a distance instead of close-up. The maximum possible resolution at the moment is 1,280 × 1,024. They are currently very expensive indeed – between £5,000 and £10,000. Current designs also consume a lot of power, and can sometimes run hot enough to cause minor burns if touched. All this puts them out of reach for home users; they are, however, of interest to businesses, where they are popular for presentations.

Standard resolutions and the necessary monitor sizes

CRT monitor size	LCD monitor size	Comfortable resolution*	Cramped resolution*	Comfortable flicker	Possible uses
14 in	12.1 in	640 × 480	800 × 600	72Hz	Letter-writing, accounts, spreadsheets (with difficulty)
15 in	13.3 in	800 × 600	1,024 × 768	75Hz	Spreadsheets, simple desktop publishing
17 in	14.4 in	1,024 × 768	1,280 × 1,024	82Hz	Image editing and retouching, large spreadsheets
19 in	15 in	1,280 × 1,024	1,600 × 1,200	85Hz	More comfortable for 1,280 x 1,024 use than a 17-in monitor.
21 in	18 in	1,280 × 1,024	1,600 × 1,200	85Hz	Multiple applications at once, very advanced word processing, huge spreadsheets
22 iin	n/a	1,600 × 1,200	1,800 × 1,440	90Hz	Advanced commercial design and publishing

*resolution is measured in the number of dots across and down

Keyboard

On PCs, the 102-key keyboard is the standard. This includes extra keys for numbers on the right-hand side and also arrow keys which are used for moving the cursor around the screen. Some keyboards feel much more pleasant to use than others. Some people prefer more of a spongy bounce, others a definite 'clack'. This is a matter of personal taste – try a keyboard before buying it, especially if you are a touch typist. 'Cherry' keyboards made by the Cherry company, often offered as an optional extra, are built to a higher standard than budget keyboards. If possible, buy a *weighted* keyboard; this includes a metal weight that makes it less likely to slide around the desk as you type.

Keyboard fashions come and go. The 'ergonomic' designs of the mid-1990s are still available, although less popular now than they once were. These models attempt to place the keys in a more accessible position than the standard flat design. As with keyboard 'feel', this is very much a matter of personal taste.

Cordless keyboards do away with connecting cables, replacing them with a local radio link. They can be used at a distance (perhaps while playing a game with the computer plugged into the TV), on one's lap while reclining, or simply as a way to help avoid the snarl of cables that typically builds up behind a PC. Compatible cordless mice are often also available.

Internet keyboards offer extra keys for Internet browsing and other useful controls, such as speaker volume, CD playback, and so on. These help make certain operations easier and quicker. Although they are gimmicks to some extent, dedicated Internet users may find them helpful.

If you do a lot of typing, a good keyboard will make a huge difference to your productivity. You will be less likely to mistype words, your hands will be more relaxed, and in general you will find work less tiring. This is one area that can repay careful research. As a rule, most of the keyboards supplied with typical retail computer systems are resolutely average, and you should find it easy to improve on them.

Cases (PC only)

IBM-compatible machines (PCs) are sold in a standard range of case styles; these do not affect the performance of your computer in any way. A big case does not mean a fast and powerful computer, but it does mean you have more room to add extras.

Externally, the influence of Apple's iMac has had an impact on case design. Where PCs were once known as BBBs (Boring Beige Boxes), it is now possible to buy models that include colours and some elements of deliberate design. Realistically, even at their best, most PCs fail to look stylish, but recent trends have at least moved them out of the 'hideously boring' category.

Internally, cases now fall into two types – AT (also known as 'baby AT') and ATX. These do exactly the same job, and look identical from the outside, but are designed to be used with the two sizes of motherboards that are now available. If buying a new PC, the ATX option is the better one. ATX systems are better designed, easier to take apart and put together, and less prone to annoying problems (for example, memory chips that are almost inaccessible because they are hidden behind an unfortunately positioned power supply).

Apart from this basic distinction, cases come in different sizes. Besides taking up more space, larger cases have more drive bays – special areas that extras can slot into. Typically, they also have more powerful power supplies to take care of the extra load.

Drive bays are used for extras that need front-panel access – floppy-disk drives, hard disk drives, tape backup systems and CD-ROM units. Other extras slot into the expansion slots inside the computer's case. Drive bays come in two sizes – 5.25-inch, which are suitable for 5.25-inch floppy disk drives and CD-ROM players, and 3.5-inch, which are used for 3.5-inch floppy drives and hard disk drives. When not in use they are screened off with plastic blanking plates. To install an extra you simply remove the plate, slot in the new drive, tighten a few screws and then make the connections to the rest of the computer. The 5.25-inch drive bays can also accommodate hard drives if an adapter kit is used; this is often supplied with drives.

Slimline cases look trim, but are only recommended if you know exactly what you want and are sure you will not need to upgrade; they typically have one of each size of drive bay. Desktop and mini-tower cases are the most common. The desktop model sits on your desk horizontally, and the monitor sits on the case. The mini-tower model stands vertically. These are designed to sit to one side of your desk, or perhaps even out of sight under it. Either model will have two of each kind of drive bay as standard. Full tower cases also stand vertically. They are used for larger computer systems and offer four or five drive bays. These cases are best left on the floor – they are too tall to be used on most desks.

Larger cases tend to have more powerful power supplies. For a typical PC anything more than 200W should be adequate, although if you plan to add a lot of extras, or are using a fast processor chip and graphics card, 250W or even 300W may be required. Power supplies are available separately and can be swapped quite easily; fitting a larger one is straightforward. However, it's usually cheaper to make sure that any case you buy has a suitably hefty power supply to start with. It's worth noting that case prices can vary significantly. Some companies in *MicroMart* magazine advertise serviceable cases for around half the price of similar examples advertised in the more mainstream computer press.

Some cases have a door which closes to hide the drive bays. Unless you are running your computer as a file server, you should avoid this design – the door only gets in the way during everyday use.

And, of course, no computer would be complete without a small array of flashing lights and numbers. These will usually include:

- a 'power-on' light
- a hard-disk activity light: this is useful – it tells you when your hard disk is working.

There will also be a handful of buttons. 'Turbo' is now only seen on very obsolete models (on very old computers this button was used to slow down the main processor chip, because certain software refused to work at the maximum possible speed – this feature has not been used since around 1994). 'Reset' forces your computer to go through its start-up sequence. *Do not touch this button without a good reason*: you will lose any unsaved work. The reset button should only be used when your computer has obviously stopped working and needs to be restarted. Switching the power on and off again strains the hardware slightly (although whether or not this makes a lasting difference is debatable); use the reset button instead.

Expansion options

Extra hardware can be added to a computer in one of two ways – inside the case, where it lives permanently, or outside it, linked via one of the connectors on the back, together with appropriate cables.

Inside the case, all motherboards offer a number of 'expansion slots'. These now come in two types – ISA (Industry Standard Architecture) and PCI (Peripheral Connect Interface). (An older standard called Vesa is now obsolete, and only appears in second-hand 486 machines. Spares and extras are no longer available for this standard.) ISA is used for slow devices, such as sound cards, modems and slow network cards. PCI is used for faster devices, such as high-performance sound cards (graphics cards use a different system again, called AGP). ISA is now being phased out, and recent PCs no longer include any ISA slots at all. Apple computers, meanwhile, have switched to a PCI-based system from a proprietary one – this means that some PC extras will now work inside an Apple machine. To install extra hardware, the relevant circuit card is simply plugged into an empty slot. Once all available slots are in use, the PC is 'full'. If you have a lot of extras installed, it is important when upgrading to check that a new PC offers a similar number of suitable slots. Otherwise you may find that one or more of your extras becomes unusable, simply because there is nowhere to plug it in.

External connectors consist of five types – parallel ports, serial ports, Universal Serial Bus (USB) sockets, a system called 'Firewire' (currently standard on some Apple machines, and available as an optional extra on PCs), and infra-red links (IrDA).

The first two are traditional computer connection options that have been used for twenty years. Parallel ports are large, chunky sockets typically used to connect printers; serial ports are smaller sockets that are more often used for modems and mice.

USB has now become a practical option, and USB-compatible devices such as scanners and monitors are starting to become widely available. Where a single connection needs to be shared or parcelled out among a number of different devices, a 'USB hub' can be used to distribute the information from a single cable to a number of USB sockets (often four, occasionally eight). Note that USB has limitations, and will stop working properly if too many items are connected to it. Using a USB cable to connect a monitor, for example, will use up most of the available connection power ('bandwidth'). USB is best used for low-bandwidth applications, such as connecting mice and keyboards, modems and sound-cards.

USB and Firewire are both attempts to overcome the rats' nest of connections that can build up at the back of a computer. They work by 'daisy-chaining' (connecting from item to item) a single cable from the PC through printers, monitors, modems, speakers and other extras. Thus, instead of multiple cables connecting the computer to individual devices, there is only one.

The IrDA system is available primarily on laptops and personal organisers, although it is also beginning to appear on desktop PCs and printers. It uses a cordless link that works rather like a TV remote control to move information from one item to another. For example, it can be used to copy a list of contact addresses from a PC to a personal organiser or vice versa. No cables are involved, although of course any devices that are to be connected have to be visible to each other and less than ten feet apart – the system will not work through walls and doors. There are plans for IrDA to start appearing in public places such as telephone boxes, airports and station waiting-rooms, where it will be used to provide a link to the Internet or some other public data network.

Some companies are experimenting with radio systems The most popular are called 'Bluetooth', which was designed to work with mobile phones, and the memorably named '802.11', originally used by Apple in its iBook. The eventual aim is to make it possible for someone to carry a laptop anywhere in a building, and have access to an Internet or network connection and all the information in base machines wherever they are. These wireless systems are popular in the US for both home and business use, and related products have started appearing in Europe. Note, however, that wireless network security is minimal. Would-be hackers can use a simple aerial on top of a car parked outside a company's offices to tap into a business network. If security matters to you, you should hire a consultant to avoid these kinds of security loopholes before installing a wireless system.

The industry is attempting to move towards USB and Firewire connectors, but until this process is finished you will continue to find older parallel, serial and PS/2 connectors for monitors, keyboards and mice on the back of computers. It's almost impossible to connect them wrongly when setting up a computer for the first time. One point to be aware of is that 'PS/2' connectors for the mouse, and perhaps the keyboard, are linked directly to the motherboard. This has the advantage of making it possible to use both serial ports, rather than having to dedicate one to the mouse.

Graphics card

The graphics card controls what appears on the monitor. It sets the maximum number of colours that you can use, the resolution and the scan rate. New computers are sold with good basic graphics cards that are perfectly adequate for most work. However, if you plan to work with a large monitor you may need to upgrade your graphics card to match. Graphics card specifications quote the amount of memory used, but in practice you are better off checking for scan rate, maximum resolution and maximum number of colours available. Better still, ask to see a graphics card in action at its highest resolution with the maximum number of colours it can produce. This should tell you everything you need to know about the speed and clarity of the display.

All graphics cards are now **accelerated**. They are built around a special chip that takes some of the load from the main processor – so, for example, the processor can ask for a rectangle to be drawn on the screen without having to do all the calculations required to make it appear. The majority of graphics cards plug into AGP slots (very rarely you may come across a much slower card that plugs into an ISA or PCI slot).

The graphics card market is now dominated by cards designed for game players. These feature impressive enhancements which make no difference whatsoever to business users. However, the development of these cards means that all but the very cheapest cards will produce excellent results with any monitor up to and including the largest available models.

One point to watch for is compatibility between cards. Cards use differing standards, including Microsoft's DirectX, OpenGL and a small selection of others, and not all games support these equally well. Any limitation is unlikely to be serious, but it can be worth checking to see which standards are supported.

Newer versions of Windows (see page 244) include a facility for using two graphics cards at once. These can provide a larger virtual working space than a single card. Some cards, notably the Matrox G400 and G400 Max, include two monitor sockets, and so offer the same facility from a single card. The same feature can also be used to provide a TV output for connection to a VCR.

A related trend has been for some graphics cards to include TV and video connections, so that video can be shown on the computer's screen, or alternatively games can be played on the family TV. ATI's Radeon Vivo (Video In Video Out) is a good example. Video-capable cards are rarely as fast as conventional game cards.

Another useful feature on a handful of cards is a direct connection to an LCD display. This provides a clearer picture than the standard video connector used to connect to a monitor, but so far is only available on a handful of cards.

SPECIFICATION CHECKLIST

Using the recommended system needed to run your software of choice as a guide, you can work out a target hardware specification based on the following:

(1) Apple or PC

(2) processor chip

(3) memory

(4) floppy disk type

(5) hard disk size

(6) monitor and graphics card

(7) operating system software: this is included as part of the hardware, as they are almost always sold together

(8) all connectors, manuals, mouse and keyboard

(9) optional extras: (i) a printer; (ii) a CD-ROM drive or DVD drive; (iii) a sound card and speakers; (iv) a modem; (v) a scanner; (vi) networking facilities; (vii) video cards, joysticks and other less usual extras; (viii) backup facilities.

When buying, check each of these items in turn and make sure that all have been included in your order.

Details of the hardware differences between Apple and IBM are discussed in Appendices IV and V.

Appendix II

Hardware extras and upgrades

Some hardware extras are entertainingly useless, such as a simulated sailing tiller which connects to your computer and lets you practise your navigation skills. Others, such as printers, are all but essential.

Like the other parts of your computer system, each extra has its own specification and jargon. Not all have specifications that are quoted with software. To some extent they depend on personal preference. Fortunately, most extras are relatively straightforward and do not demand the same kind of technical knowledge that computers themselves do.

Printers

The currently available options include:

Daisy wheel These printers are now obsolete but they were popular until the early 1990s. They occasionally appear on the second-hand market, but are best avoided, as spares and ribbons are no longer available. Daisy-wheel printers work by slamming metal dies against a ribbon, which then print letters on to the paper. The dies are arranged in a circle on spokes around a central support. The whole arrangement looks rather like the petals of a flower – hence the name.

Daisy-wheel printers are very slow, very noisy, and can only produce text – pictures, decorative borders and so on are not possible. Their only advantage is that they can produce true typewriter-quality print. With the relative affordability of good-quality laser and bubble-jet printers, however, these printers have fallen by the wayside.

> **This is an example of near letter quality (NLQ) mode printing from a dot matrix printer.**
>
> This is an example of draft mode printing from a dot matrix printer.
>
> This is 9 point Times Roman
>
> This is an example of Times 12 point output on a 300 dpi laser printer.
>
> This is an example of Times 12 point output on a 600 dpi laser printer.
>
> This is an example of Times 12 point output on a 1200 dpi laser printer.

Dot-matrix 9-pin These printers are the most basic models available. Because the printing system is mostly mechanical (a print head with 9 retractable pins scans across the paper and 'punches' dots on to it via a ribbon) these printers are slow, irritatingly noisy and produce poor-quality output. However, they are cheap (a typical example might cost around £100) and have negligible running costs. Apart from paper and minimal electricity consumption, the only extra costs are inked ribbons. These need to be replaced once or twice a year and cost under £10.

These printers are now virtually obsolete, and are usually only used where quality of print is less important than reliability, low running costs and the ability to produce multiple carbon copies – for example, invoice printing for garages. Although most printers offer a 'near letter quality' (NLQ) mode that provides sharper letters, the print quality is noticeably rough when compared with a good typewriter or laser printer.

Only the simplest block and line graphics are possible with these printers; photographic images are not. The machines can produce a range of lettering styles with appropriate software, but compared with other printers the results can look amateurish and rough.

Dot-matrix 24-pin 24-pin printers offer improved print quality compared to 9-pin printers, but otherwise have the same advantages and drawbacks. They cost between £150 and £500. The more expensive models are ideal for long inventory listings, which are most convenient when printed on continuous paper – paper which is sold as a very long strip divided into pages by perforations – and can also accommodate wider paper than cheaper examples.

Bubble-jet/ink-jet These printers have now become the standard for anyone who wants affordable low-volume colour printing. They are also adequate for text, although lettering isn't as sharp as that from a laser printer. Ink-jet printers are now the budget printer standard and work by electrostatically squirting tiny blobs of ink on to a sheet of paper. They are quiet, slightly faster than dot-matrix printers and give reasonable results at a modest cost – typically £80 to £500. Running costs are moderate for light use. The ink is supplied in the form of cartridges, which cost between £15 and £30 to replace (ink and re-inking equipment are available if you want to refill cartridges by hand, which is cheaper – although it can be messy). Many printers have separate colour and black ink cartridges. Colour cartridges can be wasteful. They contain three (sometimes more) separate ink colours, and on most models the whole cartridge must be replaced as soon as one ink colour runs out.

A bubble-jet printed page of text will always look slightly rough, although the print quality is significantly better than that offered by dot-matrix machines. (The quality can be improved by using high-quality paper rather than photocopier paper.) This makes the printers suitable for professional work, especially for sole traders working from home. For a start-up business on a tight budget a bubble-jet printer provides the best compromise between cost and print quality. Some printers are now specifically designed for photographs and high-quality images. These 'photo' models can produce excellent results. Prints were once prone to fading, but some models, such as the Epson 1270 and 1290, use special light-fast inks that are guaranteed for a decade (similar inks for other printers are available to order from specialised fine art suppliers). For dedicated fine art use, more expensive printers are available that use inks guaranteed for a century.

Colour, however, remains expensive – an A4 page of colour can cost as much as 20p – and some printers can be painfully slow, taking perhaps 20 minutes per page. (Black-and-white printing is very much quicker.) Apart from fine art and graphics, colour printing can also be used for bar charts and other business graphics, and for domestic and light business colour printing, such as cards, letters and advertisements. Some models can print on overhead transparency film. As with laser printers, fineness and accuracy are specified in dots-per-inch (dpi). However, it is impossible to compare the two different kinds of printer directly in this way. The print quality of a 300-dpi ink-jet is fairly rough for both text and graphics. From 600 to 720 dpi is better, but still not comparable to a 300-dpi laser. You need a resolution of 1,440 dpi on a bubble-jet to even begin to approach 300-dpi laser quality for text, and when used with special paper this can produce moderately satisfactory renditions of colour photographs and other images.

Some ink-jet printers can print on A3 as well as A4 paper. This is useful for posters and advertisements, and can also be a way to improve print quality for very demanding work. For certain applications printing on A3 and photocopying in colour at 50 per cent onto A4 can appear to produce a more detailed image than printing directly to A4.

If you are sure that an ink-jet printer is for you, it could be well worth considering one of the 'all-in-one' office units that are now available. These combine some or all of the functions of a scanner, a fax machine, an ink-jet printer and a photocopier in a box only slightly larger than the printer itself. However, it's important to give these units a fair trial run to make sure that each of the individual sections meets your needs.

Laser Laser printers remain the best option for anyone who needs high-quality black-and-white output for business correspondence. These printers use a tightly focused beam of light to 'paint' an image onto the surface of a special light-sensitive drum. This image is then printed to paper using a system based on photocopier technology. Laser printers give results which approach those possible with conventional typesetting and printing machinery, at a fraction of the cost. A close examination of a laser-printed page will show that the letters are slightly rough compared with work that has been professionally typeset, but for many applications the differences are unimportant.

Laser printers are no longer the expensive option they once were. Prices have levelled out at around £200, though you can pay up to £20,000 for a lightning-fast printer that can serve the printing needs of an entire office.

Running costs vary from model to model. In addition to the unit price, laser printers can be expensive to run. Not only do they consume significantly more electricity than the other printer types, they also require expensive consumables. To produce a laser-printed image, very fine dust-like particles of ink (known as toner) are literally melted on to the page. The toner is supplied in the form of cartridges which need to be replaced every 5,000 pages or so. Toner cartridges can cost up to £100. However, laser printers can still work out cheaper than ink-jets in the long run, and require less maintenance. By way of comparison, a typical ink-jet cartridge costs £20 and will need to be replaced every 500 pages.

Another cost arises from the need to replace the drum on which the laser writes the image. This is made of a special light-sensitive material which slowly wears out as the printer is used. Drums can cost up to £100 a time, but fortunately need replacing much less frequently than toner cartridges. The latest laser designs, especially the cheaper models, attempt to minimise running costs by including drum and toner in the same unit. These all-in-one cartridges cost between £30 and £50 to replace.

Laser printers can handle just about any black-and-white printing task. (Colour laser printers have now come down in price but are still very expensive. The very cheapest 'budget' models start at around £1,000 and go up to many times this, which puts the technology out of reach of most home users – although businesses sometimes use colour laser printers to check page proofs before a major colour-printing project.) As well as producing different kinds of lettering in different sizes, laser printers can also produce drawings and cartoons. Mid-range and better lasers can also produce good reproductions of black-and-white photographs.

Laser printers are specified according to how finely they can print dots on a page. A low-cost printer can create 300 dpi. This is more than adequate for most office work, although lettering produced on a 300-dpi printer does look very slightly rough when compared with professionally typeset printing. These printers are not recommended for photographs.

The next step up is 300 dpi with resolution enhancement. This process fills in the spaces between the dots with smaller dots, creating a sharper result. When buying a laser it is important to check if resolution enhancement is available, as it significantly improves print quality for little, if any, extra cost. However, these printers are still not ideal for work involving photographs.

Higher-quality printers can produce 600 dpi. This is useful for low-budget professional publishing work, as the letter quality is sharp and photographs can begin to be reproduced convincingly. Some printers are billed as having a resolution *equivalent* to 600 dpi – this is simply marketing speak for a 300-dpi printer with resolution enhancement. Top-end printers can produce 1,200 dpi or better. This begins to approach the results achieved using professional typesetting equipment. Lettering is pin-sharp and photographs can be reproduced realistically. However, these machines are significantly more expensive and are recommended only if your work needs the extra quality. For conventional word processing they are unnecessary.

An important laser-printer specification to watch for is speed. This, quoted in pages per minute (ppm), is the maximum rate at which the printer can feed paper through. Many lasers do not approach their quoted speeds. Low-cost units can usually manage four pages per minute, which is adequate for everyday business use. More expensive and sophisticated machines offer twice or even three times this rate; these are usually designed for heavy-duty work in an office environment, where the one printer is shared between many users on a network.

In addition to the printing hardware itself, most laser printers include a sizeable built-in computer of their own to manage the printing process. Like other computers, they need memory to be able to work effectively. Some lasers are supplied with the bare minimum needed to print a single page of A4 text. Graphics, photographs and other styles of lettering may well need more memory than this, and it will have to be bought and installed as an extra. Check with your dealer if you will need to do this, based on the kind of work you have in mind. Extra memory can add significantly to the cost of a laser printer.

Some lasers get round this problem by using the PC's own resources to do the preparatory work. This is a much cheaper and simpler option, but it can cause a PC to stutter while it 'thinks about' what will go on the page. It can also be a difficult option to use with older MS-DOS software.

Laser printers are sometimes advertised as **Postscript-compatible**. Postscript is an image-definition system that has become a world standard since it was introduced on the Apple Mac in the mid-1980s.

The inclusion of Postscript offers extra facilities and makes a laser printer ideal for use with the many DTP and graphics programs that support this standard.

Dye sublimation, thermal transfer and solid ink printers are all aimed at the professional colour-printing market. They are very expensive and only of interest to businesses that need to produce very-high-quality print proofs in-house.

Modems

There are three things you should know about a modem. The most important is to check for BABT approval. This means the modem has been through a rigorous programme of testing and certification and is fully compatible with the BT network. Unapproved modems are no longer common, but they are still sometimes sold to unwitting users. While they may work well most of the time, it is illegal to connect one of these modems to a telephone line, and you are more likely to suffer from minor incompatibility problems (such as not being able to recognise the BT 'busy' signal) than if you buy a fully approved model. Unfortunately, the approval process is expensive, and approved models cost slightly more than the unapproved variety. In terms of peace of mind and long-term reliability, however, the extra cost can be worth it. Approved equipment carries the green triangle mark. Unapproved equipment is marked with a red circle.

Next, check whether the modem is internal or external. To install an internal modem you will need to remove the case from your computer and slot the modem into an expansion slot. You are more likely to come across obscure problems while doing this. An external modem is a better choice if you prefer to keep things as simple as possible. You can attach this to your computer with a special cable. Any further setting up should be minimal. When buying an external model, make sure that a cable is included.

Modems work at different speeds. These directly affect your telephone bill, as the faster the modem, the more quickly it gets information. Speed is measured in baud or bps (bits per second). Often this is shown as a number – 14,400 for example. These numbers can be compared directly – so a 28,800 modem will move information twice as fast as a 14,400 modem. Since the late 1990s all modems have worked at 57,600 bps (often referred to in advertisements as '56K' or 'V.90'), which is as fast as current telephone technology allows.

Older, slower modems (14,400 or slower) are sometimes available second-hand, but these are always a false economy. The nominal cost savings possible when buying a second-hand slow modem are more than outweighed by the much larger phone bill which is likely to result. A new V.90 modem is now within the budget of most buyers, and so there is little need to compromise with a slower model.

Speed is often shown as a 'V' figure. These are industry-standard codes for different modem speeds and features. The table below lists the most common speeds and typical applications.

V.90 replaced two earlier, incompatible, systems known as X2 and K56Flex. These are still used occasionally. However, a V.90 modem should be able to work with either of them. These 57,600 modems employ special tricks to get the fastest possible connection from the ageing technology used in the public telephone system. This has important implications. First, the maximum speed is only available when the modem is receiving information – when sending information, these models work at the same speed as a 33,600 modem. As most home and small business users receive far more information than they send, this is not a drawback. Second, the top speed is only available over an interference-free telephone connection. A more realistic working speed using a typical noisy connection is around 40,000 bps. To some extent this depends on the quality of the modem – better (although not necessarily more expensive) models will be able to approach the theoretical top speed more closely. Comparative magazine reviews are a good way to check how these fast modems fare against each other.

Speed	Code	Suggested usage
2,400	V.22bis	Completely obsolete. No longer worth considering
9,600	V.32	Also obsolete. Can be used for very occasional email, but too slow for anything more demanding
14,400	V.32bis	Also obsolete. Can be used for very occasional email, but too slow for anything more demanding
28,800	V.34	Superseded almost immediately by V34+
33,600	V34+	Adequate for light use, but now superseded by V.90
57,600	V.90	The current standard, fast enough for all domestic and light business applications

Some older 33,600 modems and X2 or K56Flex models were sold with a 'flash upgrade option'. If you have one of these, it can be worth visiting the manufacturer's web site to see if this option is available to you. The upgrade is very simple and consists of a piece of software which 'reprograms' the modem so that it works with the newer V.90 standard. There is no need to open the case of either the computer or the modem.

Many modems now include answering-machine features. The best can take voice messages, and perhaps receive faxes, even if the computer they are connected to is turned off. Some even include a built-in loudspeaker and microphone, so that they can be used just like an ordinary answering machine. Speech quality in these models is not as good as that from a high-quality tape unit, but for convenience and cost-effectiveness they offer very good value.

An extra line?

Because Internet use can tie up a telephone line for long periods, many home users and businesses are now adding an extra telephone line specifically for faxes and modem use. This is usually considerably cheaper than an ISDN link (see below), although of course connection speeds are rather lower.

However, note that BT sometimes uses a 'DACS box' to split one line into two when the second line is installed. This will have the effect of limiting the modem speed to around 36,000 bps, no matter what kind of modem is used. BT has sometimes proved unwilling to take away the DACS box and replace it with a genuine two-line connection unless plenty of pressure is applied. (The usual argument offered is that the line is for speech use, not data use.) Anyone having a second line installed for Internet use should make sure that this question is cleared up before installation goes ahead.

Cable, ADSL and ISDN

These services are available to more demanding Internet users. Cable is offered by cable TV companies, and offers speeds up to 1 Mb/s (1,000,000 bps). In practice a connection is shared with a number of other houses, so it is rare for information to appear at this speed, especially during peak hours. But, even at its slowest, cable offers a huge speed advantage over a modem connection. The service typically costs £25 per month.

ADSL (Asymmetric Digital Subscriber Link) is a similar service that is available over a new, improved telephone connection. Speeds of 512 kbps (512,000 bps) are realistic, although it is possible to get faster connections. The service costs £40 per month for home users and £90 for business users, and is available direct from BT and a number of resellers. (A business user is defined as anyone who plans to use the service as part of a network. If you have a home network you may wish to clarify this with a provider before signing up for the service.)

Prices for cable and ADSL (known collectively as 'broadband' services) are fixed – there are no call charges on top of the monthly charge. These services make a significant difference to both home and business Internet use. They are always on, and there is no need to wait for a modem to connect. As a result web pages appear far more quickly than over a modem link, music and video become as practical as text, and email arrives immediately.

There are three caveats to be aware of, though. Firstly, these services are not yet available everywhere. Currently they are limited to larger towns and cities; they are not available in rural areas, and will not become available there for some years yet – if at all. Secondly, offering an always-on service leaves your computer vulnerable to hackers. Anyone using these services should install a firewall or other protection system to prevent unauthorised access (see page 159). Some providers include a firewall as part of the service.

Finally, you may find that it is not possible to use these services to put up your own web pages and make them visible to other Internet users. This is known as 'web hosting'. Usually web hosting is a paid-for service, and web pages are kept on large central computers operated by Internet Access companies. In theory, any computer with an always-on connection can work as a web host, so it should be possible to save money and do the hosting at home. In practice, however, ADSL is not always set up to allow this. Again, you should clarify the situation with your provider before signing up for the service.

ADSL providers advertise in the Internet press. BT also offers this service direct to its customers (BT's customer enquiries service will be able to supply more details). If you already have cable TV, you can find out more about cable Internet services from your cable company.

ISDN

ISDN (Integrated Services Digital Network) is ADSL and cable's poor relation. It offers a halfway house between a modem connection and these faster services. BT's standard service, known as Home Highway (or Business Highway for business users), offers two lines, which can be used for voice or an Internet connection. A single line offers connection speeds of around 60 kbps, and the two lines can be linked to provide a theoretical maximum of 128 kbps (in practice this translates to 100–110 kbps). In real terms the speed improvement over a modem connection is unspectacular.

ISDN is offered in a range of schemes, virtually all of which are almost as expensive as ADSL. This makes it hard to recommend the service, except perhaps for businesses which need faster interim access until cable or ADSL become available in their area. Those who need ADSL or cable speeds, live in a rural area and can afford to pay for a premium service should consider a satellite link (see below) instead.

Cable, ADSL and ISDN hardware

To use any of these services, you will need extra hardware. Cable uses a modem-like device, ISDN a 'terminal adaptor', and ADSL uses a special card. Some of these are specific to each provider and are not available in shops. Your provider will be able to supply you with more details.

Other technologies

Satellite links are a good choice for more serious Internet users who live in an area not covered by the cable TV companies – particularly remote rural locations. Hughes-Olivetti supplies a system called DirecPC which uses a satellite dish to receive information at speeds of up to 400,000 bps: nearly seven times faster than a V.90 modem. (DirecPC cannot *send* information to the Internet in this way – that part of the connection is handled by an ordinary modem.) At the time of writing the dish itself costs over £1,000 to install, and a number of subscription schemes are available, which depend on the quantity and time of day at which information is received. Although expensive, it can offer better value than ISDN for some users.

A number of custom satellite systems are due for launch sometime before 2005, including one in which Bill Gates of Microsoft has invested heavily. In theory, these will provide a new global network that will be available for mobile telephone, Internet and perhaps also television transmissions. If they work successfully, they will render many existing systems obsolete and offer true high-speed wireless Internet connections almost anywhere in the world. However, at the time of writing a number of technical issues remain unresolved, and it is perhaps wise to treat these systems with a certain caution until they have proved themselves in the field.

Wireless links are currently a very slow way to use the Internet. Using current technology, mobile phone users are limited to 9,600 bps. However, by about 2003 this should improve, and plans are in place for wireless networks offering between 128 kbps and 4 Mbps. If these appear on schedule, and prove to be affordable, they will effectively render BT's current connection schemes obsolete almost overnight. This will have a revolutionary effect on the way that the Internet, mobile phones, faxes and other communication systems are used.

Sound cards

These are used to add sound and music to your computer. All sound cards can record a sound and play it back if you connect them to a microphone and a pair of speakers. This can be useful if you want to add voice annotation to a letter, use voice-recognition software, or take advantage of the experimental international-telephone-like services available on the Internet.

Many also include a music synthesiser. This adds a selection of more-or-less realistic instrument sounds that are used by games and other multimedia software. (Many web pages now include information that makes this synthesiser play a tune.) Older sound cards frequently offered a connection for a CD-ROM drive, but this feature is obsolete, now that CD-ROM drives can use the same connectors as a computer's hard disk.

One final extra is a joystick and MIDI interface (a joystick is a small extra that fits in one hand and is used in games). The MIDI (Musical Instrument Digital Interface) is a computer-control system for synthesisers and music keyboards. If you decide the sound from your sound card is a bit thin, you can connect an external synthesiser to make it fuller and richer. If you want to use your computer to record and edit performances from an external music keyboard, you will need a MIDI interface (you will also need an adapter, as the connector on the back of most sound cards does not fit the MIDI standard).

Over the years a sound-card standard has emerged, based on a range of cards from Creative Labs known as the Soundblaster series. In theory a 'Soundblaster-compatible' card should work with most software that needs a sound card, though in practice this is not always the case. If sound and music are important to you it is well worth getting a genuine Soundblaster card for the best possible results.

Sound cards vary in quality. Very old models used '8-bit recording', which is roughly equivalent to telephone quality and is adequate for speech and simple sound effects. All modern cards offer '16-bit recording', which approaches CD quality, although it's probably fair to say that in practice the sound from many cards doesn't quite reach true hi-fi standards.

A handful of cards offer 'digital input' and/or 'digital output', also known as 'S/PDIF' (Sony/Philips Digital Interface). A digital input can be used to make a perfect copy of music from a suitably equipped CD player on to a computer's hard disk. A digital output can provide ultimate audio quality when connected to a hi-fi extra called a DAC (Digital to Analogue converter).

Sound synthesisers also vary. Older sound cards used the old and very thin-sounding FM (Frequency Modulation) system, which was developed over a decade ago and uses the OPL3 and OPL2 set of chips. Newer sound cards use wave-table synthesis, which uses digital recordings of real instrument sounds, which are much more impressive and lifelike.

The very latest sound card designs include 'sampling memory', which lets you use your own recordings as musical instruments, and '3D sound'. The latter is designed to enhance the sound of games by making sounds appear to move above, below and behind the listener. Although the effect is noticeable with two speakers, it is far more striking with four, and the most recent sound cards include connections for four separate speaker channels.

Synthesiser technology has also improved. Home musicians can now buy cards which include synthesisers that are comparable to those available commercially. 'Software synthesisers' (also known as 'softsynths') are another new development. Instead of using a sound card's hardware, these literally calculate the music in software as it plays.

223

Windows 98 includes a softsynth made by the Roland company. Competitor Yamaha, meanwhile, offers a very-high-quality softsynth for around £30 that can be copied from its web site. This provides exceptionally good results for a very small outlay.

Amplifiers and speakers

With all sound cards you have the option of piping the sound through your existing hi-fi system. Sometimes it is more convenient to have speakers closer to your computer. Many multimedia systems are sold with speakers which stand on either side of the monitor or clip on to the sides. Speakers and sound cards are often sold together. When buying a sound card you should always check if speakers are included. If not, check whether the sound card has a built-in amplifier – otherwise you will have to use your hi-fi, buy an external amplifier or buy powered speakers. Apart from assessing basic sound quality (which only your ears can gauge), it is important to check if speakers are shielded; this means that their heavy magnets will not affect a monitor if placed next to it.

A recent trend has been to offer more and more powerful speaker systems. 'Subwoofers' add extra bass to the sound. Some sound cards are now being sold with four-speaker (or even five- or six-speaker) systems, which attempt to mimic the all-round sound offered by an expensive home cinema system. If you are considering one of these, it's worth noting that sound quality is very much poorer than that from a proper home cinema hi-fi. There may also be problems positioning the extra speakers, as some are designed to go behind the listener, and it's rare for people to have suitable shelving (or even a suitable wall) in the right place.

MP3 players

These are digital audio players that can play 'MP3 files' copied from the Internet. MP3 is a system used to compress music so it can be copied over the Internet more quickly than true CD-quality recordings. Quality is still very reasonable – better than typical cassette recordings – but the difference between an MP3 file and the original recording is quite obvious on good speakers. All modern computers can play MP3 files through their internal speakers using software such as the Microsoft Windows Media Player or WinAmp (both available for free and regularly given away on magazine cover disks).

Hardware MP3 players are designed to make playback portable. They can store up to an hour of music in a system that uses no moving parts, and so is completely jog-proof. Unlike tape and CD players, they cannot usually be loaded with new music directly. Instead they have to be connected to a computer, which then copies a new collection of files to the player.

CD-ROM drives

CD-ROMs look and work rather like conventional CDs, but instead of music, they contain pictures, text, sounds, video clips, software and other kinds of information. To use a CD-ROM you need to install an extra called a CD-ROM drive. When buying a CD-ROM drive, the most important thing to check for is speed. Originally, CD-ROM drives were designed to supply information at the same speed as music CD players, but this soon proved too slow for computer applications. Drives are now available that work up to 48 times ('48×') faster, although 40× drives are more common. These speeds are comparable to those offered by a hard disk, but the technicalities of CD-ROM technology mean that in practice most drives work at around 24× speed most of the time.

All CD-ROM drives can play ordinary music CDs. If you have a sound card and some speakers, the music will play through them directly – you will not even need to use your hi-fi. The sound quality is not quite up to hi-fi standards, but if you want some music while you work this is adequate. Appropriate software is included with most computers.

CD-ROMs should also be multi-session – although almost all drives made today comply with this standard. This feature is specifically for use with the Kodak CD format that stores photographs on a CD (this service is available as an extra at most high-street film developers). The CD can be used again and again, so you can keep adding images from a new roll of film until the CD is full. CD-ROM drives that are not multi-session will only allow you to access the pictures from the first roll. With the arrival of digital cameras (see pages 231–2) and affordable scanners, the future of the Photo-CD format is now in some doubt, although it's worth noting that the latter does offer much higher-quality images than a typical digital camera.

Drives designed in the early 1990s used one of the proprietary formats – usually Sony, Mitsumi or Panasonic – and were most often designed to work with compatible sound cards. More recent models use the IDE system, which is more convenient as it requires less hardware – the CD-ROM can be connected in exactly the same way, to exactly the same hardware, as a hard disk. But this convenience has an important side-effect: on some computers the hard disk will be forced to transfer information more slowly. To avoid this, make sure that the CD-ROM uses its own cable and connector. (A handful of drives use the SCSI system instead. This does not suffer from the same drawback, but is not so widely available and tends to be more expensive.)

Some older CD-ROM drives were designed to work with the Video-CD system, which offered the VHS-quality playback of commercial films and other videos on a computer's screen. This feature has not become the success that was originally hoped, and it has been superseded by the appearance of DVD (see below).

At around £150, CD writers (also known as 'CD burners', 'recordable CD' or 'CD-RW' drives) have now become affordable. These write information to special CD blanks, and make it possible to produce music CDs and CD-ROMs to your own requirements. These blanks cannot be re-used – information is stored on them permanently and cannot be changed. These drives also double as conventional CD-ROM drives, although they are slightly slower – the fastest drive currently available is a thirty-two-speed ('32×'). Information can be written up to 12-speed ('12×'), although this may be unreliable compared to slower speeds.

Most CD writers can also work with CD-RW ('rewritable') blanks. These are more expensive disks that can be reused any number of times. CD-RW disks may not work in domestic hi-fi CD players or even in some computer CD-ROM drives. Note that CD-R and CD-RW disks are more fragile than traditional CDs, and require more careful handling. CD writers are becoming a de facto replacement for floppy disk drives. While less convenient than floppy disks, they offer higher capacity and lower cost than competing formats such as Zip drives (see below). Many new PCs include a CD writer as standard.

CD writers require a fast PC that can produce the steady flow of information that the writer requires. If the PC hiccups at all the writer will ruin a disk blank. Any medium-price modern PC should be fast enough, but older second-hand models almost certainly won't be.

226

BURN (Buffer UnderRuN)-proof CD writers are an attempt to work around this problem and avoid ruined blanks. In practice the technology is not completely reliable, though it does seem to reduce burn problems. A BURN-proof drive is recommended for older PCs.

DVD

DVD (officially called Digital Versatile Disk, but more likely to be known as Digital Video Disk) is a next-generation CD-like system that appeared in computer stores during 1998. The disks can store up to 17Gb of information – enough for around 15,000 copies of the text of this book.

DVD was designed as a replacement for video tape, offering much better sound and picture quality in a more convenient package, and also as a 'next-generation' CD-ROM, offering all the same facilities but with the ability to store much more information. Both consumer DVD players, which look and work like hi-fi CD players, and computer DVD drives, which look and work like CD-ROM drives, are now well established, although it is worth noting that any computer DVD drive made before the middle of 1999 may suffer from teething troubles. One other point to note is that DVD includes an anti-piracy feature that divides the world into a number of regions, with players and disks made specifically for each one. A 'Region 2' disk, for example, will not play in a 'Region 1' player. Not all computer DVD drives include this feature, thus making it possible to buy any DVD film from anywhere in the world and view it without problems.

To watch films on your computer you will need extra hardware or software. This is usually supplied when you buy a DVD drive. Note that software players require a powerful, fast computer. If your computer was bought before 1999, it may not be fast enough for the job, and DVD playback will be very jerky. Hardware players take the form of an expansion card that slots into your PC, but these cards are only included with a small number of DVD drives – software players are much more common. If you have an older computer, make sure you get a drive that includes this extra hardware. Alternatively, some graphics cards (see page 232) include similar hardware. If in doubt, check with a reliable dealer what you will need to buy.

Writeable DVD systems are starting to become available, but a number of competing, incompatible systems have confused this part of the market. DVD-RAM is the official standard, but DVD-RW and DVD+RW are also available. None of these is guaranteed to work with conventional DVD players, although DVD-RW seems least likely to cause problems. Current DVD-RAM drives are perhaps best considered as a high capacity backup option, rather than as a way to create home-made DVDs.

Other drive types

Although floppy disks are rapidly becoming obsolete, no single technology has yet appeared to replace them. A variety of systems are now available, the most popular of which are the 120Mb 'a:drive LS120' from a number of sources, and the Zip and Jaz drives made by Iomega. The latter can store 100Mb and 1Gb respectively on small removable cartridges. These and various other systems offered by other manufacturers are relatively affordable and ideal for backups, although of course none has become a standard yet. If you are buying them solely for your own use this is not a worry, but if you are planning to use them to exchange information with friends and colleagues it is too early to tell yet which, if any, of these new systems will become the most popular and widely accepted.

Scanners

These copy pictures and photographs directly from a printed page into your computer. The quality range available stretches from simple black-and-white scanning (which is more than adequate for sending paper-based faxes) to full photographic colour, with the latter rapidly becoming a new standard. As with other computer extras, scanner prices have plummeted, and equipment that was within the budget only of professionals at the beginning of the 1990s is now available for less than £60. Many scanners come with software for 'optical character recognition' (OCR). This attempts to read a page of text, rather than simply grabbing it as an image – so, for example, the words on the page can be copied into a word processor as if they had been typed. Although the results can sometimes be rough and ready, OCR software combined with a scanner can be a useful time-saving tool for applications where large amounts of text would otherwise have to be typed in by hand. Cheap OCR systems are unlikely to be reliable. You will need a good scanner and good OCR software if you want to use the system professionally. Otherwise, you will have to proof-read copy after it has been scanned and make corrections yourself. With a budget system expect an accuracy of 95 per cent at best.

Scanners come in three types. A **document scanner** is a long, thin, plastic item with a slot at the front through which you pass the document. While less bulky than **flatbed scanners** (see below), these tend not to offer comparable scanning quality, and can also be surprisingly expensive; they are very rarely found now. Flatbed scanners are more like a photocopier: you place the image on a glass plate under a lid, and the scanner does the rest. They are now very affordable and are used by both amateurs and professionals. Some flatbeds also include a transparency adapter, so you can scan in slides as well as photographs. A **slide scanner** is designed exclusively for transparencies, and is of interest to artists and graphic designers; the size and shape varies.

Scanners can be connected to a computer in one of three ways: using the same connector as a printer; with their own plug-in card, typically using the SCSI system; or using a USB connection. The last two offer much faster scanning and are the choice for more serious users. (SCSI may require an expansion card be installed in the computer, but USB is 'plug-in and go'). The printer-connector option is much slower – a single A4 page can take more than 15 minutes – and may require a printer switch box. This typically costs around £15 and connects either the printer or the scanner to the computer.

Scanners are rated according to colour depth and resolution. The best offer 24-bit colour, which makes them suitable for colour photographs. (A handful of professional-quality scanners offer 36-bit colour, which is better still but only relevant in a professional publishing context.)

Resolutions are specified in dots per inch (dpi). They are often quoted as 'interpolated' (mathematically enhanced) rather than 'native' (i.e. copied directly from the scanning hardware without further processing.) Interpolated scans can be less sharp than native scans. In practice, however, this is only likely to matter to design professionals. For general use 1200dpi interpolated is a good starting point, and 2400dpi is adequate for most work. Higher resolutions will produce very detailed but also very large images, which can be difficult to work with and are unlikely to be needed outside a professional setting.

Check also that a scanner uses the TWAIN standard. This makes it possible for the scanner to scan images directly into most image-processing software.

Mice

A mouse is a hand-held pointing device that fits under your palm. In order to use it correctly, the connecting lead should be at the top of the mouse, by your fingertips, as opposed to under your wrist. As you move it from left to right and up and down, a pointer on the screen tracks your movements. There are one or more buttons under your fingers at the top of mouse. When you have moved the pointer to an active area on the screen you can make something happen by clicking one of these buttons.

PC mice have two or three buttons (although the middle one is usually ignored by most software) and are connected to the computer's serial port, or directly to a special socket on the motherboard (the PS/2 standard). Mice vary in comfort and ease of use. Some are sculptured to fit under your hand, while others are simply blocks of plastic.

A number of companies now offer 'wheel mice', which include a tiny wheel in between the buttons. This can be used to work the scroll-bars at the side of a window. Many mice are also available in sculpted 'ergonomic' designs. As with keyboards, these are very much a matter of personal preference. One person's favourite can literally cause pain and cramp for someone else.

The latest designs are rounded and easy to use. Optical mice use a non-mechanical system to track movements, and are less susceptible to grime and dust; the best optical mice are more reliable and long-lasting than traditional mice, because they have no moving parts to accumulate dirt and debris. An interesting alternative is offered by cordless mice. Like cordless keyboards, these dispense with any kind of physical connection and so help cut down on unwieldy wiring.

In general one mouse is much like another, and unless you find the one you have been given intolerable, or feel the need to personalise your computer in some way, you will not need to change your mouse for another.

Trackballs are upside-down mice, and some users find these preferable, especially if they are working in cramped conditions without enough desk space for a standard mouse. Like mice, trackballs are available with a number of extra buttons and special features that make them easier to use.

Digital cameras

Digital cameras use no film. Instead, they store images in computer memory. These images can then be copied – 'downloaded' – to a computer. No developing costs are involved, which means that images can be seen very quickly. This makes these cameras ideal for anyone who wants to get images into their computer in a hurry.

The current generation of cameras offers much-improved optics and image quality compared to their predecessors. However, it remains true that quality is usually equivalent to that on a film camera costing perhaps half or even a third as much. This makes most of these cameras more suitable for dabbling and semi-professional work than for professional photographers who need very high-quality results. (Cameras to suit professionals are available, but at prices that vary between £2,000 and £20,000. A standard digital camera is more likely to cost a few hundred.)

A number of systems are used to store and transfer images. A handful of camera designs write information on to standard floppy disks, which can be used in a computer in the usual way; more commonly, images are transferred over a cable link, which can be slightly fiddly in practice. Camera memory is always limited. The best models can store up to 36 shots, although many models offer a trade-off between the number of shots that can be remembered and the detail and picture quality of each image. Sometimes it is possible to expand the memory in a camera by adding 'flash cards' – thin wafers that add extra memory in a very small space. Additional memory is always expensive, and can add between £50 and £100 to the cost of a camera. Check whether or not you need extra memory, and if so how much it will cost you, before buying. Battery life can also be a problem with some models, and this also should be checked before purchase.

Note that some printers now include a flash-card slot. Images can be printed directly from the card without being copied to a PC first. While this option might seem very useful, basic retouching on the PC, for example as colour and contrast control, can make such a big difference to the effectiveness of a digital photo it is all but essential. In practice, therefore, a direct-print facility is perhaps only useful for very casual snaps.

A useful feature on some cameras is the ability to preview and check images with a display on the back of the camera. If an image isn't satisfactory, it can be deleted immediately to make room for a new one. A more advanced version of the same idea is the digital video camera. This has two applications – videophone links, which make it possible to see someone while you are talking to them on the telephone, and true digital video, which in effect offers a computerised tapeless camcorder. Videophone cameras are usually designed to sit on top of a monitor, and cannot be used without a connection to a PC. They offer poor image quality, can double as cheap still cameras, and at under £150 are relatively affordable. With prices between £500 and £2000, true digital video cameras have started to become relatively affordable. Apple's FireWire connection system makes it possible to transfer video directly from one of these cameras to the computer's hard disk, where it can be edited further.

Advanced graphics cards

Where once graphics cards struggled to produce a detailed image in the maximum possible range of colours, now most cards take this task for granted. Progress has moved on to adding features for games, and in some cases for home video editing. In general, the card supplied with a PC when it is bought will be adequate for most uses, and the following will only be of interest to more demanding users.

Specialised games cards make it possible to play a game at a high resolution. They both speed up the rate at which images appear and also make the gaming environment appear more detailed. The technology used to do this is very complex, and a description of all the relevant details is outside the scope of this book. One point to note, however, is that cards develop at an overwhelming rate. The current market-leading card may be considered an also-ran as little as six months hence. The only way to keep up with this technology is to watch out for comparative reviews in magazines.

Video editing systems are available as optional extras for some cards. These typically add a TV output, so that the picture can be made to appear on a conventional domestic TV set. They often also include *S-Video* connections, which can be plugged into a video recorder for transferring pictures with minimum loss of quality. Not all cards include connections both ways. Sometimes it is only possible to get S-Video information into a card; for playback, the TV output is used. Finally, most systems include some form of editing software. (Adobe Premier is the best choice here, but is only available on more expensive systems.) There may also be a TV tuner built in, with a suitable aerial connection. This makes it possible to record video 'live' from standard broadcasts. Both TV tuners and adapters are sometimes sold as stand-alone extras for those who do not need all the other features offered by these cards.

The latest development is affordable cards that can work with DV and MiniDV cameras, copying information to the computer and back to the camera digitally, with no loss of quality, using the Firewire system. Basic editing kits are now available for around £100, while more advanced models, which include professional software as well as special hardware for digital special effects, cost around £1,000. These use the Firewire system to copy video to and from a MiniDV camcorder. These camcorders are now available for between £500 for a very basic model with mediocre optics, to £1,500 and more for a semi-professional model with much better picture quality.

Games accessories

The number and complexity of the hardware extras available for dedicated games players is increasing steadily. *Joysticks* allow game players to navigate around their virtual world by pulling and pushing a single controller. The most complex and expensive designs include extra buttons which can be pre-programmed to shoot weapons or move in a special way. Some also include 'feedback' – a built-in electric motor which sometimes shakes the joystick to make the gaming experience more tactile.

Steering wheels are a popular choice with players of driving simulations. These are literally smaller-than-normal plastic steering wheels which clip on to the front of a desk. Floor-standing brake and accelerator pedals are often also included.

Game pads are simple button pads, similar to the ones used on games consoles, that are simply used to translate the console experience to a PC.

Graphics pads

Used by artists and illustrators, these are large, flat, plastic surfaces that are used in conjunction with a stylus. The stylus can be used as a pen, so you can draw, write or trace on the pad, and the result goes straight on to your computer's screen (it can also be used as a replacement for the standard mouse). The best pads are pressure-sensitive – as you press harder, the stylus responds. You should always try out a pad for yourself before buying. This is a small market with few competitors. In tests, the most highly rated pads are usually those made by Wacom.

Pads are available in sizes from postcard-sized A6 to huge A2; A3 or A4 are adequate for most applications. Larger pads are not necessarily better – if they are too large you can strain your arms through excessive movement.

Network cards

Apple computers can be connected together very simply using the built-in network features and appropriate cables – Apple dealers will be able to advise you how to do this.

PCs are more complicated and require extra networking hardware as well as the cabling. Although creating a medium-sized or larger network (typically involving more than five machines) is a job for an expert, it's possible to use the features in Windows 95/98/ME, together with some network cards, to create a smaller working network very quickly and easily. A number of dealers now supply 'network kits' which include everything required to link two or more PCs for less than £100.

Network cards offer two speeds – 10 Mb/s and 100 Mb/s. Two very similar systems, called 10baseT and 10base2 (the former is more popular), offer 10Mb/s. This speed is adequate for light use, such as copying a letter from one computer in an office to another, but rather slow for any applications that regularly use large amounts of information. For these more demanding applications the 100baseT system, which runs ten times faster, is recommended; such systems should ideally plug into the faster PCI slots in your machine, as the slower ISA slots can slow down the performance of the connection.

Networks based on network cards can sometimes be a little fiddly to set up. For someone who simply wants to connect two PCs together, it is quicker and cheaper to simply link the PCs using a USB cable and a copy of some suitable software, such as Travelling Software's LapLink.

The most recent versions of LapLink make it possible to transfer information from one PC to another, to control one PC remotely using the other's screen and keyboard, and even to print on the remote PC's printer.

Other network hardware

At the time of writing wireless networking systems using the Bluetooth and 802.11 systems (see page 208) are due to arrive very soon, but have been delayed by technical and political wrangles. Wireless networking makes it possible to connect a laptop to a desktop computer anywhere within a radius of a few tens of meters. No cables are required.

A small number of systems are available that will create a network over standard house telephone wiring. Computers can be connected wherever there is a telephone socket. Connection speeds are not as fast as with standard network hardware, but the approach has its advantages for anyone who has more than one computer but does not want to wire their house or office for Ethernet.

Operating systems

Most software is designed to help you with a specific job – writing a letter, sending a fax, and so on. An operating system, however, works on a more fundamental level. It manages the smooth running of your computer: it takes your commands, passes them on to the hardware and software, and then sends the results back to you.

By choosing the software first you will not need to worry about which operating system to use. It will be given as part of the software's required system specification, together with all the hardware details. Apart from the basics needed to get the software running, it is not usually necessary to deal with the operating system directly.

There is one exception: all software is written to match a specific operating system. Any new software you buy has to match the operating system you already have on your machine. If, for example, you have a spreadsheet that works with (the technical term is 'runs under') the popular Windows system, then buying software written for a different system, such as Unix, is a waste of time and money. It will not work. Find out which operating system your computer uses, and make sure that new software is compatible.

Ease of use

Operating systems work on two levels. The most visible level is the **user interface** which you use to work with your machine. It determines the 'look and feel' of your computer, and also how easily you can get work done.

Some operating systems use pictures on the screen to show what your options are. These systems are known as GUIs (Graphical User Interfaces) and are designed to be as easy to use as possible. Software that works with GUIs has on-screen 'buttons' and other controls. You use these with a mouse that is plugged into the computer (see page 230). Most GUIs also include a drag-and-drop facility. To move a sentence or paragraph in a document you simply highlight it with the mouse, then 'drag and drop' it by holding one of the buttons down, moving the pointer to a new location and releasing the button. The sentence disappears from the old location and appears in the new one. This makes editing very quick and easy. Drag-and-drop features are used in all kinds of software.

Older operating systems work on a text-only basis known as a **command-line interface**. To work with one of these older systems you have to learn a set of commands, such as COPY, which moves information from one place to another, and DIR which lists all the information on your hard disk. To use these commands you type them on the keyboard, hit the RETURN key and the computer responds to your request. Editing tends to be much slower with this kind of operating system.

Text-only systems date from a time when computers were much less powerful, and text was all they could handle. This is no longer true today, and text-only systems are all but obsolete. However, they are still preferred for some kinds of work. They give you more control and have the advantage of working with cheaper and less powerful hardware.

The less visible level of an operating system is the system interface – a complex set of connections to the hardware. This standardises the way the hardware works. This part of the operating system is completely hidden from users.

All modern operating systems let your computer do more than one thing at a time. You can start off a long calculation, compose a fax, send it, write a letter, print it out and log a phone call, all while the computer continues with the calculation 'in the background'. This useful ability is known as pre-emptive multi-tasking (usually shortened to multi-tasking.)

A multi-tasking operating system is – nominally – more reliable. Each task is managed so that it works independently of the others. If the task runs into problems or attempts something impossible, the computer as a whole does not hang or crash. The problem task can be stopped while the others carry on regardless.

Multi-tasking became an option during the mid 1990s. Before then a simpler system known as task-switching was sometimes used. This allowed you to switch between different applications quickly and easily and could be very useful. You could be working on a letter, decide you need to check an address in your information manager, switch to it quickly, and then come back to the letter which remains exactly as you left it. Without task-switching you would have to unload the word-processing software, load in the information manager (time-consuming even on a fast machine), unload the organiser, load in the word processor and return to your place.

Before the arrival of task switching, operating systems worked on a strict one-job-at-a-time basis. The best they could manage was a feature called **print spooling**. You could print a letter without having to wait for the printer to finish – the printing itself continued in the background while you got on with other work. This feature was usually part of the software, rather than of the operating system.

Like other software, operating systems evolve and go through different versions. Some are radically different from their predecessors; for example, Windows version 1 and Windows version 3 were completely different operating systems. The differences between Windows 95 and Windows 98, though, are far less obvious. It is important when looking at operating systems to include the version number, as the differences between versions can sometimes cause problems.

Only a handful of operating systems are available today. The ones you are likely to come across are listed below.

MS-DOS (PC)

MS-DOS (Microsoft Disk Operating System) is the original PC operating system. It is still sold by Microsoft, the world's leading PC software company, even though it has now been made obsolete by Windows 95/98. MS-DOS was devised in the late 1970s but has maintained its position because so many people use it. MS-DOS (often shortened to DOS) is a command-line system. It can only do one thing at a time.

In terms of modern computing, MS-DOS is a throwback to the age of the dinosaurs. It can be something of a nightmare for beginners, as it does not appear user-friendly or accommodating. However, it is the lowest common denominator between different PC machines. A program written to use MS-DOS on a very early PC will work on an up-to-date model.

The one great advantage of DOS is that it is simple and unfussy. It will work on the oldest and least impressive hardware and will place minimal demands on it. In general, though, it is ham-fisted and obstructive. It was designed when computers were basic and slow, and users had to be forced to work them in a way that suited the computer, rather than the user. Graphics are minimal and crude, and the software can seem clumsy when compared with later examples that use a more modern operating system.

MS-DOS is no longer being developed. The last available version as a separate product is 6.22. Earlier versions (such as 6.0 and 5.0) are very occasionally sold by stores that cater to computer enthusiasts, but they are unreliable and should be avoided. Any new computer will be supplied with a recent version of Windows, rather than MS-DOS.

Windows 3.1 and 3.11 (PC)

Like MS-DOS, Windows was created by Microsoft, although it is based on earlier products from Apple and Xerox. The name derives from the way in which the screen is split up into areas or 'windows', each of which has a frame. Each window can be moved, opened, closed, resized and hidden without affecting the others. This makes it possible to have a word processor in one window, a spreadsheet in

Windows 3.11

239

another, some Internet software in a third, and so on. To switch
between them you move the mouse pointer to the window you want
to work with, click on it once and it becomes active.

Windows 3.1 and 3.11 (which are known generically as 'legacy
Windows' or Windows 3.1x) are not quite true operating systems,
because they exist on top of MS-DOS to make it easier to use and
more appealing visually. Both are obsolete now, having been replaced
by Windows 95 and 98 (see below). However, they are still available to
special order and can also be found on second-hand machines, where
they offer certain advantages for anyone on a tight budget. They can
be used successfully on older, cheaper and less impressive hardware.
While less robust in some ways – if something goes wrong, they can
stop a computer in its tracks until it is switched off and on again – they
are also easier to troubleshoot.

Windows 3.11 is almost identical to 3.1, but has extra features that
make it easier to use on a multi-user network. It is sometimes known
as Windows for Workgroups (WfWG.) Both systems offer task-
switching and very limited multi-tasking.

Windows 95 (PC)

Windows 95, released in 1995, was a major rewrite of the Windows
system that attempted to bring it up to date. It included all kinds of
useful extras (such as built-in Internet support, improved
information handling, proper multi-tasking for Windows 95-
compatible software and overhauled screen layout designs) and was
intended to be much easier to use. From a technical point of view
though, it still relied to some extent on a special version of MSDOS
(version 7), although this had been hidden away even further.
Windows 95 could also be used to work with applications written
for Windows 3.1x, albeit with some reduction in effectiveness. It also
included 'Plug and Play' features that made it easier to add new
hardware to a PC (although these were still not as developed as they
could be).

There were two versions of Windows 95. The more recent was
known as OSR2 or Win95b, and offered some improvements over the
original. OSR2 was never sold as a separate product, and could only
be bought as part of a PC package. All its improvements are included
in Windows 98.

Windows 95

Windows 98/SE/ME (PC)

Windows 98 – released during the summer of 1998 – was a minor update of the Windows system. Some of the parts of Windows 95 that didn't work properly were fixed, and a variety of other cosmetic changes were made. From a practical point of view, Windows 98 was the first version that could work properly with USB computer extras (see pages 207–8). It also included a feature called FAT32 (first introduced in Windows 95 OSR2) that made it possible to use larger hard disks more efficiently. Anyone who is still using either version of Windows 95 but doesn't find these two extras essential is unlikely to gain much from upgrading to Windows 98.

The most obvious difference is that Windows 98 uses a special version of Microsoft's Internet Explorer web browser to find and work with information inside the computer as well as outside it on the Internet. While this replaces the older and less flexible way of working available in Windows 95, it also makes much heavier demands on a computer's speed and power. This in turn makes Windows 98 a problematic upgrade for anyone who is using a pre-1998 computer.

Microsoft originally planned to kill off Windows 98 as soon as it could, and replace it with a consumer-oriented version of its new Windows 2000 system (see below). However, Windows 98 has been temporarily reprieved because this proved impractical. Two new versions have been released in the meantime. Both 'Second Edition' (Win98 SE) and the later 'Millennium Edition' (Win98 ME) fix some of the more obvious problems and add a small selection of features, such as the ability to share a single modem over a network. They do not, for most people, offer enough to justify upgrading from the first version of Windows 98. In any case, many of the enhancements can be copied and installed for free from Microsoft's web site.

Microsoft has systematically and deliberately stripped out some networking features from Win98 ME, with the goal of forcing business users to switch to Windows 2000. Any business using an older version of Windows 98 would be well advised to continue using it until a switch to Windows 2000 becomes practical.

Windows 98 looks very much like Windows 95. The biggest difference is that it uses a browser-like system to find and display information

Windows NT (PC)

Where Windows 95 and 98 – sometimes known in the computer press as 'Windows 9x' ('x' is often used as a wildcard in computer jargon) – are designed for consumer and very small business use, Windows NT ('New Technology') has been aimed at more demanding professional users. From the user's point of view, NT looks and works very much like other versions of Windows. Internally, however, it works very differently. All versions include extra features that are designed to be used on networks of computers. It is also one of the few systems that can use more than one computer chip at once in the same machine – a feature known as Symmetric Multi-Processing (SMP), which is sometimes available on expensive, powerful hardware.

For a home or small business user, the extra expense, computer power and degree of skill needed to install and use Windows NT is probably wasted. It is also completely unsuitable for game players or other 'hobby' applications. But it can be worth considering for companies that need network security features and enhanced reliability.

NT 3.51 looked like Windows 3.1 externally. It was the first commercially successful version of Windows NT and, although it is still used in some companies, it has been superseded. NT 4 was the next version, updated to look like Windows 95, and is still used today, although it too has been superseded by Windows 2000 (see below). NT is more secure and reliable than Windows 9x, and also has better networking facilities. On the minus side, it needs more powerful hardware and more memory to work effectively. NT users should make sure that they check with Microsoft for the latest 'service packs'. These are updates to NT that are supplied to fix various problems. They are available on CD from Microsoft for a nominal cost, or can be copied from the Internet. Business-oriented magazines often include them for free on their cover disks.

Windows 2000 (PC)

Windows 2000 is the latest version of Windows NT. It is a complete rewrite of the NT system, and so much has changed that some Windows 9x and older NT software may no longer be compatible. Windows 2000 is designed for heavy-duty business use, such as

Windows 2000

maintaining the records of a very large company, as well as for smaller business systems.

Windows 2000 has been designed with the 'look and feel' of Windows 9x, and also includes its 'Plug and Play' features which should – in theory – make it easier to set up. In practice, though, the installation or upgrade process is still more technically demanding than it might be, and early releases were incompatible with a wide range of common hardware. While the latter situation is improving slowly, it remains the case that Windows 2000 is not suitable for home use, as home-oriented hardware (such as graphics and sound cards) may not work reliably with it. On the other hand, its networking facilities are a great improvement over both Windows NT and Windows 9x. Taken together, these changes mean it should be considered seriously for business computing – where reliability is more important than the ability to play games – but not seen as an upgrade that is suitable for home use.

Windows XP (PC)

Released in 2001, Windows XP is Microsoft's attempt to streamline its product line so that both business and home users use versions of the same operating system. Internally it is based on Windows 2000, with some enhancements to make it more suitable for domestic use. Externally it uses a new look and feel (called 'Aqua') in an attempt to simplify the Windows 95 look and feel and make it even easier to use. Business users can buy a 'professional' version that includes more advanced networking facilities than the cheaper domestic version.

Older software and hardware designed for use with Windows 9x may, or may not, work with Windows XP. This makes it a problematic upgrade for owners of older computers, especially those who have made a big investment in both software and information for their Windows 9x computers. Where possible check with the relevant manufacturers and dealers before upgrading.

One controversy associated with XP is its product activation system. Where previous Windows could be installed on multiple computers and registration was a formality rather than a necessity, Windows XP will not work unless it is registered over the Internet and supplied with a code. This code is keyed to specific computer hardware. If you upgrade your computer by putting in a new processor or motherboard, the code will no longer work. At the time of writing Microsoft has yet to clarify what this means for users, and many people consider the system to be unworkable. Clearly if your computer won't start, it becomes impossible to connect to the Internet. Similarly, it is hard to see how Microsoft can police the system effectively. Taken together, these issues mean that XP should perhaps be treated with a certain amount of caution by users of older software and hardware. Some industry commentators have suggested that Windows 2000 is a better choice for both home and business users.

.NET (various)

For some time now Microsoft has been trying to move away from Windows towards a more complex Internet-based system known provisionally as .NET. This is still being developed and discussed, and if and when it becomes a commercial product it may not bear much resemblance to the system that is being considered today. The information that follows should be considered provisional, and is included only for completeness.

In outline, .NET is an attempt to rework PC use so that services are provided remotely. Instead of paying for a word processor and installing it on your computer, the word processor will be made available on the Internet, and you will use it by hiring time on it. This guarantees that you always have all the latest features available – and, of course, guarantees the software developer a more reliable source of income. It has even been suggested that information will also be stored on the Internet instead of in home computers. The scheme also includes plans to make it easier for users to share information. For example, patients will be able to book a dental appointment directly from their computer, and the booking will appear automatically in the dentist's diary.

Many people are uneasy at the prospect of having letters, emails and finances stored outside the home or office. Similarly the idea of hiring software rather than owning it has encountered a degree of resistance. In the opinion of many in the industry, Microsoft has yet to offer a convincing rationale for how any of these changes will significantly benefit the consumer. Time will tell whether or not the system can be brought to market, and, if so, whether it will prove to be as successful as Microsoft's other products.

Windows CE/Pocket PC (various)

Windows CE was an attempt to create a 'pocket' version of Windows 9x that worked well on small hand-held computers and PDAs. The rationale was that a familiar environment, and the ability to copy information easily from 'pocket' versions of typical Microsoft applications such as Word and Outlook to their larger and more powerful desktop counterparts, would be an irresistible combination. Unfortunately, it was not a notable success in this part of the market, and so in early 2000 Microsoft redesigned the system and rebadged it as 'Pocket PC'. Pocket PC is slimmer, simpler and has improved Internet facilities, but it remains to be seen if these changes can bring it success against competing products.

OS/2 and Warp (PC)

Warp was IBM's competitor to Windows 95. Despite an 18-month lead and a number of technical advantages (such as the ability to run software written for Windows 3.1), Warp became a historical curiosity instead of a serious alternative – although a professional version of Warp, known as OS/2, can occasionally be found in a business setting. Neither OS/2 nor Warp can be recommended, even when supplied with a second-hand machine. They are included here only for completeness.

Unix (all computers)

Unix is widely considered (with reason) to be a computer professional's operating system, and hence something of a challenge for non-technical users. Unix is a command-line system, and much of its notoriety stems from the way in which command names seem to be obscure and confusing. Fortunately, a graphical extension called X-Windows is available, which works rather like Windows or the Macintosh Operating System. Unix is always fully multi-tasking.

Although Unix is used mainly on powerful machines in large companies, on smaller machines it tends to be the preserve of the hobbyist. Consultants may recommend it for certain applications, as at its best it can be much more powerful and reliable than Windows, and perhaps even Windows NT. It is not recommended for beginners.

Linux (various)

Linux is a version of Unix that was developed as a co-operative effort by computer hobbyists on the Internet. Unlike other operating systems, Linux is supplied with a licence which makes it clear that it is completely free. You can copy a version to your computer from the Internet and install as many copies as you like on as many machines as you like without owing a penny to anyone. (Compare this to systems such as Windows, which are usually charged on a per-user basis, causing very significant expense to businesses.)

Commercially packaged versions of Linux on CD – Red Hat, Mandrake and SuSE are among the most popular and highly regarded – are now widely available in larger computer stores under similar licence terms. These include the core Linux software and typically also feature plenty of extras, including Internet software, simple games, and so on. Corel supplies a free version of its Wordperfect Office Suite with some of these commercial packages. A related product called Star Office is also available for free. Windows-like systems such as Gnome and KDE are also available, which helps to make Linux easier to use for beginners.

Compared to Windows, Linux will work well even on very old hardware (a 386 computer with 8Mb of memory is a recommended minimum system). It also uses available computer power very much more efficiently, which makes it useful for scientific and mathematical research. In general, it seems to be more reliable and robust than Windows. From a computer professional's point of view, Linux is unique in that it is supplied with its *source code* – the actual raw programming details that are used to put it together. This makes it ideal for customised business projects, or for anyone who wants full control over what is happening inside their computer. Unlike Windows, which is a completely prepackaged system, Linux allows, and even encourages, users to change it to suit their own needs. Improvements are typically posted on the Internet, so that others can benefit from them.

The main drawback of Linux is that it is currently too complex for complete beginners to set up – although, once running, it is no more difficult than Windows to learn and use. It is also unlikely to work with unusual hardware. Finally, it lacks some of the safety features that Windows includes to prevent beginners damaging their hardware. It is perfectly possible to accidentally set up Linux so that it destroys a monitor. While this is very unlikely – and the newer commercial packages do their best to make it as unlikely as possible – this level of control makes Linux inappropriate for anyone who lacks a good working knowledge of computer hardware and software.

Linux has been touted as an alternative to Windows, but it still has some way to go before it can compete on similar terms. While Linux can be persuaded to look much like a Windows PC (only with

---

THE FUTURE OF WINDOWS
At the time of writing, Microsoft's future is uncertain. It is involved in an anti-trust (anti-monopoly) lawsuit with the US government over alleged illegal business practices designed to take unfair advantage of the success of the Windows system. The government has won the first round, but still has to fight its way through appeal. If successful, the government hopes to split Microsoft into two competing companies, with a view to opening up the market for both operating systems and business software. What this will do for consumers – if it happens at all – remains unclear

improved reliability), the underlying organisation is much more complex, and the degree of computer expertise required to understand how to manage and maintain the system remains much higher. Linux also lacks equivalents of the better software available on both PCs and Macs. Leading packages – such as Microsoft's Office, Adobe's Photoshop and Illustrator and Quark Xpress – are not only not available, but are unlikely ever to become available. This makes Linux a popular choice for hobbyists and computer professionals, but it is less likely to appeal to someone who simply wants to write letters and use email with the minimum of fuss.

BeOS (PC and Apple)

Created by an ex-Apple employee, BeOS is a very specialised operating system that is aimed at anyone who works with music, art or video. It is designed to use the available hardware more efficiently than other operating systems, and so effectively turns existing computers into more powerful machines. However, the range of software available for the system is currently very limited. At the time of writing BeOS seems to have been unsuccessful in carving out a niche for itself, and so it is included here only for completeness.

Mac OS (Apple only)

Apple's proprietary operating system, which is designed to work exclusively on Apple's own machines, swerved an unsteady and unpredictable course during the 1990s. But in the early years of the new decade it finally appears to have settled into a more predictable and rationally planned niche.

At the time of writing, Apple has started selling its long-awaited Mac OS X (pronounced 'ten'). This is a complete rewrite of the old Mac OS, and is based on the UNIX system. It offers a wide range of improvements including enhanced reliability and ease of use.

Apple is hoping that all users will eventually switch to OS X; in the meantime, though, it is also continuing to sell version 9.1 of Mac OS. Whether or not your Mac will work with OS X depends on how old it is, and what hardware is installed. Deciding whether or not to upgrade is a complicated issue, and prospective buyers should talk to a Mac dealer before attempting to change.

Note that it is possible to buy products known as 'Windows emulators' for MacOS. These effectively turn the Mac into a simulated PC that can use most standard Windows software. Because of the simulation process, the software runs rather more slowly than on an equivalent real PC, but for dabbling, and even for more serious business applications, Windows emulators give Mac users a chance to work in the best of both worlds.

Appendix IV

The IBM PC

When you start looking at different computer makes and models, you will find that by far the most readily available and widely publicised brand of computer on the market today is the IBM-compatible PC.

PC stands for 'Personal Computer', and in this context the term denotes a computer that is designed to be used by one person at a time and to fit conveniently on a desk. This can apply to any small computer, but in practice the letters 'PC' have become synonymous with IBM-compatible machines.

IBM-compatibles are manufactured from standard parts manufactured in the US and south-east Asia. Smaller dealers simply assemble these to order. Larger manufacturers, notably IBM, Dell, Compaq and Gateway, put together their machines from parts they have designed and manufactured themselves. Whatever their origin, all PCs conform to the same design standard originally defined by IBM (International Business Machines). In practical terms, this means that any software that is 'written for a PC' will work on any of these machines. It also means that it is easy to exchange information between machines.

Over the years the PC standard has undergone a number of revisions. Newer models can do everything that the older models could and usually much more quickly. Each aspect of the design has been refined and updated, and this process continues today. The full range of machines is still available, although the older models can only be bought second-hand.

Instead of brand names, PCs are distinguished by the model of computer chip at their heart. This master chip – also known as the processor or central processing unit (CPU) – is rather like the engine in a car: it is the main component that does most of the work. All the other parts of a computer exist to get information into and out of this chip. Some computer chips work faster than others. A chip's speed is quoted in MHz – millions of cycles a second. This means that a 500MHz chip runs twice as fast as the same model of chip that runs at 250MHz, but not, unfortunately, that the computer will work twice as fast – the speed of a computer system as a whole depends on a number of other factors. All the same, the processor speed does give a basic indication of a computer's power.

Here is a guide to the PCs you will see advertised, together with ratings out of ten for cost (a higher rating means a cheaper machine), performance (a higher rating means a faster computer) and value for money (a higher rating means a better price/performance ratio).

Note that second-hand prices are variable, and the ones shown below can only offer a very rough indication. Sellers often lack a realistic idea of what an older machine is worth. Put simply, all computers but the very latest are worth very little compared to their purchase price. The constant stream of improvements in new machines also means that there is a huge backlog of outdated technology available. With this in mind, it is always worth looking out for technology of a more recent generation when buying second-hand. The difference in price between an old 486 model and an old Pentium machine is likely to be only around £25–£50. But the Pentium is a significantly faster and better computer.

8088/8086/80286/80386

All these models are now effectively obsolete. None of them will work with new software or with newer versions of Windows, and they are too slow for Internet use. They are not recommended, even as second-hand machines, and are included only for completeness.

80486SX & SX2 (25MHz–66MHz)

Cost: 9/10
Performance: 2/10
Value for money: 2/10

Suggested applications: Light office work. Can work with older Windows software but slow with Windows 95/98. Suitable (but slow) for Internet use.

Pros: Reasonable value for those on a very tight budget.
Cons: Very slow at arithmetical work (such as spreadsheets).
Expansion: ISA and VLB slots.
Floppy disks: 3.5-inch 1.44Mb as standard.
Hard disk: Standard between 250Mb and 540Mb.
Typical memory supplied: 4Mb, sometimes 8Mb.
These machines are best avoided, even on the second-hand market. They are outperformed by 486 DX models (see below), which will be sold for a very similar amount.

80486DX, DX2, DX4, DX5 (33MHz–150MHz)

Cost: 9/10
Performance: 2/10
Value for money: 3/10
Suggested applications: Good basic business machine, now outdated technically but still a competent performer when used with suitable software. Adequate for Internet use.
Pros: The faster models especially are good budget machines.
Cons: Sluggish when working with Windows 95 software. Difficult to upgrade to a modern specification. Not suitable for very latest multimedia software. Unlikely to work with Windows 98.
Expansion: ISA and VLB slots. Some machines offer PCI slots.
Floppy disks: 3.5-inch 1.44Mb as standard.
Hard disk: Standard, between 250Mb and 540Mb.
Typical memory supplied: 4Mb, sometimes 8Mb.
The DX4/120 and DX5/150 models are faster than a slow Pentium machine. On the second-hand market they offer reasonable value for anyone whose needs are modest. For Windows 95, 16Mb or even 32Mb of memory are strongly recommended. As an upgrade this will offer better value for money than a faster processor chip.

Pentium P60 and P66 (60MHz and 66MHz)

Cost: 8/10
Performance: 3/10
Value for money: 2/10
Suggested applications: Average office work. Adequate for Internet use.
Pros: Faster than an equivalent 486 processor, especially for work

253

which involves lots of numerical calculations (for example working with large spreadsheets).

Cons: Not good value compared to other Pentiums.

Expansion: ISA and PCI slots.

Floppy disks: 3.5-inch 1.44Mb as standard.

Hard disk: Typically 420Mb fitted as standard.

Typical memory supplied: 8Mb, sometimes 16Mb.

The 60MHz and 66MHz Pentiums were introduced at the end of 1994, but were soon left behind by faster models. These early chips may suffer from the Pentium bug (see note at the end of this Appendix). Not recommended under any circumstances, as other Pentium models offer better value for money.

Pentium (75MHz–200MHz)

Cost: 7/10
Performance: 5/10
Value for money: 4/10

Suggested applications: Office and home use and advanced applications such as large spreadsheets, image editing and sound and video work. Adequate for Internet use.

Pros: Now firmly in the recent category, these models are reasonable, low-cost, second-hand machines.

Cons: Sluggish compared to more recent machines.

Expansion: ISA and PCI bus slots.

Floppy disks: 3.5-inch 1.44Mb as standard.

Hard disk: 540Mb, up to 1Gb (SCSI).

Typical memory supplied: 8Mb, 16Mb, sometimes 32Mb.

Although these computers are all but obsolete, the faster models – from 133MHz upwards – are still perfectly usable for word processing, light office work and occasional Internet use. Intel deliberately killed off this range in mid-1997 to make way for its new Pentium MMX computers. However, only game players and dedicated Internet users are likely to notice much of a difference between MMX and non-MMX computers.

Pentium MMX (166MHz–233MHz)

Performance: 5/10
Value for money: 4/10

Suggested applications: Basic business and home use.

Pros: Reasonable second-hand machines.

Cons: MMX features only make a difference with suitable software.

Expansion: ISA and PCI slots. Recent models include USB and AGP.

Floppy disks: 3.5-inch 1.44Mb as standard. Some systems supplied with LS120 120Mb drives as well.

Hard disk: 1Gb to 3Gb, plus 24× CD-ROM drive.

Typical memory supplied: 16 Mb, 32Mb, occasionally 64Mb.

Originally designed for serious home and business use, these models have been left behind somewhat, but are still suitable for those who want a second-hand computer with reasonable performance for undemanding work. Adequate for the Internet, but will struggle with recent games.

Celeron & Duron (266MHz–900MHz)

Cost: 5–6/10

Performance: 5/10

Value for money: 8–9/10

Suggested applications: Less demanding work, including office work and Internet use.

Pros: Cheaper than an equivalent Pentium II model, and often only slightly slower.

Cons: Not ideal for games and very demanding work.

Expansion: ISA and PCI slots. Recent models include USB and AGP.

Floppy disk: 3.5-inch 1.44 Mb as standard.

Hard disk: 8–10Gb, plus 32× CD-ROM drive.

Typical memory supplied: 32Mb to 64Mb.

The original 'Celeron A' range of chips was based on a very crippled Pentium design. It was supposed to offer low power at a low price, but the slow speed and relatively poor value for money persuaded Intel to kill the design and replace it with the technically more advanced and less crippled standard Celeron, which is often significantly cheaper than a Pentium II but offers very similar performance. Celeron machines are ideal for undemanding home users, but are a little sluggish with the latest games. AMD's Duron range of chips offers better value than the Celeron, both new and second-hand.

Pentium II or AMD K-6II (233MHz–450MHz)

Cost: 5/10
Performance: 6–7/10
Value for money: 8/10
Suggested applications: All general-purpose computing work, including demanding applications such as multimedia design and editing.
Pros: Fast, and good value second-hand, if sold at a realistic price (i.e. around £300).
Cons: None.
Expansion: PCI, USB and AGP. ISA is no longer available on some models.
Floppy disks: 3.5-inch 1.44Mb as standard. Some systems supplied with 120Mb LS-120 drives, or the Iomega Zip system.
Hard disk: 3Gb to 10Gb, 40× CD-ROM or sometimes DVD drive as standard.
Typical memory: 32Mb, 64Mb, occasionally 128Mb.

Now only available second-hand, these models offer extremely good value for money for anyone who isn't interested in the latest games or editing audio and video. They are fast enough for typical Internet use, and most can be upgraded with faster components and more memory.

Pentium III (500MHz–1GHz)

Cost: 1–3/10
Performance: 8–9/10
Value for money: 4/10
Suggested applications: All computing work, including demanding applications such as multimedia design and editing.
Pros: Very fast.
Cons: Expensive.
Expansion: PCI, USB and AGP. ISA is no longer available on some models.
Floppy disks: 3.5-inch 1.44Mb as standard. Some systems supplied with 120Mb LS-120 drives, or the Iomega Zip system.
Hard disk: 9Gb to 20Gb, plus 40× CD-ROM or DVD drive as standard.
Typical memory supplied: 64Mb, 128MB, occasionally 256Mb.

These chips contain a 'next-generation' version of MMX called KNI (Katmai New Instructions). Despite Intel's advertising campaign suggesting that these models can speed up access to the Internet, the reality is that most users will notice barely any difference between the performance of a Pentium II and a Pentium III running at the same speed. As with MMX, software needs to be specially rewritten to take advantage of the KNI features. Only certain games, a small selection of multimedia editing titles (such as Adobe's Photoshop) and Microsoft's Office 2000 suite include the changes. KNI instructions are also used to speed up games and other applications, such as voice recognition.

AMD Athlon (750MHz–2GHz)

Cost: 1–3/10
Performance: 8–10/10
Value for money: 5–6/10
Suggested applications: All computing work, including demanding applications such as multimedia design and editing.
Pros: Currently the fastest chips available. Cheap.
Cons: Overpowered for undemanding work.
Expansion: PCI, USB and AGP. ISA is no longer available on some models.
Floppy disks: 3.5-inch 1.44Mb as standard. Some systems supplied with 120Mb LS-120 drives, or the Iomega Zip system.
Hard disk: 9Gb to 30Gb, plus 40× CD-ROM or DVD drive as standard.
The original Athlon (sometimes known as the Classic) is a slightly better performer than the Pentium III. An advanced model, known as the '266MHz DDR', is significantly faster, and currently offers the best performance of any processor chip available today. Although AMD chips lack Intel's KNI instructions, they make up for this by being faster in other areas, as well as cheaper.

Pentium III /4 Xeon (500MHz–2GHz)

Cost: 1/10
Performance: 9/10
Value for money: 3/10

257

Suggested applications: Professional business servers.
Pros: Very fast.
Cons: Very expensive and relatively poor value for money.
Expansion: PCI, USB and AGP.
Floppy disks: 3.5-inch 1.44Mb as standard.
Hard disk: 10Gb or more, plus 40× CD-ROM drive.
Typical memory supplied: 256Mb upwards.
Intended solely for serious business users, and with a price to match, the Xeon range is overspecified and overpriced for home or small business use. Performance can also be relatively disappointing. The difference between a Xeon processor and a standard Pentium III is not as significant as might be expected. Business users looking for server hardware should investigate a system based on the cheaper technology before investing in these more expensive models.

Pentium 4 (1.3GHz to 2GHz)

Cost: 1–3/10
Performance: 8/10
Value for money: 4–5/10
Suggested applications: Video and some games.
Pros: Very fast.
Cons: Expensive, poor value compared to Athlon machines.
Expansion: PCI, USB and AGP. ISA is no longer available.
Floppy disks: 3.5-inch 1.44Mb as standard. Some systems supplied with 120Mb LS-120 drives, or the Iomega Zip system.
Hard disk: 9Gb to 20Gb, 40× CD-ROM or DVD drive as standard.
Typical memory supplied: 128Mb, 256Mb, occasionally 512Mb.
The Pentium 4 has been a disappointment for Intel, as performance in many areas is eclipsed by AMD's Athlon machines. A relatively tiny number of applications (notably certain kinds of video work) show it to best effect. For almost all other work the Athlon offers better speed at a lower price.

THE PENTIUM BUG

In computer-speak, a 'bug' is a design flaw and, whether found in hardware or software, can cause reliability and/or accuracy problems. Bugs cause your computer to stop working or give you the wrong answer to a calculation.

Early versions of the Pentium processor (specifically those produced before February 1995) included a bug which gave the wrong result for certain long-division calculations.

For most users this bug is more of an irritation than a major worry. The error introduced is slight – of the order of a few pence in a calculation working with tens of thousands of pounds – and happens only with a small range of numbers. For engineering, medical and other professional applications the chip should be replaced. This is a free service from Intel.

You should use a simple test program called CPUIDF.EXE, which is available directly from Intel. For more information call Intel's customer support line on 0800 374838.

Appendix V

The Apple Macintosh

The Apple Macintosh (the 'Mac') computer has a long and colourful history. Unlike the IBM PC, which has always been something of a corporate design, the Apple Mac was conceived as an attempt to make a computer that was easy to use and appealing to non-business people.

Apple machines are the computer of choice for many artists, graphic designers and publishing houses. They are less popular with businesses, which tend to choose the more widely used IBM PC-compatible machines.

The Apple Mac offers a number of important advantages for absolute beginners. Firstly, it is undoubtedly easier to use and set up. Upgrading a PC is usually best left to a specialist, but almost anyone can upgrade a Mac. Older PCs need to be set up after some new hardware has been installed, but a Mac will often accept the upgrade and work out what needs to be changed for itself. This can save time and temper in a professional setting, and can also help build confidence among users.

All modern Macs include networking facilities as standard. It is possible to set up a simple network – which can share information among users and make the best use of common resources such as printers – for little more than the cost of a few cables. A simple email facility, called QuickMail, is also available, and this can be used to exchange messages between different computers on one site.

All Macs are built to a high standard, whereas PCs can vary greatly in build quality and reliability. The Mac looks good and works well.

After the range became established, Apple split the product line into two areas. Domestic Macs are aimed at home users and professionals working at home. Professional Macs are targeted at publishing houses and professionals who need power and can afford to pay for it.

Domestic models tend to cost roughly as much as an equivalent PC. Professional models are usually significantly more expensive. At the top end of the market many Apple Macs are fitted with extras that speed up certain kinds of work. These specialised upgrades have no equivalent in the PC world, and so it is difficult to compare the two kinds of computer on a like-for-like basis. The top-level Macs are recommended for computer-intensive work such as image manipulation, photo-retouching and professional magazine publishing.

The best way to decide whether or not a Mac system is suitable for you is to find a local Apple dealer – many advertise in *Yellow Pages* or in local directories – and try out a system for yourself. Explain your needs to the dealer, try out some relevant software and then do the same with a similarly priced PC system.

Current range

The following Mac models are currently available:

'iMac' range

The iMac comes in a range of very striking translucent case styles. It returns to the original Apple all-in-one design, with a built-in screen. The iMac is aimed at first-time buyers, and is sold with a collection of software and other extras, including a built-in modem and network connections. There is no floppy-disk drive; if one is needed it has to be purchased separately. Most buyers seem to be very happy with their iMacs – apparently because of the combination of styling and convenience. It's worth noting, though, that at the time of writing iMacs are only average games machines; more dedicated players may find them frustrating, and may find a professional model is a better choice.

The Cube

Sold as the ultimate designer computer, the cube looked like no other machine available, making much use of transparent perspex and a novel cube shape for the main system unit. Performance was pitched mid-way between that of the iMac and Apple's more powerful G-range. Perhaps best thought of as an iMac for those with more money to burn, its lack of expandability has made for disappointing sales. At the time of writing Apple is still selling the Cube, although it's likely that it will be discontinued very shortly.

'G'-range

Starting with the now obsolete G3, and currently up to the G4, this is Apple's professional range. Case designs have varied from original Mac beige, to a striking blue and white fold-out case for some models in the G3 range, to a more restrained graphite grey for the G4. The latter includes the 'velocity engine' chip, which speeds up certain operations, especially those used in programs such as Photoshop.

Speed comparisons with fast PCs remain problematic and controversial. It's perhaps fair to say that the G4 is faster for certain specialised applications, such as graphic design and photo editing, but the PC is faster for more general-purpose work. Prospective buyers should compare machines in person, as other factors, including the Mac's improved ease of use, affect productivity as much as absolute speed.

Powerbook range

Essentially portable G-range computers, these are designed for those who need a powerful computer on the road. Apple has again made styling important. The latest titanium-cased models have sold extremely well. For simple work, such as email and letter-writing, these machines are somewhat overspecified; however, they are popular with designers and music and video artists, who can work who can make full use of the available power.

iBook range

These are the portable equivalent of the iMac, with similar quirky design, and with more attention paid to battery life and robustness. In the US they are popular in schools and colleges, although this has been less true in the UK. They are ideal for note-taking and basic Internet use, but may be underpowered for more demanding applications – including games. An optional 'AirPort' wireless networking system is available, which makes it possible to exchange data with a fixed computer, such as a G4, without the need for a physical connection.

Mac history

Over the decade and a half or so that Macs have been available, Apple has released a regular stream of new product announcements and name changes. A complete list would take up many pages, so a summary is presented here.

Mac Classic series – Classic, Colour Classic, 128, 512, SE, SE/30 and Plus

These are the original Macs in the original all-in-one case. Memory is minimal – a mere 128K in the '128' version, and no more than 4Mb in the SE/30. Hard disks are either small or absent. These models are suitable for word processing, but otherwise belong in the 'vintage' category. There are no internal expansion slots.

Mac II range – Mac II, IIx, IIcx, IIci, IIsi, IIvi and IIvx and IIfx

These were powerful machines in their day, especially the IIfx, but are now somewhat dated. They were aimed at professional users. Memory was expandable up to 32Mb in some cases, and hard disks are standard. NuBus slots were included to allow for expansion.

Mac LC range – LC I, II & III, LC460, LC475, LC520 and LC630

These are all domestic Macs and are now very dated. The LC was roughly equivalent to a Classic. The LC II was only slightly more powerful. The others are dated, second-hand machines and are suitable for light business use. The 630 was sometimes fitted with a TV tuner card and NICAM stereo decoder system.

Performa range – Performa 630, 5200, 5300, 6200, 6500

These are the previous-generation domestic Macs. All except the 630 offered PowerPC performance at a reasonable price. The 5200 and 5300 were single-box models that contained the computer and colour monitor in a single case, which helps reduce unsightly cabling. The Performas were designed very much as home entertainment centres, and CD-ROM drives, TV tuner cards (which could also grab 'stills' from TV programmes) and NICAM stereo decoders were either available as options or included in the basic price. The 6500 was the only Performa model to use a PowerPC chip, making it still usable today, although it is very slow by modern standards.

Quadra range – Centris 610, 650, 650AV, Quadra 605, 610, 650, 700, 800, 840AV, 900 and 950

These were aimed at professional users and were the top of the line until the PowerMac models were introduced in 1994. The AV models included extra hardware to record and play back sound at CD quality.

PowerMac range – 6100, 7100, 8100; 7200, 7500, 7600, 8200, 8500, 9500; 4400, 8600, 9600

These machines significantly boosted the performance of Macs by switching to a new and more powerful chip called a 'PowerPC'. The 6100, 7100 and 8100 were the original models, and are now very out of date. More recent models, especially the 9600, are still very usable today, although they have been eclipsed to some extent by the latest G-range models.

PowerMac clones

For a short period, Apple licensed its technology to a number of other manufacturers. This is no longer the case, and these 'clones', as they were known, are now only available second-hand. In general, however, they are a poor choice, as servicing and spares can be problematic.

Original G3 range

With the G3 range, Apple decided to give up its complicated naming scheme and distinguish models according to the speed of the processor chip and the available memory. These models used the 720 and 740 chips. Although outdated, they are still usable today.

'Blue' G3 range

A recent Apple model using a striking blue-and-white case design. Inside, a fast 750 chip made these computers unusually powerful. The trend was to increasingly PC-like technology, with IDE drives being used instead of SCSI, and a PC-standard graphics card instead of a proprietary model. Note that the 'Blue' series lacked a SCSI connector, which meant that users of older Apple equipment needed to buy a SCSI card if they upgrade to a blue G3. The G3 also lacked a floppy-disk drive; USB floppy-disk drives had to be bought as an extra.

Powerbook 100 series – 100, 140, 145, 145b, 150, 160, 165, 165c, 170, 180, 180c, 190, 190cs

These were first-generation portable Macs. All are now obsolete, although they can still be used for word processing and note-taking. Models with the 'c' suffix included a colour screen.

Powerbook Duo series – 210, 230, 250, 270c, 280, 280c

These were 'docking-station' computers; most extras were external and could only be accessed by plugging the computer into a 'docking port' when it was deskbound. Unlike the other models, they were lighter and easier to carry around than the other Powerbooks, and could be used as normal desktops if connected to a docking station (see Appendix VII). This allowed a normal keyboard, a floppy-disk drive and a printer to be connected.

Powerbook 500 series – 520, 520c, 540, 540c

These were Powerbooks with the same speed and power as the Quadra range. They have a 'PDS' (Processor Direct Slot), which means that in theory they can be upgraded to a more modern specification. In practice, however, suitable extras are no longer readily available. Unlike earlier Macintosh portables, these use a trackpad system, which responds to finger pressure.

Powerbook PowerPC series – 1400 range, 2400 range, 3400 range, 5400 range and G3 range

These Powerbooks used the PowerPC chip, and were as fast as some of the PowerPC desktop models. They were far too powerful for the kind of simple word processing and contact management for which most notebooks are used. On the other hand, these machines made it possible to continue with almost any kind of work away from the office, including DTP and CAD.

Appendix VI

Other brands of computer

In terms of sales alone, PC and the various versions of the Apple Macintosh account for almost all the market. There are other brands, however, most of which date back to the early 1980s, when the computer market was split between machines that were used for serious work and those that were used for games and entertainment. Most such machines are no longer available new, but they are still available on the second-hand market.

The main disadvantage of these brands is a lack of service and support, and the fact that they have become increasingly marginalised as the home-computer market has matured. PCs and Apple Macs are an industry standard, and information and software for both are all widely available. These other brands therefore cannot be recommended – except, perhaps, for someone who would like to dabble with computers without making a huge investment.

Stand-alone word processors

For around £200 it is possible to buy an all-in-one word processor that includes a printer, keyboard, and simple editing software. These machines offer an interesting alternative to anyone who doesn't want a full-sized computer. Their main disadvantages are slightly less straightforward ease of use – instead of a screen they typically only offer a small text window – and a lack of Internet facilities. It is worth bearing in mind that, while novels are still submitted to publishers in printed manuscript format, journalism and short-story submissions now rely heavily on email, and anyone planning to use one of these machines for serious writing is advised to check whether or not printed submissions will be acceptable.

Acorn Archimedes

Descendants of the original BBC Micro of the 1970s, the Archimedes range sold well to schools and colleges up to the end of the 1990s. Technically these computers were far more advanced than the more popular PCs of the day, and they were also very much easier to work with. The most recent models included a 'PC on a card' which gave users the best of both worlds. Unfortunately, Acorn lacked the marketing resources needed to push them effectively, and the company bowed out of the market in 1998; spares and extras have subsequently become very thin on the ground. Despite their technical credentials, it is no longer possible to recommend these computers as second-hand machines.

Atari

The Atari ST series was originally designed as a games machine, but found favour in the professional music market, largely as a result of the chance inclusion of the music industry-standard MIDI control system.

The Atari range never lived up to its potential as a business machine. The early games-oriented machines had a clunky, rubbery keyboard that was integrated with the main system unit, and this made them unappealing to anyone who needed to do a lot of typing. The floppy disk drives had to be bought separately and were housed outside the main system unit. This often led to a tangle of wires.

The models that are worth serious consideration for business use are the Mega ST and Mega STE ranges. Both have a more usable detached external keyboard and come with a built-in floppy disk. Hard disk drives are available as an extra. One of the best features of the Atari range was the excellent black-and-white monitor, which is more than adequate for prolonged use and matches or even betters some of the monitors available today.

In terms of software, Write On! and First Word Plus are good choices for word-processing applications, while Calamus offers powerful DTP features as well as simple word-processor-style editing features. First Word Plus is adequate for light-duty work, but does not have any of the features needed for professional use.

Other applications are not widely available. Although spreadsheets and communications packages do exist, they can be hard to find. Most

Atari machines are sold second-hand with large collections of games or music software. To find an Atari machine for serious use, it is best to look in some of the mainstream computer magazines and on the Internet.

Amiga

The Amiga started life as another games machine. It found favour with some programmers, but on the whole was more of a leisure than a business computer. For all this it had some impressive features, and in some ways was more advanced than comparable computers at the time.

Commodore Business Machines, which marketed the Amiga, foundered in 1994. In spring 1995 Escom, a high-street retailer and PC manufacturer, bought the rights to the Amiga range. However, Escom, too, ceased trading in 1996. A number of attempts have been made to resurrect these computers since then, but to date none has been entirely successful. As a result, this machine is now something of a museum piece, and spares are becoming increasingly difficult to get hold of.

Amstrad Word Processor Range

These machines, known as the PCW range, were very popular when they were released in the mid-1980s. Combining basic word-processing software with a keyboard, monitor, disk drives and printer, they were the ideal all-in-one solution for anyone who wanted to write letters but did not have the expertise to take on a complete computer system. However, they are true computers, rather than just word processors, and can handle a range of applications beyond simple word processing.

The biggest problem with the PCW range is the non-standard floppy disk format used on earlier models. These used 3-inch disks, rather than the more usual 3.5-inch variety. Supplies of these disks are now drying up, but a number of companies offer a 3.5-inch disk upgrade option which allows normal disks to be used.

Realistically a PC will do far more than one of these machines, and do it faster and more conveniently. PCW machines are more or less obsolete and cannot be recommended as a second-hand purchase, even when available at a very low price.

Amstrad PCs

In the mid-1980s Amstrad released a range of PC-compatibles which created their own mini-standard at the lower end of the market. Much of this was due to marketing – these were the first machines that were widely available in the high street. Technically they were simply cheap IBM-compatible machines. The 1512 and the 1640 are now very much in the 'vintage' category. Many people still use them for word processing and simple tasks. They cannot run modern software or easily be upgraded. But they were popular in their time and are widely available on the second-hand market. They are very limited and slow by today's standards, and so cannot be recommended.

Emulators

Atari, Amiga and PCW owners can to some extent replicate their machines inside a standard PC or Mac. A special piece of software called an 'emulator' simulates the older machine in software. Many emulators are produced as amateur projects. While these are available for free, they may not be 100 per cent reliable. However, commercial products are sometimes also available (for example Cloanto's AmigaForever product. The advantage of emulators for users of older computers is that they can keep all their old information and software, while using them in a more modern environment.

Appendix VII

Portable and 'laptop' computers

A good option for the business user is a powerful, expensive computer at work and a relatively cheap portable machine for use everywhere else. It is rare that a portable can take the place of a proper office system, as the limited battery life means that its uses are restricted in practical terms. But for light use – letters, invoices, faxes and so on – a cheap portable can be ideal. Portables are also an excellent choice for making presentations. Most portables can be hooked up to an external display, which means it is possible to prepare a presentation at home, or even on the road, and then present it on location.

Portables, especially in the form of laptops, are becoming more and more popular. Battery technology is improving all the time, and as batteries get smaller and lighter, portables will replace desktop machines. Some of the most exciting developments will be in the field of on-line services. It is now possible to buy modems that work with the cellular phone network, and this means that users can send and receive email messages away from their base of operations. This is likely to transform the way that people communicate with each other.

For now, portable computing still has limitations. It is recommended for anyone who needs to be away from his or her base, be it home or office, while maintaining access to records and other information stored back at base. It is also recommended for users who find existing monitor designs difficult to work with. Portables use a different display system that does not flicker in the same way, and some users find this easier. However, while many newcomers feel that a portable will be right for them, the disadvantages should be considered carefully. Cost is a major factor. A portable will cost perhaps one and a half to two times as much as an equivalent desktop machine. Reliability appears to be more of a problem, and any problems that occur outside of the warranty period can be extremely expensive to fix. Weight also remains a problem.

Portables come in a variety of shapes and sizes. The larger machines are now dated and almost obsolete; newer models are getting smaller and lighter each year. Within the portable family you will find the following kinds of machine:

'Luggables'

These are typically the size of a pilot's briefcase. They were once common, but are no longer found outside specialist areas, where they are typically combined with extra hardware to produce a package designed for a very specific task, such as sound recording and video editing. Older luggables are sometimes sold second-hand. They cannot be recommended, as the technology they offer is now obsolete.

Portables

'True' portables are still unwieldy, although they can be carried quite a distance. They tend to be large and bulky and, like luggables, are rapidly being superseded by more modern designs. Because many of these models are now obsolete they cannot be expanded in the way that more modern machines can. Battery life is poor and, like luggables, they are better suited for desk work than for use on trains and planes. Like luggables, these machines are now extremely rare.

Laptops

Laptop machines are much more manageable in size and weight. They are usually more or less A4 size, but offer features similar to those found in desktop machines. All-in-one models, which include extras such as modems and CD-ROM drives within the case, are now available, although it is doubtful whether these are light enough to be easily carried a long way. Modern notebooks are expandable using the PCMCIA system, which allows tiny extras such as modems and soundcards – some of which are literally credit-card size – to be plugged into the case. Notebooks have become the portable standard since the early 1990s.

Sub-notebooks

These are even smaller versions of the standard notebook design. Sub-notebooks are an excellent choice for a general-purpose information manager and portable word-processing tool. They can be used for most of the tasks a desktop computer can, but they are light enough to carry around with ease.

At the time of writing, there has been a spate of very slim, style-conscious, light machines. With these machines it is important to check which extras – such as a floppy-disk drive, or a CD–ROM drive – are included inside the case and which need to be used and carried externally (and perhaps even bought as extras).

Electronic organisers, palmtop computers, and Personal Digital Assistants (PDAs)

Those who do not want the size, weight and expense of a true laptop can choose one of a growing range of smaller computers. At the bare minimum, these include an electronic notepad, address book, diary and planner, and clock with alarm and time-zone facilities. More advanced models include email and web-browsing facilities (although these are very limited compared to those available on a full-size or laptop PC and usually need to be used over a slow and expensive mobile phone connection). Some models can also be enhanced by adding and installing extra software.

The very smallest models have no keyboard. Instead, notes are entered by 'writing' on the display with a stylus. Some of them use a form of handwriting recognition to make sense of the writing; others expect users to learn a form of written shorthand with separate and distinct letter shapes. Another common option is a tiny 'virtual keyboard', with letter keys that appear on the display and are selected with the stylus.

More advanced models use some form of mini-keyboard. These are usually quite hard to work with for long periods, although they may be adequate for note-taking. The most sophisticated – but also large and expensive – offer a true keyboard that is only slightly smaller than that on a standard laptop.

All models offer some form of exchange system that makes it possible to copy information to and from a PC for backup purposes, and (in some cases only) integrate it easily with an existing address book or diary. Note that only a small subset of the available organisers offers the same facility for users of Apple computers.

The following models are popular:

The 3-Com Palm Pilot series Also sold as the **Handspring Visor**, these are tiny units, approximately the size of a wallet, with a large display panel/writing area that is operated with a stylus. The software is very simple, and users are required to spend some time learning how to 'write' individual characters before they can start to use the machine. Simplicity, low cost and ease of use have made these models very popular. An infra-red link makes it easy to exchange electronic business cards with other Palm users. A surprisingly large range of software is available for these machines.

The Psion series The Psion 3 has been a popular PDA since the early 1990s. The more advanced Psion 5 has built up a similar following since it was released in 1996. The Psion 7 and the netBook are very small laptop models, with a colour display and a full-sized keyboard. Although larger than a PDA and also more expensive, they are cheaper and lighter than most laptops, and offer much longer battery life. They are a good choice for note-taking, typing and even basic spreadsheet work on the move. Email and web browsing are also available. Psion machines are popular with business users because of their very slick design, flexibility and ease of use. Email and data-exchange software is included as standard, together with a relatively sophisticated word processor, spreadsheet and database. A wide range of software is available. Uniquely, Psion includes features which make it possible for users to write their own software to suit individual needs.

Windows CE/Pocket PC models These are made by a number of companies, and offer similar features to the Palm range. However, they use a simplified version of the Windows system, which includes 'pocket' versions of a Windows-standard word processor, address book, and so on. Handwriting recognition is usually available only as an extra. Otherwise there is little or no extra software available. To date, these have not had the success of the Palm or Psion ranges, although certain models in Hewlett Packard's Jornada range offer a full-size keyboard, good display and long battery life, which give them a competitive edge over most laptops when used for note-taking and undemanding business work.

Larger Windows CE models These are also made by a number of manufacturers and, like their Windows CE/Pocket PC counterparts, use a variant of the Microsoft Windows system. The main difference is that they offer a built-in keyboard. The quality, usefulness and value for money of these machines varies hugely. At worst they are very heavy compared to smaller organisers, and have poor displays and poor keyboards. At best the very largest offer a reasonable alternative to a PC laptop, by including all the features required for note-taking and simple office work in a package with a high-quality keyboard, a reasonable display and a much longer battery life.

Expanded mobile phones A very small number of portable phones include a built-in PDA. Nokia and Alcatel are two names to watch for. To date they have offered products which include a notepad, address book, web and email software, and fax facilities, sometimes with a small typewriter-style keyboard. The case typically hides the PDA features when the unit is being used as a phone. While these models are rather heavier and bulkier than most phones, anyone looking for a PDA with mobile phone facilities will them find worth considering.

Cellular communications

Although on-line services such as the Internet are just starting to become popular, the real revolution will happen when email and other communication systems are freed from their reliance on physical phone lines. Portable modems that use cellular technology to provide an integrated communication system are now available without using telephone lines. However, cellular modems are relatively expensive and slow compared with their more conventional equivalents. But, as the technology develops and systems become cheaper, it is very likely that portables will come to replace desktop machines altogether, and that it will be possible to arrange meetings and dinner dates away from the phone, directly from organiser to organiser. At the time of writing the wireless/cellular networks are hinting that much higher speeds and cheaper access may become available around 2002. If this proves true, cellular communications may even start to compare favourably with fixed telephone lines. As and when this happens, it will make the Internet accessible from everywhere, rather than mostly from homes and offices, as it is now.

GPS

The Global Positioning System (GPS) offers a kind of electronic compass which uses a network of satellites to define positions on the Earth's surface to within 10 metres. Certain route planners (see page 115) are now sold with an option for connecting to a GPS receiver to create a 'live' road map that literally shows you where you are. GPS hardware for laptops is relatively affordable (around a few hundred pounds) and is already being used by certain haulage companies and sales forces. One drawback is that few route planners are completely geographically accurate, so a map may show your car in a field when you are really on the adjacent motorway.

Docking stations

Some portables can be plugged into a larger base unit – a docking station – when used on the desk. This base unit contains extras – expansion slots, an option for a better keyboard and perhaps a better display – which will not fit into a standard portable. The idea is that, when 'docked', the whole system becomes a substitute for a proper desktop unit.

Docking stations are now extremely rare and are only available for a very small number of PC and Apple laptops. Most laptops now include all the facilities that would once have required a docking station, so the idea is becoming obsolete.

Buying tips

When buying a notebook you should remember to check with your dealer the level of support and service offered. Will the dealer's service scheme cover you if something goes wrong when you are on the road?

Check what software comes with the portable. A very useful extra is a data-exchange program, which enables you to transfer information to your main PC. On some machines this will need additional hardware. Other features to check for include:

Maintenance and service options Laptops and portables are not currently outstandingly reliable. According to some estimates, as many as one user in three will suffer some kind of failure during their first year of use. As a result, technical support is even more important than usual. Check to see what support is offered, and how long it will take to get the work done in total. If possible, also phone the support line to see how easy it is to get through during office hours. A permanent engaged tone is unlikely to bode well.

Weight How easy is it to carry the portable? Is it as portable and light as an organiser, or is it more 'luggable' and unwieldy?

Display quality Try the computer out and look closely at the display. Watch out for mouse pointers that disappear when you move them, and for overall brightness and clarity. Will the display still be visible in bright sunlight? In general, TFT (thin film transistor) displays give the best results but are between £100 and £300 more expensive than the less impressive DSTN (Dualscan SuperTwist Nematic) displays that are also available. Colour is now standard on all laptop models, although for technical reasons this usually means 64,000 colours, rather than the more useful 16.7 million. This in turn makes accurate image-editing a problem.

Size and resolution are also important. Some displays now offer a resolution of 1,024 × 768, which is ample for most work. In general, a 12-inch display is usually adequate, although 13.3-inch and even 14-inch displays are available at extra cost. When checking the displays, look for *stuck pixels*. These are tiny dots, the colour of which is fixed because of a manufacturing flaw. An ideal display would have no stuck pixels at all, but for reasons of cost most manufacturers accept a small number – typically five or fewer – as an unavoidable side-effect. Any more than this and the display can be considered faulty.

Keyboard Does the keyboard suit you? Check the 'feel' – its stiffness and clickiness – and also whether or not you think you can work with the keyboard layout. There is much less room on a portable than on a desktop machine, so the keys have to be fitted into a smaller space, and this inevitably means that some keys do double or even triple duty. The ideal layout is one that is not too dissimilar to your current desktop machine, if you have one. Beware of 'bargains' that offer a US keyboard layout instead of the UK standard. On these machines the £ key may be absent, or only available with an obscure combination of keystrokes.

How does the mouse work? On portables, mouse pointers come in all shapes and sizes. The most popular are *trackpads*, which track finger pressure on a special rectangular area. Cheaper track pads are prone to static, which has the annoying effect of sometimes keeping the pointer moving after you remove your finger from the pad; more expensive models work more reliably. *Trackballs* are inverted mice: the ball is fixed in place, but can be rotated by hand. *Trackpoints* are tiny plastic stubs that usually sit between the G, B and H keys on the keyboard.

If you are left-handed, check to see how conveniently placed the pointer system or the mouse buttons are. Some models have a definite right-handed bias, which may prove inconvenient over long periods.

Battery life Battery life is uniformly poor on laptops. Four hours is exceptional; three hours is good; two hours is average. Older laptops used nickel cadmium (NiCad) and nickel magnesium hydride (NiMH) batteries, which were heavy and also offered poor charge/discharge characteristics. (NiCads, for example, had to be fully discharged before recharging – a 'top up' was likely to shorten battery life.) New lithium ion ('lion') designs do not have these drawbacks and offer improved power capacity and lighter weight.

Externals, connectors and built-in extras On some machines a floppy-disk drive is an optional, and external, extra. If you can connect your laptop to a desktop machine you may not find this is a problem. Other extras to check for include sound cards and speakers (these are almost always built into laptops now, although the speakers are often very poor), CD-ROM drives, DVD drives, Zip drives, network cards and TV/video connections (the last are very useful for presentations). USB ports are now standard on laptops.

It can also be worth checking the number of available PCMCIA slots. Some extras – such as combined modem/network/cellular modem cards – can use all the available slots. If your laptop features less than the usual complement of slots, you will not be able to make use of these.

Basic specification and expansion options Processor chips, memory and hard disk size should be selected in the usual way. Note that the memory and hard disk units used in laptops are smaller than usual, and so more expensive. It makes sense to get a generous specification when buying, rather than finding yourself forced to upgrade at a later date.

Infra-red links The very latest organisers include an IR information transfer system. This makes it easy to exchange information with other organisers and suitably equipped PCs.

Using laptops abroad

Below are some practical points worth considering when using a laptop on your travels.

The first is power – always make sure that you travel with suitable power adapters for the country or countries you are visiting, and that your laptop's power supply can work with the local voltages. General-purpose adapters are available in many airports and travel stores.

Similar considerations apply to foreign telephone systems. If you plan to use your modem abroad, you will need a suitable phone adapter. You will also need a modem that can be 'homologised' to work with the local telephone system, so that it can create and respond to the correct dialling and other tones that are used there. Not all modems do this, and if you plan to travel widely it is essential to make enquiries about this.

Although in theory airport X–ray machines are safe, in practice they have been known to cause occasional data loss, especially with older hardware. So, where possible, try and avoid putting your machine through this process. It can also be worth stocking up on spare batteries for long flights – *and you should not use your laptop during take-off or landing, as it can interfere with a plane's radar and communications systems.*

Appendix VIII

The Internet and bulletin board systems

The Internet

The Internet originated as a series of experiments designed to create a computer network that could survive nuclear attack. From these rather unpromising beginnings it has evolved into a global computer network linking people in almost every country in the world.

The most useful service available on the Internet is email. Other networks may have a mail gateway to the outside world but are geared towards exchanging mail internally. With the Internet, however, you can send mail to anyone who has an Internet mail address anywhere, no matter what kind of computer the addressee uses or which system he or she subscribes to.

To access the Internet you need to open an account with an **Internet Service Provider (ISP)**. This allows you to connect your computer directly to the Internet. You can also access all the other Internet services listed in Chapter 6. Some providers offer a service to a certain geographic area, but the majority offer local-call or free access from anywhere in the UK using special telephone numbers.

Finding a service provider

The number of providers is growing all the time. For an up-to-date list of ISPs look in one of the Internet magazines listed in Appendix XIII. More detailed information on the Internet is given in *The Which? Guide to the Internet*.

When choosing a provider, it is important to check what kind of software you will be given, and also how good the technical support is. The software should be easy to use, easy to install and offer the full range of services. The most important elements are news (Usenet),

America OnLine is a popular on-line service

email and access to the Web. All providers now offer web space as well. This can be used to publish your own web pages, which will then become visible to everyone on the Internet. Note that some providers prohibit commercial use of this facility, and that the amount of space available is always limited (although in practice most people are unlikely to need more than 5Mb for their pages) .

While some providers charge a flat rate per month, typically between £5 and £15, others now offer a completely free service. (Instead of charging you, they take a percentage of the phone bill that you run up while using their service.) The range of companies offering free connections includes many household names, including Dixons (which pioneered free connections with its Freeserve service), various banks, football clubs, supermarket chains, and so on. A few have started to offer free calls at certain periods, such as evenings or weekends (they aim to make money from advertising on their main web site). Such providers are obviously worth investigating, especially for dedicated Internet users.

In general, service from different providers, both free and paid for, can be variable. The slowest and least efficient can have a disastrous effect on your phone bill; not only can it take a number of tries to get a connection, but the connection itself can be very slow. For anyone who uses the Internet for more than occasional email, the importance of finding a fast provider cannot be overstated. In tests, slower providers can literally take four times longer than the fastest to deliver the same web page. *Internet* magazine publishes a regular league table of the best and worst services available.

On-line services offer both an Internet connection and access to a range of information and services that is not available elsewhere. To date there are no free on-line services. The best example is perhaps AOL (America OnLine) which offers huge quantities of information on every subject imaginable, as well as the ability to send internal emails to other members, and also 'chat' with them live (in practice this means typing messages live on a one-to-one basis). AOL is popular with beginners, although more experienced users sometimes find its approach too watered down and simplified.

Which? launched its own Internet service – Which? Online – in November 1996. For a monthly fee, Which? Online offers unlimited Internet access plus exclusive access to regularly updated Which? information from its magazines, books and specialist publications. In addition, ProductPicker lets you create your own Best Buys, which can then be purchased from the on-line shopping centre at guaranteed lowest prices. There are discussion forums, where *Which?* experts are on-line to give personal advice; plus details of campaigns, product recalls and safety information. Every subscriber gets five email accounts and 5Mb of personal webspace.

Cable, ISDN and ASDL

If your home is wired for cable TV, you may be able to avoid the phone charges associated with Internet use. Some cable providers offer free local calls for some or all of the day, which makes them ideal for Internet access (although a handful prohibit this because it places a strain on their services). If in doubt, check with your cable company. If the service is available it can save you a fortune in phone bills.

Some cable companies also offer a much faster Internet connection than that available over a phone line. Competing with this are BT's ISDN and ADSL services, which provide a faster link and a much faster permanent link respectively (see Appendix II).

Access without a computer?

A computer is no longer essential for Internet access, although it still offers the most efficient and flexible way to use the Internet. *Mobile*

281

phones now include Internet services. Newer phones use a system known as WAP (Wireless Access Protocol) to provide text-only summaries of useful information that can be viewed from any phone compatible with the WAP standard. (At the time of writing the Nokia 7110 is one of the most popular examples.) BT also offers an email service to and from mobile phones.

While WAP has its attractions, there are some long-term doubts in the industry about whether or not it is an ideal solution. WAP services are often very simple, and while in theory it will eventually be possible to book theatre tickets, deal in shares, check timetables, read the latest news and make restaurant reservations using the system, at the moment the reality is somewhat more rudimentary.

An alternative approach is offered by Nokia's Communicator range of phones. These combine a PDA equipped with email and web browsing facilities with a mobile phone, in a package that is smaller and lighter than many competing PDAs. Although hampered by the slowness of the mobile network, the resulting product can easily be used to send and receive emails, check web sites, maintain contact details, and take notes on the move, as well as offering all the usual features of a mobile phone.

In the home, both games consoles and some satellite TV systems offer Internet access as an option. In both cases a telephone link is still involved, although the console or satellite decoder takes the place of the computer, and information is shown on the home TV instead of on a separate screen. While relatively clumsy compared to a computer-based system, these services are still very usable, and they are worth investigating as an alternative for anyone who doesn't want a computer in their living-room.

Bulletin board systems (BBSs)

There is now very little that BBSs can offer that is not available on the Internet, often more conveniently and at lower cost. They have now been largely superseded by the Internet, but are still popular with a die-hard collection of enthusiasts, and so are likely to survive for some time yet.

Bulletin boards are used for playing games, exchanging messages and software. Games are often multi-player and can prove costly in terms of phone bills. Many boards include large public areas that contain shareware and freeware software, as well as other information: pictures and computer art, sounds and so on. All of these can be accessed via the telephone to your computer, often for free. To find out more about UK BBSs do an Internet search on 'UK BBS'.

Appendix IX

Tackling computer DIY

This appendix is intended for readers with a practical bent who have become familiar with the basics of computer ownership and would like to know how to save money on upgrades and modifications. While it may be quicker to pay a local dealer to maintain and modify a computer, it certainly will not be cheaper. Service charges can vary from £25 to £50 an hour. 'On-site' modifications (an engineer comes to you) are likely to be even more expensive, if they are available at all.

Besides the financial incentives, there are practical reasons why computer DIY can be worth mastering. If something goes wrong, you can be less reliant on outside support, and therefore at less risk of 'down-time' – time wasted while your computer is not working properly. And as with conventional DIY, some people find the process of learning these new skills offers a satisfaction all of its own.

Of course, this approach will not suit everyone. However, if you are practically minded and capable of basic domestic DIY, very little about computer DIY should faze you. In this Appendix the tasks have been graded according to difficulty and experience, and it is strongly recommended that you master the simpler ones before attempting the more advanced.

Most of the information given here applies to recent IBM-compatible PCs, such as those built from 1995 onwards. Certain tasks are also relevant to Macintosh and PowerPC computers, and – to a lesser extent – to older PCs.

The electronics inside the different models of Apple computer are not as standardised as those in PCs, and for reasons of space it is impossible to include the relevant details here. Because Apple system components are not available to the general public, it is not possible to build an Apple computer from scratch.

Older PCs and also laptops require more detailed instructions before they can be upgraded. The possible options, especially those covering hard disk drives, new processors and motherboards, are too complex to be listed in full here. If you own an older PC and would like to find out more about upgrading it, you may wish to start by discussing this with a knowledgeable dealer who can advise you on which options to pursue.

And some PCs are designed not to be opened by non-engineers at all. If your model has a 'warranty void if broken' sticker anywhere on the case, then it is advisable to leave the hardware alone – at least until the warranty runs out, or you find you feel confident enough to deal with any problems that may arise.

Consumer issues

PCs can and do behave in quirky and unpredictable ways that require trained professional help to sort out. For obvious reasons, it is impossible to cover every single eventuality in a book like this. Any modifications carried out by the reader are done so at his or her own risk.

Warranties

Opening up your computer may or may not void the warranty. This depends very much on the policy of the dealer or manufacturer. A few companies have a cast-iron policy that states that any unauthorised work voids the warranty immediately. Other dealers, especially some of the larger and better-known names, will continue to offer warranty support if they can talk you through the upgrade process themselves. Some do not seem to mind either way. Before attempting any work detailed in this Appendix, **always check to see where your dealer stands on this issue and** *read the small print.*

Getting support

Most dealers who sell upgrade hardware will be happy to provide basic telephone support to customers who are attempting their own modifications and upgrades. Smaller, local computer stores may do this at no cost to you, and some medium-sized dealers and mail-order companies may offer free technical support lines on a special telephone number – although you are unlikely to find them helpful unless your query is specifically about the products they sell. As usual, it pays to do as much research as possible – if you appear to be 'one of the trade' you will be treated with more respect than someone who is a complete beginner. But even beginners can get useful support this way.

Finding spares and upgrade hardware

These are advertised throughout the computer press. One of the best sources is *MicroMart* magazine, which contains advertisements from a large number of component specialists who tend to sell more cheaply than some of the larger industry names. Before buying any extras it is essential to check that they are suitable, preferably by reading through magazine reviews. If in doubt about which particular brand or model of extra is best, it can pay to phone a selection of suppliers and ask their opinion. This can help to weed out those suppliers who can't provide technical backup. For example, if you are trying to choose a hard disk drive, a supplier who says 'We supply whatever brand we have in stock at the time' is best avoided. One that can quote different makes and model numbers and recommend one or more items is much more likely to be worth dealing with, and may also be able to provide useful technical support.

First steps – a practical primer

Before you start work on your PC, *you should read through this section carefully*. It introduces the most useful practical points involved in computer DIY, explains some of the more advanced jargon, and describes how you can work on your computer safely.

Backups

Wherever possible, back up all the information in your PC before attempting any of these tasks. While it's unlikely that anything will go wrong, accidents do happen, and you may be left with a completely dead machine. Having a backup copy of everything can save the day in situations like this.

Tools

The following should be sufficient:

- A small Phillips (crosshead) screwdriver OR an electric screwdriver
- A small standard screwdriver

- A pair of pliers
- A small torch or Anglepoise desk lamp
- A grounding strap (see below)
- Notebook and pen or pencil.

Many people assume that they will need to use a soldering iron or complex electronic test equipment. This is not true. All basic upgrades and modifications consist of nothing more complicated than clipping or screwing the correct parts into place and – occasionally – pushing plugs and cables of various kinds into suitable sockets. Most of the items in question are designed so that it is impossible to do this the wrong way – for example, memory modules will only fit into their sockets the correct way round. Where this is not the case, parts are clearly marked to show which way round they should be fitted.

The most challenging aspects of computer DIY are not electronic, but mechanical. It can be a very tight squeeze inside a computer's case, and in some machines certain vital areas can be hidden under other parts (the most common example is the main memory, which often seems to be hidden underneath the power supply). This can turn a simple upgrade into a challenging three-dimensional jigsaw puzzle.

For this reason it is always worth opening up your PC before attempting this kind of work, to acquaint yourself with its innards and try to foresee possible problems. You may decide that the work you were planning looks too complicated and is best left to a professional. This is a perfectly sensible decision to make. While you are unlikely to damage your PC if you follow the precautions outlined below, you may find yourself in a situation where putting the computer back together may not be as straightforward as it first appeared. To avoid this, it is an excellent idea to make notes and sketches as you work, especially where you suspect that reassembly may be less than obvious.

Note that if you plan to do a lot of computer DIY (or even standard DIY) an electric screwdriver is a worthwhile investment. It can cut down assembly time dramatically.

Static electricity

The electronic items used in computers are extremely sensitive to static electricity. While most people have experienced a jolt of static after getting out of a car or walking across a carpet, it takes much less than this to damage an electronic device. Your fingers can build up a charge of tens of millions of volts without any obvious symptoms, and when this is earthed through a computer chip the results can be disastrous and expensive.

Before starting work on a computer, it is important to invest in a **grounding strap**. This is a strip of special plastic that conducts electricity, which you wear as a bracelet round your wrist. The strip plugs into a wall socket which 'grounds' static before it can do any damage (note that only the earth lead in the socket is connected to anything!). These straps are available from larger computer stores and from electronics hobby shops, such as Maplin Professional Supplies.

All computer spares are sold in bags made of a similar plastic. It is important never to remove an item from a bag before you are ready to use it, and never to place it on a non-conductive surface of any kind (particularly not a carpet or a plastic kitchen table top) while you are working. Always put chips and circuit boards on the metal parts of the frame of your computer when you are working with them, or on top of the bag they were supplied in. Try to avoid touching any of the exposed electronics with your fingers, even if you are using a grounding strap. It can even be worth buying a grounding tray – a plastic conductive tray which can also be connected to earth, and provides a completely safe working area for static-sensitive components.

What's inside the case?

When you open up a PC, you should be able to see three main parts: the motherboard, the drive cage and the power supply.

The **motherboard** is the large circuit board that holds most of the electronics. In modern PCs, the processor chip, which is the most prominent item on the motherboard, will be hidden by a small fan or a large metal structure with fins called a *heatsink*. This board also holds the memory (RAM).

Everything inside the PC is connected to this board with cables. Arranged in a row at right angles to the board, plugged into a line of long thin sockets – known as the *expansion slots* – are various extras such as a sound card, a graphics card and perhaps an internal modem if one is fitted. Expansion slots present two rows of metal 'teeth' inside a plastic strip. These teeth grip the corresponding bare metal terminals on an expansion card.

On ISA slots the teeth are fairly wide apart. On VLB and PCI slots they are much closer together. (All ISA slots are electronically identical, but on some PCs the PCI slots differ. You may find that a particular item will work only in a certain slot; this will be noted in the documentation.) ISA slots are black, PCI slots are white. VLB slots look like extended ISA slots, with more connecting points in the slot. AGP slots (see page 207) are short and brown. There will only ever be a single AGP slot on a motherboard. In all cases these slots back on to *blanking plates* – small metal plates fitted to the back of the computer with a single screw.

The **drive cage** sits behind the front panel of the PC. This is where the hard disk drive(s), the floppy disk drive and the CD-ROM drive are fitted. If you are adding a new drive, free space must be available for it in this cage. These spaces come in two sizes – 5.25-inch for larger hard disks and CD-ROM drives, and 3.5-inch for floppy-disk drives and standard hard disks (you can fit a 3.5-inch item into the larger space with the aid of an adapter pack, which your dealer can supply). The number of free spaces for each size of item varies depending on the case your PC came in. Full tower cases will have plenty of free spaces of both sizes, while slimline cases may not have any. Before attempting to add a new CD-ROM or hard drive to your PC it is essential to check that a suitable space is available.

The **power supply** is the large self-contained, shielded metal boxes with a mains connector and perhaps a master power switch at the back, a fan at the bottom. From its front protrudes a tangle of wires (mostly red, black and yellow) leading to large, flat, plastic power connectors.

All modern computer power supplies are earthed, which means that unless something has gone very seriously wrong there should be little danger of stray mains voltages anywhere within easy access. (The power switch at the front of the case simply carries a nominal small voltage that should offer no more risk than a battery.) A common trick among engineers is to work with the mains cable plugged in and the power switched off; this earths the whole case, and makes damage from static less likely. However, things do sometimes go wrong, and so **for reasons of absolute safety it is strongly recommended that you work with the mains cable removed completely, and the case earthed using a separate grounding strap**.

Cards that slot into the motherboard draw their power from it directly and do not need any further power connections. However, certain extras have to be connected to the power supply by hand. You will need a free power connector for this. If none seems to be available, ask your dealer for a power cable splitter (this splits a single connector into two). You can then connect one back to an existing item, the other to the new extra.

Power connectors are designed to fit tightly into their sockets, and you will need to use considerable force to detach them. This reduces the chance of their coming loose by accident. However, it does mean you need to take care when trying to disconnect one. A triangular notch on the connector's socket makes it impossible to fit it back to front.

Ribbon cable

Many computer extras — such as hard disks — use **ribbon cable.** This is a long flat strip of cable fitted with thin plastic connectors that have two rows of tiny sockets. The cable is made of a number of much finer cables laid flat and welded together at their sides. One edge will be marked in some way — typically with a red line, or with a fine mist of red paint. This marking tells you which way round the cable fits into its socket. It is often referred to as 'Pin 1'. The plugs that match these connectors have two corresponding rows of tiny pins. 'Pin 1' will be indicated in some way on the circuit board near the plug — with an arrow, a dot, or some other marker.

One of the biggest problems with computer DIY is getting ribbon cable to behave itself. The connectors can easily be pulled out of their sockets by accident, or they can be fitted wrongly, either by plugging in one row of pins instead of two, or by misaligning the connector so that some pins are left unconnected. In some instances — especially when working with a full tower case — the cable is simply too short, and the only solution is to move the item it connects to closer to the motherboard. Or the cable may need to be twisted and threaded in a clumsy way through the PC.

If something doesn't seem to be working, always double- and even triple-check that you have the ribbon cable fitted properly. Getting it wrong will not usually cause any permanent damage, but it may mean that your PC refuses to start. This, which can be heart-stopping for beginners, can usually be solved by refitting the connector properly.

Jumpers

Some computer items use small plastic-coated links that have to be pushed onto or removed from tiny pairs of pins. These links are known as **jumpers,** and have to be fitted or removed by hand. Jumpers perform different functions on different items of hardware – for example, on a motherboard they are often used to set the correct operating speed for a given processor chip. Documentation supplied with the item will explain how and where jumpers should be fitted. Happily, this rather crude technology is slowly becoming obsolete, but jumpers are still found regularly on items such as hard disks.

Where a pair of pins should be left unconnected, it is standard practice to fit the jumper so it only covers one pin of the pair. Never detach jumpers from an item completely, just in case you need to change the operating settings for the hardware again (jumpers are very easy to lose, and replacements are hard to find).

Drivers

Many items of computer hardware require **drivers.** These are small items of software supplied on floppy disk or CD-ROM that tell your computer how to 'talk' to the hardware. They are specific to the hardware involved – for example, each kind of sound card comes with its own unique set of drivers. Always follow the installation instructions *exactly* as specified.

If you buy an item marked 'OEM' in a computer magazine, you may not get any drivers with it at all. In theory, OEM ('Original Equipment Manufacturer') items are aimed at computer manufacturers. In practice the OEM label simply means that you get the same product for less money, albeit in a plain box instead of a colourfully decorated one, and most often with no supporting documentation or software.

The way around this is to copy the latest drivers from the Internet. This can often be a useful thing to do even for non-OEM 'consumer' items. By the time an item has been shipped, stored and sold, it may be months old, and the drivers supplied with it may no longer be the most current.

All the major manufacturers have their own web sites. Sometimes you may need to do a web search to find them, but you are likely to find the most recent drivers, as well as frequently asked technical-support questions. Copying the drivers to your PC is a relatively simple procedure that takes half an hour to an hour. Usually it is simply a case of clicking on a web link and telling your PC where to store the resulting driver information. Once it has been copied, you can install the drivers in the usual way.

It is not just hardware extras that require drivers. Motherboards sometimes benefit from a driver update. In theory, Windows includes all the drivers that are needed. In practice, these may not be up to date, and so it can be worth visiting your motherboard manufacturer's web site, and that of the manufacturers of the chipset it uses (often, but not always, Intel), to see if any updates have been made available. Doing this can sometimes solve serious problems, such as mysterious random crashes.

Simple tasks

The following tasks are very straightforward, and a relative novice should be able to tackle them successfully.

Installing a sound card

This is a relatively simple procedure, especially on PCs that are not already heavily burdened with extras. The step-by-step approach given below can be applied to most circuit-card upgrades.

1. Turn off the power to the PC, open the case and identify the expansion slots.
2. Pick a suitable expansion slot. (You may find that in some slots the sound card is blocked by the processor chip. This is an unfortunate design flaw in some PCs that limits your choices.)
3. Remove the blanking plate from the slot you have chosen. Keep the screw to hand.
4. Push the card into the expansion slot. You might have to use a fair amount of force – but be careful not to apply too much, as the motherboard may crack. Try lining up the card and then wiggling it into place. The row of bare metal terminals fits into the teeth of the slot, and the metal bracket on the card takes the place of the blanking plate. Make sure that the card is pushed in fully.
5. Double-check that the card is slotted in properly. Most of the metal on all of the card's terminals should be hidden by the plastic strip of

the expansion slot. The terminals should be pushed in evenly, so that the bottom of the card is horizontal. If it is uneven, take the card out and refit it.

6. Fit the blanking plate screw so it holds the card's bracket in place.
7. Keeping clear of the PC's innards, turn on the power and install the drivers. Test the card by connecting speakers, microphones, and so on.
8. If everything seems to be working, turn off the power, and refit the PC's case.

Where an existing sound card is present, remove the old sound card before installing the new one. This is simply a case of pulling the old card out of its slot. The same slot can be used for the new card. You may also need to remove (uninstall) the old drivers before installing the new ones.

Installing a graphics card

To install a faster graphics card follow the same procedure as for a sound card. The card slots into one of the PCI or AGP slots instead of the ISA slots, but otherwise the procedure is identical. (If your PC has VLB slots instead of PCI slots, it will probably be impossible to find a suitable card, as VLB graphics cards are very, very difficult to get hold of now.)

Installing graphics card drivers can often be a fiddly process. It is useful to make sure that you always have the very latest drivers to hand (see page 291–2).

Drivers aside, graphics cards in PCs use a part of Windows known as DirectX, which is supposed to make games and other demanding software work more efficiently but often causes problems of its own. When you install new hardware or software, it sometimes assumes that you also want to install a version of DirectX. However, the version that comes with the product may be *older* than the version you already have installed. Or the installation may reinstall older drivers for some other part of the system, such as the graphics or sound card. If you run into any of these problems, first make sure that you have the latest versions of both DirectX (which is available free on the Microsoft web site) and the relevant drivers to hand. Then try reinstalling one or the other till the system appears to be stable again.

Installing a faster IDE CD-ROM drive

If your PC dates from around 1996, the existing CD-ROM drive may be on the slow side. Faster drives are relatively inexpensive and very easy to fit. Note that the procedure below only applies to IDE CD-ROM drives. These are connected to the motherboard, usually by way of a ribbon cable that goes via one of the hard disk drives.

If your PC was made before 1995, the drive probably will not figure in the 'frame' of information that appears when you turn your PC on (see below), and you may find that the CD-ROM drive is attached to the sound card instead of the motherboard. This makes the process more complicated. Treat this as similar to 'Installing a bigger hard disk', an advanced task described on pages 299–304.

Like hard disk drives, CD-ROM drives can work in 'master' or 'slave' mode. This is a way of connecting two items to the same cable so that they can work together. To ensure your new CD-ROM works properly, you have to set it up the same way as the one that is currently installed. This usually involves setting a jumper on the drive. You can tell how it has been set up by looking at the 'identification frame' that appears after you switch on your computer. This is a list of hardware settings and includes master/slave information for your hard disk(s) and CD-ROM drive. If your CD-ROM doesn't appear here, you will need to check the jumpers on the back of the drive after you have removed it and read through the drive's manual to discover which way it has been set up. If all else fails, contact your original supplier for help.

1. Turn on your PC, and watch for the 'frame' that appears. Look for the item near the bottom left of the frame that refers to the CD-ROM drive. Note whether the word 'master' or 'slave' appears.
2. Turn off the power, open the PC's case, and identify the drive cage (see page 288).
3. Find the CD-ROM drive. Undo the screws that hold the drive in place on the metal frame of the cage. Keep the screws in a safe place.
4. Remove the connectors at the back. Tie or tape them together to stop them disappearing into the rest of the PC.
5. Slide out the old drive.
6. If the word 'master' appeared in Step 1, slide in the new drive. If the word 'slave' appeared, find the jumper that sets slave mode

operation. (This will usually be on the back of the drive near the connectors. You may need to refer to the drive's manual or talk to a technical support person to find it.)

7. Slide in the new drive, and screw it into place. Refit the connectors.

8. Turn on the PC. If the CD tray slides out immediately, or if your PC does not work or appears to stop after a minute or so, you may have plugged in the ribbon cable at the back of the drive the wrong way round. Turn off the PC and refit the cable correctly.

9. If the PC still refuses to start, you may have failed to set the 'master' or 'slave' operation properly. Double-check the jumper and set it appropriately.

10. When the PC is working properly install the drivers and check the system by trying out a CD. If it works, refit the case.

Intermediate tasks

The following tasks require more detailed specialist knowledge and are prone to technical or mechanical complications. They are within the reach of adventurous beginners, but are realistically best left to those with more experience.

Adding more memory

Computer memory is supplied in the form of long, thin, green or brown wafers called SIMMs (Single In-line Memory Modules) or DIMMs (Dual In-line Memory Modules), which have varying numbers of attached black plastic chips. These wafers fit into slots that use a similar, but smaller, version of the 'teeth-and-terminals' system used for expansion cards. (Note that memory slots do not have any blanking plates, and the memory 'cards' themselves are very much smaller than a typical expansion card.) Four or six slots will be available. Modern PCs use slots with 72 holes for SIMMs and 168 holes for DIMMs. Older models have 30 holes, which are used with a larger (now nearly obsolete) kind of SIMM.

SIMMs are supplied in pairs, and each pair can offer 1Mb, 2Mb, 4Mb, 8Mb, 16Mb, 32Mb or 64Mb of memory. (Note that the physical size of the SIMMs doesn't vary, even though the memory capacity does. However, the number of attached black plastic chips will.) By fitting different-capacity SIMMs into different pairs of sockets you can expand the memory up to a limit set by the design of the motherboard – typically 768Mb or 1.5Gb. DIMMs are usually fitted singly. (Some portables use yet another type of memory called SO – Small Outline – DIMMs. They are much smaller than the DIMMs used in desktop PCs, and again need to be fitted in pairs.)

Installing more memory can be straightforward enough to count as a beginner's task, but a number of problems can complicate the process. Perhaps the most aggravating is discovering that the memory has been hidden by the power supply. In this situation the task is perhaps best left to someone with extensive PC experience, as typically you will have to unplug all the cables from the motherboard and lever it out of the PC's case so that you can get at the relevant slots.

The other problem is working out what kind of memory you have installed already, and deciding whether there is room to fit more. Once all the slots are filled, some memory has to be removed before more can be fitted. As an example, one popular upgrade is to remove two SIMMs that offer 8Mb in total and replace them with two that offer 32Mb.

All memory modules of whatever variety are graded according to speed and memory type. When fitting new memory always use the same type, and a speed that is equivalent to or better than your existing memory. Speeds were once measured in nanoseconds (nS), varying from 60nS to 80nS, but are now measured in MHz (100MHz or 133MHz) or with a 'PC' rating (PC100 or PC133). Faster memory will work perfectly well in slower computers, so if you always use 60nS or PC133 memory you should have no problems. Types include standard, EDO SDRAM, DDR and Rambus (see page 196). You may need to refer to your PC's manual to work out which to use, or you may even need to call the manufacturer's technical support line.

1. Turn off the power, open the PC's case and find the memory. You should be able to see a number of wafers slotted in vertically somewhere on the motherboard.
2. If it is easily accessible, either find two free slots or remove two of the existing SIMMs (if working with DIMMs, remember these are used singly, rather than in pairs). To do this push the clips at each end of the slot outwards until the memory moves freely. Then lever it out.

3. Slot in the new SIMMs. Make sure they click into place firmly. If they do not, turn them round and try again.
4. Switch on the PC and watch for the memory test that appears almost immediately. The numbers should stop at the total amount of memory you have fitted. (Note that 1Mb = 1024Kb, not 1000Kb. So, for example, if you fitted 80Mb of RAM this counter would stop at 81920Kb.)

Installing a faster processor chip

Before starting this task, you may want to consider whether or not installing a faster processor will be a cost-effective upgrade. In terms of value for money, expanding your PC's memory to 64Mb or even 128Mb is much more likely to make a noticeable difference to your work than replacing a 300MHz Pentium II chip with a 400MHz Pentium II. However, if you have already expanded your memory to a reasonable amount and still feel your computer is sluggish, then a faster processor is a valid alternative.

Like adding more memory, this upgrade can be a relatively simple task, or it can involve disassembling and reassembling most of the PC. This depends on the motherboard that is installed. Most motherboards will only work with a given range of processor chips, and some will only work with a subset of that range that works within a certain speed band. If you want to fit a better chip inside your computer, and you find your motherboard cannot cope with it, you will need to replace the motherboard as well. For example, if your current PC is a Pentium, and you want to fit a Pentium III, you will need to buy and install a new motherboard. While this has its attractions – you will end up with a much faster PC without the hassle of copying all your information from one machine to another, or buying a new case or even a whole new system that you don't want or need – installing a new motherboard is an example of advanced DIY and should not be attempted by someone with limited experience.

However, if your motherboard *can* work with a faster chip than the one you have now, the upgrade is relatively straightforward. If you are not sure whether your motherboard is compatible, ask your supplier. Guessing the answer and getting it wrong can leave you with a useless – and very expensive – dead processor chip.

A handful of newer motherboards are 'jumperless' and can assess automatically what kind of processor chip needs to be fitted. If you have a jumperless board – check the documents that came with your computer or ask the retailer – you can skip the steps below that refer to changing the jumper settings. Otherwise you will need manually to set any jumpers to match your processor chip's model and speed rating. Information about how to do this is invariably included with the manual supplied with the motherboard.

1. Check your motherboard's manual to try and identify the jumpers that set the processor chip's speed. If you cannot find these, refer to your original PC supplier. If you still can't find them, STOP! You will not be able to perform this upgrade and should consider buying a new motherboard.
2. Turn off the power to the PC, open the case, and locate the jumpers on the motherboard. You may find they are hidden under a nest of cables. If so, carefully push your way through the cables until the jumpers become visible. Be especially careful not to pull out any of the cables by accident.
3. Set the jumpers to the speed of your new chip.
4. Remove the old chip. On PCs where the processor is hidden under a square heatsink, unclip the processor from the socket using the plastic or metal arm next to it; lift out the old chip. On PCs which use a long slot, pull the whole unit out of the slot, removing any mechanical restraints first.
5. If your new chip uses a clip-on heatsink, fit it first.
6. Insert the new chip (you won't be able to fit it the wrong way round). On PCs with a plastic socket, lower the arm to clip it firmly into place again. On PCs with a slot, refit the mechanical restraints if present.
7. Turn on your PC and check for signs of life. If everything seems to be working properly turn off the power and refit the case. Otherwise turn off the power, double-check the jumper setting, double-check any connectors around the chip, and make sure that the new chip has been seated firmly.

Advanced tasks

These tasks require a reasonable amount of technical background knowledge and should be attempted only by those who understand the issues and principles involved. If you are a complete beginner you are strongly advised to do some thorough research first to familiarise yourself with the various technical and mechanical settings involved. Getting these settings wrong can create a PC that appears to have stopped working. At the very least you should understand enough of the theory to be able to retrace your steps in case of trouble.

Installing an extra hard disk

Typically, new PCs are supplied with a single hard disk drive. This can fill up remarkably quickly, and almost everyone who uses a PC finds that adding a larger hard disk soon becomes essential.

Most PCs built after 1995 can be fitted with up to four hard disks and/or CD-ROM drives. These are fitted to two connectors on the motherboard – one labelled 'primary' and one 'secondary' – using pieces of ribbon cable. The two drives that can be attached to each of the primary and secondary cables are further distinguished by being set up as either the 'master' or the 'slave'. As explained earlier, this is simply the way the PC tells them apart even though they use the same piece of cable.

These designations appear on the information frame when you turn on your PC. The primary master, primary slave, secondary master, and secondary slave disks are listed there, together with their capacity and their 'mode' – a measure of the way they transfer information. (Modern hard disk drives use 'Mode 4'. CD-ROM drives use 'Mode 1'. These are identified automatically, and you don't need to worry about what they mean.) If any of these designations appears blank it simply means that there is no drive connected in that position.

In most PCs you are likely to find a single hard disk drive as the primary master, and a single CD-ROM drive as the secondary master. If your PC has been set up like this you should fit your new hard drive as the primary slave.

Occasionally you may find that the main hard disk is the primary master, and the CD-ROM is the primary slave. If your PC has been set up like this, you should complain to the manufacturer. The rule of thumb with drives of any sort is that if two drives share the same cable, information will move at the speed of the slower drive. Since a CD-ROM drive can be as much as ten times slower than a hard disk, the speed of your whole PC will suffer as a result. Ask your dealer to modify your PC to make sure that the hard disk is the primary master,

and the CD-ROM drive is the secondary master before you proceed
any further – and install your new drive as the primary slave as above.
Setting jumpers and connecting ribbon cables is still only part of the
story. The PC needs to be told about the specification of the new hard
drive, once it has been fitted. And the drive itself needs to be prepared
('formatted') before it can be used.

The first part of this process requires an exploration of what are
known as the 'BIOS settings'. (BIOS – short for Basic Input Output
System – is pronounced BYE-oss.) These appear on a set of special
screens that can only be accessed after you turn on your PC. When
you see a message that says 'Hit DEL to enter SETUP', hit the delete
key, and the main BIOS screen will appear. (Some systems use a key
other than delete; the message will indicate which key to press.)

The BIOS settings are the heart of the PC, and changing these
settings can cause your PC to appear to stop working. These settings
have to 'match' the exact hardware used in your PC, otherwise the PC
may not work, or will only work erratically. If you change anything by
accident – or don't know the numbers that match your hardware, and
type in the wrong ones – your PC will most probably not get any
further than the 'Hit DEL to enter SETUP' message when you turn it
on. This is unlikely to cause any permanent damage, but if you can't
work out for yourself what the correct setting should be, you will need
professional technical support to get your PC working again.
Changing these settings should not be undertaken lightly!

All the settings – and there are over a hundred in a typical PC – are
arranged on different pages. Each page shows the settings for a specific
part of the PC – for example, the speed of the memory, the
specifications of the hard disks, and so on. The first BIOS page is an
index to the other pages. The mouse will not work while any of these
pages are shown, so to look at, or change, anything on one of the other
pages, move the highlight to a page's name using the arrow keys and
hit the 'Enter' key. This will show all the settings for that page. To select
a setting, use the arrow keys again. To change it, use the 'Page Up' and
'Page Down' keys (when you have to choose one of a fixed list of
options) or the number keys (when you have to type in a number). To
get back to the main index page hit the 'Esc' key.

Because these settings are so critical, you have to confirm any
changes you make before they take effect. If you change something on
these pages by accident, as a last resort you can always turn off your PC

immediately to recover the original settings. A more elegant solution is to learn how to confirm or cancel the changes. The 'save and exit' option on the main index page confirms the changes. The 'exit without saving' option cancels them, leaving all the settings unchanged. As a double-check each of these brings up a further question, asking you to confirm your confirmation, or cancel the cancellation. Respond with a 'y' for yes and 'n' for no, depending on which you require. If you hit 'enter', the changes will not be confirmed.

Always make a note of the old BIOS settings before changing them. If you get into trouble you can get back to where you were by going back to the relevant pages and typing in the old settings again. While this may not always solve the problem, it is invaluable information to have to hand if you need to make a technical support call.

Although there are a number of BIOS pages, there are two particular pages to look out for. The first will be called something like 'Basic CMOS setup'. The other may be something like 'Auto IDE HDD identification' (the wording may vary). The first is where you set the numbers that define each hard disk's operation by hand. The second attempts to guess the correct numbers automatically. Details of how to use these options are given below.

The second part of the setup process requires **partitioning** and **formatting** the new drive. Partitioning divides up the drive into sections (known as **logical** partitions) which appear as separate letters in the list of hard drives – for example d: and e: can both be on the same disk drive. You will be forced to partition your drive if it is over a certain size. If you don't, you will waste a large proportion of the drive's available storage space. The size depends on the version of Windows you are using. You will discover what the maximum size is on your machine when you attempt to create partitions on the drive for yourself. Formatting prepares the drive so that Windows can store information on it. In effect, it creates a framework for the information and makes it possible for Windows to keep track of where all the information is stored on the drive's surface.

One final practical note – when buying a larger drive, always ask for mounting screws and ribbon cable to be included. Otherwise you will be sent a bare drive with no way to fit it into the PC, or connect it to the motherboard. If you do find yourself with a drive but no screws or cables, a small local computer store will usually be able to help you with these extras.

1. Restart your PC and note which of the primary or secondary, master or slave designations are free.
2. Turn off your PC and open the case. Identify the drive cage. Check that there is space available inside the cage for a new drive, and whether or not you will need a mounting bracket to fit a small drive into a 5.25-inch mounting space.
3. Install the new drive into the cage. Fit a power connector and the appropriate ribbon cable, making sure that the latter is fitted the correct way round. (When the cable is plugged in, Pin 1 always goes nearest the power connector.)
4. Turn on the PC and hit the relevant key to enter the BIOS setup screens. Find the IDE auto-detect page if one is available. This scans each hard drive in turn and reports back the correct settings for it. Where more than one setting is available the one marked 1(Y) is usually the correct one. Hit 'Enter' to scan the next drive. Where no drive is fitted, the scan will report back with a row of zeros. Hit 'N' to skip a failed scan – unless the scan has found a CD-ROM drive, in which case hit 'Y'.
5. If there is no auto-detect option, go to the Main CMOS Setup screen and type in the numbers by hand. You will find these in the manual that comes with the hard drive. If this is missing, or if you are not sure which numbers to type in, call your hard disk supplier's technical support line and ask them to talk you through this part of the process.
6. Hit 'Esc' to take you back to the main BIOS screen, and then 'save and exit.' This last option is designed to confuse you and make you think twice about what you are doing, so that you don't save a new setting by accident. Confirm with 'Y' or 'N', as appropriate, to make sure that the new settings are saved.
7. Your PC will now restart. If you have entered the settings correctly it should start up as normal. If not, it will stop and wait at the screen that says 'Hit DEL to enter SETUP.' Hit the delete key (or whichever is appropriate for your machine) and double-check the settings. Save them as before.
8. Once your PC restarts properly, you will need to be in DOS to partition the disk. If running either version of Windows, quit to DOS or use the MS-DOS prompt option. (For Windows NT/2000/XP see the on-line help features that describe partitioning and formatting, and follow the steps listed there instead of the ones that follow.)

9. Type FDISK. Follow the prompts to set a physical partition and then one or more logical partitions on the new drive. **Be very, very careful here. If you delete a partition on an existing drive, all the information on it will be lost and you may also cripple your PC by deleting the operating system.** The latter is not fatal; the operating system software can be reinstalled. However, there is no remedy at all for the former – except to avoid the problem in the first place. Triple check that you are working with the correct drive before proceeding. Since it is new it will be completely blank. If you see a partition listed, you are likely to be looking at the wrong drive.

10. Restart the machine and format the new hard disk. You can do this from within Windows or DOS, using the relevant format commands. Again, be careful – if you format the wrong drive you will lose all the information on it.

11. When the new hard disk is ready, close the case again. You can now start to copy information to it, or install new software.

'Cloning' an existing hard disk

Sometimes it is more convenient to move all your information to a larger hard disk and then install that as a replacement for your current one. This approach means that in addition to having extra space, your main disk will be faster and newer than the original, and all your software and settings will remain unchanged. The most convenient way to do this is to use a program called Partition Magic. This can copy, format, and otherwise maintain disks of all types. To clone a disk:

1. Fit the new hard disk using a spare connector. Make sure it is set to the correct master/slave setting as usual.

2. Do not format it or partition it. Instead, start Windows, then start Partition Magic.

3. If you have more than one partition on the original disk, use Partition Magic to create the same number of partitions on the new disk.

4. Copy all the partitions from the old disk to the new one.

5. Resize the new partitions ad lib, to give yourself extra working space.

6. Make sure that the partition that now contains the operating system is marked 'bootable' (the documentation supplied with

Partition Magic will explain how to do this, and why it is important).

7. Turn off the PC, and fit the new disk to the connector used by the old disk, setting it to the correct master/slave setting (this will usually be 'master' mode).

8. Restart your PC. The operating system should start as normal, only you should now have more disk space available.

9. If everything appears in order you can optionally turn off the PC again, then fit the older hard disk to a different connector, to give yourself still more disk space. (Note that, if you have more than one partition on the disks, doing this will change the order in which the various disks and partitions appear within Windows. This is usually undesirable, and will – almost inevitably – cause problems. However, if you simply use all the partitions other than the first to store information rather than for software – for example, if you have a large collection of music, images, animations or video clips – then this becomes less important.)

Installing a new motherboard

This is a rather more complex process than installing a new hard disk. In effect, you will be taking your old PC apart and putting it back together again. Do not attempt this unless you have plenty of experience.

There is usually little reason to buy a new motherboard unless you buy a new processor chip at the same time. When buying a combination, check to be absolutely sure that your motherboard is compatible with the chip you have in mind, and also with its clip-on heatsink (remarkably, it is possible to buy a heatsink from a dealer that cannot be fitted successfully to certain motherboards sold by the same dealer). Check also that it matches the kind of memory you are using. If you have a lot of extras installed, ensure that there are at least as many ISA slots on the new motherboard as in your existing PC – otherwise you may find that you run out of slots, and so have to do without one of your extras. Also check that you buy the same size of motherboard – either AT, or ATX. Otherwise you will need to buy a new case and transplant your entire PC to it, motherboard, disks and all.

When fitting a new motherboard you will need to keep track of all the connectors on the back of the PC, including the parallel (printer) port and the serial (mouse and modem) ports. On newer hardware all these connections live on the motherboard, and so cannot be moved. On older models, however, they typically take the form of ribbon-cable links to connectors that have to be fitted to suitably sized slots on the PC's case. If your PC offers USB you will need to keep track of these connectors too. While not difficult, it pays to identify the relevant connectors on your new motherboard so that you don't miss anything out. As with other jobs, you may find that fitting all of these inside the case is a tight squeeze. Unfortunately this is an occupational hazard, and you may need to use your powers of ingenuity to re-route the various cables until all the connections can be fitted in correctly.

1. Restart the PC, enter the BIOS screen and make a note of all of the drive settings. You will need to supply your new motherboard with this information later.
2. Shut down the PC, turn off the power, open up the case.
3. Disconnect all the wires and cables from the motherboard, making a note of what they are connected to. Do this slowly and carefully.
4. Either remove all the other cables and connectors, or tie or tape them to the inside of the case so that they do not get in the way. Pay particular attention to the two big power connectors at the edge of the motherboard.
5. Remove all expansion cards from the board.
6. Remove the screws that hold the old motherboard in place and remove the board itself. You will usually need to jiggle around the small plastic pins that hold up the board to do this.
7. Place the old board on a static-safe surface, such as a static-protective bag.
8. Remove the memory from the old board and install it in the new motherboard.
9. Install the new board using the plastic pins and appropriate screw fittings saved from the old board. The position and number of pins and screws may well be different from that on the original board.
10. Refit the expansion cards.
11. Referring to the motherboard's manual, set up any jumpers on the new board to match the processor chip you have chosen, and install the processor and its heat sink.
12. Refit all the connectors, bearing in mind the notes above.
13. Double-check that the expansion cards are seated firmly in their slots, the jumpers are set correctly, the memory is fitted correctly,

and that all the connectors are attached properly – especially the power connectors for the board. Triple-check these connectors using the diagram in the motherboard's manual.

14. Turn on the PC. Enter the BIOS setup screen. Set the hard disk specifications. All the other settings – include those you haven't checked yet – will usually work correctly.

15. Check to see if the PC starts. If nothing at all happens, double-check the BIOS settings, the processor jumpers on the motherboard, and all the hard disk connectors. If you get memory errors or the PC seems very erratic, you may need to change the BIOS memory setup. Get a support person to talk you through this.

16. If the PC starts up with a beep but stops at the 'Hit DEL to enter SETUP' screen, repeat step 15, leaving out the jumper check.

17. When all is working properly refit the case.

'Flashing' a BIOS

Sometimes it can be cheaper and quicker to upgrade a motherboard by upgrading its BIOS. This is known as 'flashing the BIOS.' (Technically the BIOS is stored in a special kind of memory known as 'flash memory', which can be modified electrically and keeps its settings even when the power is turned off.) BIOS upgrades are sometimes necessary to fix problems such as random crashes, or to make it possible for the BIOS to work with larger hard disk drives.

Note that **flashing a BIOS can be dangerous**. If the process fails, you will be left with an irretrievably useless motherboard that will have to be replaced. Even professionals approach this operation with a certain caution, so you should attempt it only if you are fully willing to accept the risks as your own responsibility.

To flash a BIOS you need two items of software – a BIOS flashing program and an updated BIOS 'image'. During the flashing process, the former simply copies the latter into the flash memory on the motherboard. Both can typically be obtained free from the motherboard manufacturer's web site. Make sure you choose the ones that are directly relevant to the make and model number of your motherboard. Then copy both items to your computer, unzip them if necessary, copy them to a Windows startup disk which has had all the other files deleted, and then start the computer from the startup disk. From there run the flashing program and follow the instructions.

If possible, connect your computer to a UPS while you do this. If the power fails at any point in the flashing process, the process will also fail, and you will be left with a broken motherboard.

Very advanced tasks – building a PC from scratch

If you have mastered the earlier tasks, then building a PC from scratch should present few problems. However apart from putting the PC together, you will also need to install an operating system (OS) from scratch. In doing this, you have two options. If the operating system is supplied on floppy disk (which is unlikely if you are installing a modern OS such as Windows 95/98) then start by installing MS-DOS, and install the other OS over the top. If the operating system is supplied on CD-ROM you will need to install MS-DOS, install the drivers for the CD-ROM, and then run the installation program from the CD. The rest happens automatically.

The following is a 'shopping list' for constructing a DIY PC. If you buy all these items together you should be able to negotiate a discount on the total. Remember to check for compatibility – for example, that the motherboard is designed to work with the processor chip you have in mind. Most retailers will be able to help you make these decisions.

Surprisingly, the DIY route may not save you money. Even with a discount, the total price is likely to be greater than that for an off-the-shelf PC. However, you will end up with a machine that you know inside out, and will be able to repair if something goes wrong.

Some suppliers are now offering complete PC kits, which include all the relevant parts, complete with instructions, for a slightly greater discount. If you have computer DIY experience these can be worth considering as an alternative to buying everything separately. Even so, the benefits of building your PC from scratch are in the realm of personal satisfaction and acquiring new skills, rather than financial gain.

Hardware (main PC unit)
- Motherboard
- Processor chip
- Memory
- One or more hard disk drives

- CD-ROM drive (optional, but strongly recommended)
- Sound card (optional)
- Graphics card
- Floppy disk drive
- Case

Hardware (other)
- Keyboard
- Mouse
- Monitor
- Modem (optional)

Software
- Working copy ('boot disk') of DOS on floppy disk. You will also need a part of DOS called FDISK on the same floppy. A Windows startup disk will typically provide both of these, as well as CD-ROM drivers (see below).
- Main operating system, such as Windows 95/98. (If the operating system is on CD-ROM, you will need drivers for the CD-ROM on floppy disk as well.)
- The latest drivers, where relevant. Motherboards, sound cards and graphics cards will often be sold with drivers that (most probably) work, but may not be the best available. Windows also includes a collection of drivers, but again these are unlikely to be the most efficient or reliable. To get the best from a PC it can be useful to obtain the latest drivers before starting work.

1. Open up the case.
2. Fit the motherboard. This is supported on small plastic pins and screwed into place with one or more screws. Make sure the board is well supported.
3. Fit the memory on to the motherboard.
4. Fit the processor to the motherboard. Fit the heatsink to the processor.
5. Set any drives that require it to slave mode, and fit them all into the drive cage. You may find that you need to remove part of the cage (typically the 3.5-inch part) to make it possible to fit screws on both sides of all the drives. If this is so, simply refit that part of the cage when you have finished. You may need to remove one or

more metal blanking plates. These are plates fixed to the front of the drive cage behind plastic panels, and can only be removed permanently. Push out the plastic panels at the front of the PC where you need access to the drives – i.e. the floppy disk and the CD-ROM.

6. Plug in all the relevant power connectors. Be especially careful with the power connectors to the motherboard, as you can plug something in the wrong way round and cause damage. Double-check the connections in the manual before proceeding.

7. Plug in the ribbon cables for the hard drive(s), floppy drive, CD-ROM, printer and serial ports, mouse, and any other connectors on the back.

8. Fit the graphics card into an expansion slot.

9. Plug in the mouse, monitor and keyboard and turn on the PC. Check for signs of life. If nothing happens, double-check every single cable and connector and also the graphics card, and try again. Your PC won't start properly, but you should get a single 'beep' and a message that says 'Hard drive failed...'.

10. Restart the PC and set up the BIOS so it recognises the hard disk(s) and the CD-ROM drive. Restart the PC again with the MS-DOS floppy in the slot.

11. Run FDISK to partition the hard disk(s), and then FORMAT to format them.

12. Restart the PC, install MS-DOS to the hard disk, and then install the CD-ROM drivers.

13. If installing an operating system from a CD-ROM, run the SETUP program on the CD-ROM. Everything else should happen automatically. If the operating system is on floppy disks, then you will need to swap these in and out by hand as it loads.

14. Shut down the PC, and install the other expansion cards and drivers for all the cards. (Up to this point the graphics card will have been working in a 'bare minimum' way that doesn't make use of all of its facilities. Installing the drivers for it will allow it to operate at its full potential.)

15. Install your favourite software.

Various things can go wrong during the assembly process. The most likely place for problems is the installation of Windows. The Windows setup disk occasionally does unexpected things, such as trying to install

Windows to the CD-ROM and complaining that there is not enough available disk space, or simply stopping or crashing before full installation is finished. In many cases problems can be solved by simply repeating installation till it works correctly. If all else fails, it may be necessary to call for technical support, or perhaps even to send back the chosen motherboard and try again with a different model.

Overclocking

There is no physical difference between similar chips with different speed ratings. After manufacture each processor is tested to determine its maximum reliable operating speed, and it is then labelled appropriately and sold at that rating. Often this rating is a conservative estimate. Because of minor random variations, some chips work reliably at higher speeds than others. In practice many chips can be made to run 10–20% faster by making some simple adjustments to a motherboard's BIOS settings, This is known as overclocking. It is a popular pastime with computer hobbyists who want to get the maximum possible speed from their hardware, particularly for games and other applications. Overclocking is most commonly attempted with processor chips, but video cards and motherboard components can also be overclocked.

Overclocking can have serious side effects, even when it appears to be working well. As a chip runs faster it produces more heat, and also works less reliably. At best this means that overclocking can lead to random crashes and other failures. Operating life may also be reduced. At worst it can cause a chip to fail completely and permanently.

Any attempt at overclocking will void your warranty, and is done entirely at your own risk. It's useful to weigh up the costs against the benefits. Very few applications genuinely need the small speed boost that overclocking supplies, and no applications benefit from an unreliable or dead PC. Overall, then, this is a task for experts and dedicated hobbyists who feel confident that they can handle any accidental damage, and don't mind paying for replacement parts if their attempts are unsuccessful.

To cope with the extra heat, many overclockers resort to powerful heatsinks and other heat dissipation tools. In extreme cases this can mean adding extra fans to a computer's case, or even bolting a small refrigeration unit onto the processor. This is known as active refrigeration and can improve the speed rating by 20–50%. But the noise and extra complexity make this an option that only appeals to the most dedicated hobbyists. Even for less ambitious overclocking projects, the extra heat and noise generated by additional cooling hardware can be a serious drawback.

The details of overclocking depend on the hardware involved, and a full summary is too complex to include here. For more details an Internet search on 'overclocking' will produce a wealth of tips and practical advice for anyone who wants to experiment with their computer in this way.

Computer troubleshooting

Computer problems are many and varied, and providing a usable list of faults and possible solutions is beyond the scope of this book. However, the following rules of thumb are useful:

1. Keep notes of all the changes you make. Sometimes installing a piece of software will cause some other piece of software to stop working. Uninstalling the new software may undo the damage – at the very least it can provide some hints about where to find the problem. Note that sometimes problems caused by software installations may be obscure. For example, installing a media player may cause email software to stop displaying text correctly. Even if the problem seems unrelated, the rule of thumb still applies – the last change made to the system is likely to be the culprit, even if it isn't at all obvious how or why this should be the case.

2. Make complete system backups regularly, and especially before making any major changes. The best way to do this is by cloning the hard disk that contains Windows (see page 244.) If something goes seriously wrong – perhaps so seriously wrong that Windows refuses to start – you will be able to undo the damage by copying the cloned disk back to its original location.

3. Windows includes a *registry*, which holds all the relevant hardware and software settings. Delving into the registry by hand is something that even experts do with caution, and that requires at the very least an understanding of the registry's format and structure. However, both Microsoft and Norton provide registry repair tools that can, in some cases, fix damage and solve problems. Norton's registry tool is

sold as part of Norton Utilities; Microsoft's tool is called RegClean, and is available for free on Microsoft's web site (*http://www.microsoft.com*). (At the time of writing, RegClean and other free updates can be found by selecting 'All products' on the main menu, then 'Downloads', then 'Windows 98', and 'Windows 98' again from the individual product menu. Unfortunately there does not seem to be a version available for Windows 95.)

4. When adding a new PCI card, a card that doesn't work correctly in one slot may work perfectly well in a different one.

5. Many problems are caused by *drivers* (see page 291). Random crashes can sometimes be solved by copying the latest motherboard, hard disk ('EIDE'), graphics card and perhaps also sound card drivers from the Internet, and installing them.

6. Sometimes hardware simply doesn't work properly. For example, a computer may crash regularly when the USB connectors are turned on ('enabled') in the BIOS settings, but works perfectly reliably when they are turned off. Even commercially assembled computers may suffer from problems like these. There is little that can be done in such cases, apart from asking for a working system or – if there is some certainty about where the problem lies – a different, problem-free component such as a motherboard.

Trouble-shooting games

Games can be notoriously difficult to get working. Typical problems include lack of sound, lack of CD music, stuttering, slow animations, and even complete crashes which freeze the PC. Sorting out the many possible problems is not an easy task. It is a good idea to start by making sure that you have the very latest drivers for all the hardware you are using. This includes the latest version of Microsoft's DirectX (see page 293).

Next, visit the game manufacturer's web site and see if there are any updates (sometimes known as 'patches') for the game itself. Usually there is literally no other way to get the same information, so without access to the Internet you may, unfortunately, be left with a non-working game and no chance of fixing it. Manufacturers will often include a list of frequently asked questions about the game on their web site, and one of these may solve any problems you are experiencing. Typically, you will also find details of a contact email address or phone number here, or else in the manual for the game. Over time manufacturers build up a database of common problems, and if you contact them directly they can sometimes help.

However, it is always possible that your particular problem will be new to the manufacturer, especially if the game is relatively new. At this point, your options are very limited. It can sometimes be worth looking at the more obscure settings offered by your graphics card and experimenting with any setting that uses terms such as 'Direct Memory Access' or 'Bus Mastering' (if these exist, they may be hidden away behind a button labelled 'advanced').

If the game still fails to work, you are perfectly within your rights to take it back to the shop you bought it from and ask for a refund.

Appendix X

Computers, your health and the environment

Can computers damage your health? It seems bad working practices (sitting in a fixed position at the keyboard for long periods, making awkward or repetitive movements with your arms, head or body) contribute to a variety of ailments ranging from eyestrain to pain and discomfort in the limbs. Fortunately these are easily preventable. Taking time to ensure that your desk, chair and screen are positioned correctly can save days, even months of frustration and fatigue.

Health issues

Repetitive strain injury

Repetitive strain injury, or RSI, is a blanket term used to cover a collection of strain- and sprain-related health problems. Although there is some disagreement in the medical profession about whether or not RSI really exists, and if so exactly what causes it, a number of RSI sufferers are in no doubt that it is a work-related health issue. In extreme cases it can cause significant loss of flexibility in the hand and fingers.

If caught early and treated, the effects can sometimes be reversed. But there is no guarantee that this will be possible; the damage produced by some kinds of RSI may lead to a permanent incapacity.

From the point of view of working at a screen, RSI seems to be related to tendonitis and carpal tunnel syndrome (CTS), a disabling injury which can affect anyone who uses their fingers or wrists for long periods. Concert pianists and professional keyboard players have been known to suffer from CTS, which can sometimes be treated by surgery, though not always with success. It is much wiser to avoid the problem in the first place.

Keyboard

One of the biggest problems facing anyone who uses a keyboard every day is the way that the standard QWERTY keyboard is arranged. Conventional touch-typing can place severe strain on the wrist and finger joints. The hands can be cramped and often unsupported for long periods, the fingertips can be in almost constant use, and the finger joints may be held in a strained position as well as being continually flexed.

One simple but effective solution is a wrist support. This is a simple foam pad placed in front of the keyboard on which the wrists can be rested comfortably between bouts of typing (while typing the wrists should not rest on anything). A wrist support is highly recommended for anyone who works with a computer keyboard on a regular basis.

A more adventurous solution is to use another keyboard layout. The Dvorak keyboard – named after its inventor, John Dvorak – uses a different and more logical letter arrangement. Not only is it faster to work with, it is also easier to learn and produces less strain when used over long periods. Most keyboards come with keytops that can be detached with nothing more complicated than a small screwdriver, so the keyboard can be rearranged into the Dvorak layout. Some software, such as Windows for the PC, includes support for the Dvorak system as well as the QWERTY layout.

Another alternative is ergonomic keyboards. These are designed to fit the hands better and provide built-in wrist support, although they still use the standard QWERTY layout. Apple sold an ergonomic design in the mid-1990s but this is now only available second-hand. Microsoft's ergonomic keyboard is still current.

A company called Maltron offers ergonomic keyboard designs for the UK market. These look even stranger than the Microsoft and Apple models (and are not designed to the standard QWERTY layout), and cost between £200 and £400, which makes them very expensive. However, many users report that these keyboards can make a difference to anyone with persistent RSI.

Opinions about ergonomic keyboards are mixed. Some users find they make a huge difference, others find they do nothing at all. Try out a keyboard at your local computer store and see for yourself before you decide whether or not to pay the extra.

VDU emissions

A computer screen is also known as a VDU or visual display unit and, like a television, emits radiation, although levels likely to be generated are well below officially imposed limits. A simple but expensive way to avoid the problem is to buy a good portable computer or a flat-panel display. These have screens which do not produce the same kind of hard radiation. Unfortunately these screens are still relatively expensive. The next best option is to choose a monitor that has been fully certified to the MPRII or TCO95/99 standard (you may see an appropriate marking e.g. MPRII on the back of the monitor). This ensures that any stray radiation is below background levels (see page 201).

A glare filter – a plastic, glass or mesh panel that fits over the front of the VDU – will not affect 'hard' radiation such as X-rays, as these need proper shielding, but advanced models can help with static electricity. This tends to collect as charge on the screen – hence the 'crackling fingers' effect – and can, in extreme cases, have an effect on the operator's face and skin. (If this is a problem, you might consider investing in an air ioniser, which adds a complementary charge to dust particles that balances out the positive charge from the screen.) Glare filters can also be helpful in improving display quality and contrast, and hence lessening eyestrain. Generally speaking, correct position will do more for glare than a bolt-on filter. However, the problem of glare should be treated at source, for example, angling the screen, rearranging the work station, using window blinds, and other options before resorting to glare filters. Before buying a monitor look very thoroughly at it – with a glare filter fitted, if you feel you need one. A good – or a bad – monitor can make a huge difference to the amount of stress you feel when using your computer.

A useful way to help avoid eyestrain is to set up software so that it shows very large type. Microsoft Word, for example, has a Zoom feature which can show letters on the screen much larger than their usual size. Setting Zoom to a size larger than 100% can be a surprisingly effective way of making working at the computer less stressful. Choice of foreground and background colours can also make a difference. Black text on a grey background is easier to read than grey text on a white background. It can also be helpful to look away into the distance regularly, ideally at an object or scene a very long way away.

Printers

Early laser printers produced ozone, a gas which can be harmful in high quantities. Some newer models use a slightly modified printing system which is ozone-free. Always make sure that the printer you are using is in a well-ventilated area.

Another health hazard is toner spillage. The toner for most printers is a very fine powder and can be messy if spilled. Spills – which are unlikely unless the toner case is broken – should always be cleaned up immediately, wearing protective gloves. Be careful not to have your head too close to the powder when cleaning up spillage. Inhaling this powder can be uncomfortable and harmful; it is best to wear a simple dust mask if you think there is a risk of inhaling the dust.

The problem with dot-matrix and daisy-wheel printers is one of noise. Many computer accessory stores sell acoustic hoods, which you place over the printer to deaden the sound. These are strongly recommended for daisy-wheel printers in particular, and worth considering for dot-matrix designs. The print head on a dot-matrix model can become very warm. When changing a ribbon avoid touching the print head until it has cooled down.

Bubble-jet printers are relatively safe. Apart from the very minor problem of ink spillage if you try to refill an ink cartridge, bubble-jet and ink-jet printers have no notably unhealthy side-effects.

Noise

Your computer should run quietly. The cooling fan should not be distractingly loud. Although this may seem like a minor point, unwanted noise can aggravate stress levels. If you plan to spend a long time in front of your machine make sure that it is quiet enough to enable you to work with some tranquillity. Also, arrange your work to ensure you leave the screen for frequent short breaks *before* the onset of tiredness.

Posture

To prevent long-term problems you will need to maintain a good posture. According to EU suggestions, this means adjusting your working environment so that knees, hips and elbows are at ninety-degree angles, the wrists and neck are straight, and the monitor is at a five-degree angle below the line of sight.

HEALTH CHECKLIST

Monitor
Clean! (and easily cleaned)
Low radiation, MPRII-rated
Adequate letter size and display contrast
Comfortable flicker rate (i.e., 72Hz or better for smaller screens, 90Hz or better for screens larger than 19-inch)
Comfortable on-screen colour scheme
Tilted and swivelled to a comfortable viewing position
At the right height
Fitted with a glare filter if necessary
Located out of direct sunlight, with brightness and contrast set comfortably

Keyboard
Fitted with a wrist support
Easily movable
Weighted to prevent sliding
Optional Dvorak layout
Optional ergonomic design

Desk
Worktop at a comfortable height: this varies from person to person. First get the height and position of the chair right and then either raise the desk surface and/or use a footrest. Concentrate on the body position and adjust accordingly
Matt, non-reflective surface
Sufficient free space (at least 6 sq. ft) around the computer for papers, etc.
Located out of direct sunlight
Supplied with a comfortable footrest if necessary
No unnecessary obstructions underfoot (such as papers, wastepaper bin)

Chair
Stable, moves easily
Good back support, including the lower back

Fully adjustable; should be adjustable to a height which allows the forearm to be horizontal to the desk in order that the fingers fall naturally on the keys. This may mean you need to use a footrest

Document holder
Easily adjustable; should be at the same height as the screen and on the same plane

Printer
Acoustic hoods where necessary
Located in a well-ventilated area
Toner spills are cleared up immediately

System unit
No buzzes, squeaks, squeals or hums
Accessible without user having to strain

Lighting
No glare or direct lighting from any source shining into user's eyes

Electrical
All power connections made safe
Unavoidable trailing wires placed under flat rubber floor conduits
When ceasing work always switch off at the unit, then at the mains supply at the socket

Air ioniser
To remove positive ions from the immediate environment if necessary

Working practice
Regular breaks of at least ten minutes an hour, spent walking around rather than stretching at the desk
Regular relaxation periods, based on professional relaxation techniques.

For further information contact the Health and Safety Executive

It also helps to relax regularly while working. Take short, frequent breaks from keyboard work. A helpful scheme to follow is a one-minute break every ten minutes, a ten-minute break every hour and a forty-minute break (at least) every three hours. Stress-management consultants and some alternative health practitioners are sources of advice on how to relax while still working effectively.

EU directives

The European Union's set of directives designed to prevent operator discomfort while working with DSE (display screen equipment) became mandatory on 1 January 1997. If you are an employer you are required to follow these. In outline this means you must:

- provide a monitor that has clearly formed and well-defined lettering, no reflective glare and negligible radiation
- provide a footrest for anyone who asks for one
- provide a document holder which can be positioned so as not to require unnecessary movements
- provide a wrist support that enables the operator to adopt the correct posture.

These regulations can be ordered from good bookshops and, though in part quite vague, they will go some way to ensure that as an employer you are aware of health issues and of your responsibility to act on them.

How 'green' are computers?

You may see computers advertised as 'green', and in this context the word means something very specific. 'Green' features imply a range of power-saving options. The computer only draws maximum power while you actually use it. After a period of inactivity it starts to shut down – the monitor, the main processor chip and perhaps the hard disk go into a low power 'standby' mode. This saves electricity and – in theory – has less of an effect on the environment.

To get a computer with power-saving features, you should watch out for the 'Energy Star' rating. This was introduced by the US government in an attempt to save energy on a national basis, but is now available in the UK as well. A computer with a full set of Energy Star features will use less electricity than one without. But the differences are likely to be minor.

Appendix XI

Legal aspects of computer use

Certain areas of everyday computer use are regulated by law. These are, the holding of information about individuals, and the copying, or use of illegal copies, of software. It is important to be aware of the legal implications as ignorance could prove to be costly.

The Data Protection Act

In March 2000 the Data Protection Act 1998 came into force. The new law replaces the Data Protection Act 1984. It increases some obligations on data users, gives individual new rights of access to information and changes registration requirements to a simplified system of notification.

Under the new law, if you maintain any kind of information about identifiable living people on your computer, you may be liable to notify the Office of the Information Commissioner. Notification is a relatively painless process, which costs an annual standard fee of £35. The penalties for not notifying are much stiffer – up to £5,000 in a Magistrates' Court, or an unlimited sum in the higher courts.

However, this is the exception. If you maintain and use personal data for personal, family and household purposes you will **not** need to bother. Likewise, if you only use personal data for staff administration, advertising, marketing and public relations or accounts and records. However, even if you don't have to notify, under the new law you may still have to comply with the requirements contained in the Act on the use of personal data.

You should notify even if the information is kept on a computer that you do not own. If you contract out the maintenance of a list of details to a computer bureau, then you are still the person who is determining the purpose and the way in which the data is to be processed and should notify accordingly.

If you are subject to the Act, you must comply with eight principles of good information-handling practice. Broadly, these state that personal data must be:

1. obtained and processed fairly and lawfully
2. maintained and processed for limited purposes and not used in a way incompatible with those purposes
3. adequate, relevant and not excessive in relation to the purpose for which the data is held
4. accurate
5. kept only as long as is necessary
6. maintained and processed in line with the individual's rights under the Act
7. secure
8. transferred only to other countries that have adequate data protection.

There are also special provisions for the use of sensitive data, such as racial or ethnic origin, political opinions and religious and other beliefs. These can be processed only under strict conditions and may mean that you have to obtain explicit consent from the individual for any use.

If you have to notify, you may have to convince the Commissioner that you are not collecting information unnecessarily. This can sometimes have surprising implications. It is difficult to say what approach the Commissioner will take under the new law. However, in a previous case a video hire shop that was collecting the passport and driving licence numbers of its customers as a security measure was advised to stop this practice, as collecting this information was inappropriate in the circumstances. Notification will require you to look at the records you keep and to ensure you have good reasons why you need to continue keeping them.

For information on whether you need to notify and what you need to do to ensure you are using and processing personal data fairly, contact the Office of the Information Commissioner (see Addresses) or *www.dataprotection.gov.uk*

Software piracy

Software piracy ranges from the organised, black-market copying of software and manuals, to the use of illegal copies of a word-processing package in an office because 'no one need ever know', to the installation at home of a single copy of software obtained from a friend who bought it legally.

If you use pirated software – and some estimates suggest that almost half of all the software in use in the UK today is pirated – you are liable for prosecution. Although the police tend to concentrate on organised pirating operations, if you use a disk supplied by a friend, in theory you are still committing a theft and are liable for prosecution.

Software is usually sold on a licence rather than an outright purchase basis. This usually means that your rights are limited to:

- using the software on one machine at a time
- possibly making backup safety copies

You are not allowed to:

- use the software on two different machines at once (e.g., desktop and laptop)
- pass copies to a friend
- sell the software on, even second-hand.

Any of these actions could leave you liable to prosecution. Passing copies to a friend is particularly dangerous. All software includes a unique serial number. If copies with your number turn up in an investigation then you could be held responsible.

In general, then, it is unwise to pirate or to use pirated software. This applies especially in an office situation, where the software is spread across a network or is installed on a number of PCs. This kind of semi-organised piracy is being vigorously pursued by the industry, and agencies such as FAST (Federation Against Software Theft) (see Addresses) even run a hotline service where the public can provide tip-offs about piracy (see Addresses). In short, the best advice is – don't.

What to do with your old computer

What do you do with an old computer? Getting rid of it can be a headache. You could just throw it away – leave it outside the house with the other rubbish, or take it to the local tip or recycling centre. However, by throwing away the computer you could also be throwing away any value that it may still have. Simple disposal is also ecologically unsound. It therefore makes sense both from a financial and ecological point of view to recycle or sell your hardware if possible, or to give it to a deserving cause if not.

Second-hand value

Many computers still have a second-hand value. But you must be realistic in your pricing. A machine that cost £1,000 five years ago is likely to be worth perhaps a tenth of that today. It can be more appealing to prospective buyers if the computer is sold as a complete package with all software and a printer included (although you should, of course, bear in mind that caveats about software piracy and licensing apply in this situation). You could advertise it for sale in the local newspapers and in newsagents' shop windows. Another option is advertising it on the Internet, for example on auction services such as eBay (www.ebay.co.uk).

Selling the parts

More experienced users may want to consider dismantling the computer and selling the pieces individually. Breaking up a computer in this way is only worth considering if it is so outdated that it is unlikely to interest anyone looking for a complete second-hand machine. Depending on size, hard disks are worth between £10 and

£100 second-hand. Experienced buyers will want to know if there are any damaged or 'bad' sectors or flaws on the surface of the disk that will affect its ability to hold information reliably. The Partition Magic package can check for these, and a hard disk that is completely free of them can be sold with some confidence. Other components can also be sold off one by one. Cases are worth up to £30, again depending on size and 'form factor'; floppy disk drives around £5; and CD-ROM drives between £10 and £20, depending on speed. Processor chips can fetch up to £300, depending on speed and age, although in older machines a more realistic asking price might be between £10 and £50. Used motherboards, especially obsolete ones, are very hard to dispose of, and are unlikely to fetch more than between £10 to £20.

If you do decide to sell your computer in bits, the best place to advertise all the parts is in the local free advertising papers, and in computer specialist magazines such as *MicroMart* and *PCMart*.

Deleting information

Before disposing of a computer, it is important to remove any sensitive information from it. Normally, deleting the information (which in Windows 95/98 means making sure that it is also removed from the 'recycle bin') will offer enough security. However, business users and those with confidential personal information should be aware that deleted information can be reconstructed, albeit with some time and effort. Anyone worried about business or personal details falling into the wrong hands may want to use a 'professional' delete tool, which not only removes the information but makes it utterly irretrievable. For example, Norton Utilities has a military-standard deletion tool which removes all traces of deleted information so thoroughly that not even removing the hard disk from its case and surrounding it with specialised electronic equipment makes it possible to retrieve it.

Donating to charity

You may want to consider donating an old computer to charity, or to a local school. Secondary schools tend to standardise on systems from one manufacturer, and so may be less keen to take an older machine. However, primary schools are often less fussy, and it can be worth asking head teachers if they are interested in a free machine In the UK,

Computers for Charity and Gifts In Kind (see Addresses) are two organisations that specialise in taking away old machines and passing them on to worthwhile causes.

Finally you may know of friends or relatives who would like your old machine. Even if it is of no further use to you, it may be very useful to friends, or perhaps their children.

Appendix XIII

Further reading

Although most computer magazines cover the same territory, there is a huge difference in readability, usefulness and value. At one end of the market are the unashamedly technical magazines aimed at readers who already have a good grasp of the subject and need the latest information to keep up with the rest of the industry. At the other end are the magazines which specifically cater for the uninitiated. In between are the new family-oriented lifestyle magazines. A recent development is titles specialising in the Internet.

Many magazines include software in the form of one or more CD-ROMs or DVDs on the cover. These can be an invaluable source of product demonstrations and free software. Magazines sometimes publish separate CD-ROM and DVD versions of the same issue, with the latter offering more extra free software. You will also find free booklets that give further information on some aspects of computing. These can be an excellent source of information for beginners and a very good way to equip yourself with a 'free' set of tutorials and a reference library.

The magazine market is rather volatile, and titles appear and disappear regularly. For the latest information visit the web sites of the major publishers, as listed on page 339. (The Ziff Davis and the *Wired* sites are particularly interesting as they include topical industry news and commentary.) A more detailed list of Internet titles can be found in *The Which? Guide to the Internet*.

What follows is a brief survey of the magazines available in May 2001.

Monthly professional PC titles

These are usually heavy on advertising and make few concessions to the absolute beginner. Many articles will be all but incomprehensible to anyone without a good grasp of the subject, although there will sometimes be a couple of pages – but no more – devoted to absolute beginners. A handful of titles try much harder to present information in a way that does not exclude readers without a technical background.

Computer Buyer (Dennis Publishing)
An all-round general-purpose title, although sometimes perhaps too technically advanced for complete beginners. The main emphasis is on hardware and software news, comparisons and reviews. The comprehensive Buyer's Guide is unusually good.

Computer Shopper (Dennis Publishing)
There are useful sections devoted to computers other than the PC and Mac but much of the content is highly technical. A regular beginners' feature ('Ivan Iwannado') does its best to demystify a different part of computing each month, but is perhaps still a little technical for absolute beginners. The large question-and-answer section is a reliable source of technical hints and solutions.

PC Direct (Ziff Davis UK)
This magazine is aimed particularly at mail-order buyers of PC equipment. Otherwise it is very much a typical PC enthusiast's monthly title.

PC Magazine (Ziff Davis UK)
PC Magazine specialises in in-depth comparative reviews. Hardware reviews are presented in simple bar-graph form, and software reviews include usability and productivity studies.

PC Plus (Future Publishing)
This magazine has the usual opinion, news, reviews and educational sections. It is best suited to readers who have a middling level of technical expertise, and includes information about computer programming and other more advanced IT skills. There is an informative, if not quite comprehensive, buyer's guide which lists

most of the widely available software and hardware products in any month.

PC Pro (Dennis Publications)
This title is aimed at the computer-literate professional user. It includes a comprehensive buyer's guide and list of industry contact numbers and addresses.

Personal Computer World (VNU Publications)
This is one of the longest-running computer titles on the market. Apart from the usual blend of industry news and product reviews there are also company profiles and interviews, as well as occasional more general computer- or information-technology-based features.

What Laptop and Handheld PC (Crimson Publishing)
Details of the latest laptop and PDA hardware and software, with reviews, news and relevant Internet-related information.

What PC? (VNU Publications)
This is a very basic and straightforward monthly that is unusually useful to beginners. Each month a new topic, such as printers or portable computers, is covered in some detail. While not as thorough as some of the more professionally-oriented monthly magazines, it is a good place for complete novices to find explanations of jargon and other useful information.

Fortnightly professional PC titles

Computer Active (VNU Publications)
Among the best of the beginners' titles, *Computer Active* includes news, reviews, step-by-step how-to workshops and a range of other general PC-interest features. The contents seem to be chosen as much for practical as technical interest, and the magazine as a whole tries hard to be accessible to non-experts – it is recommended by the Plain English Campaign.

PC Mart (Maze Media)
A fortnightly paper containing classified ads. Good source of bargains and computer-book reviews, but not much solid buying advice.

Monthly leisure PC titles

Leisure titles concentrate on games and entertainment. They are written in a much friendlier and chattier style than the professional titles, and this can make them much less intimidating to beginners. They are also likely to include reviews of non-business multimedia software, such as animated story books for children, encyclopaedias, and other general-knowledge and specialist-interest software products.

A relatively recent development is a range of leisure titles aimed at home and family users. These cover a wide range of computer-related subjects and include many articles pitched at beginners.

PC Advisor (IDG Media)
Aimed specifically at beginners and family users, it is very reasonably priced and also reasonably comprehensive. However, the presentation is perhaps not as clear and focused as it could be.

PC Answers (Future Publishing)
This is a general leisure title.

PC Basics (Paragon Publishing)
A slightly more technically oriented title than other beginners' titles, *PC Basics* includes how-to columns, reviews, news and a technical answers section.

PC Format (Future Publishing)
This title concentrates on games and is aimed largely at younger readers, but also includes general-interest articles, interviews with writers, artists and musicians as well as computer professionals, and reviews of leisure software.

PC Gamer (Future Publishing)
A title devoted exclusively to PC gaming, and aimed at younger readers. It offers plenty of game reviews, hints and instructions on how-to find the built-in cheats in popular games, and complete game puzzles solutions. However, there is not much general PC advice.

PC Guide (Future Publishing)
Originally a family-oriented monthly, this has now changed course and become a more general-interest PC magazine, with simple 'how-to' features for beginners and information and stories about colourful

and creative computer applications that affect everyday life, such as computer-generated special effects in films.

PC Home (IDG Media)
Similar in style and content to *PC Format*, but without the general-interest articles. Concentrates on games and multimedia titles.

PC How To (Live Publishing)
Forty 'how-to' step-by-step tutorials every month, covering PC maintenance, creative applications, business use, and so on. No news or other editorial content.

PC Explorer (Live Publishing)
General news and other industry information, how-tos, commentary, and other standard content of a low-to-middling technical standard.

Linux Format (Future Publishing)
A brave attempt to bring Linux to a larger market, this monthly often includes free give-aways of various versions of Linux, plenty of free software, and information about how to set up and use your own Linux PC.

Linux Magazine (Linux New Media)
General Linux commentary, projects, background information and discussion. Not recommended for beginners.

Windows Made Easy (Paragon Publishing)
Aimed at the relative beginner, *Windows Made Easy* consists almost entirely of heavily illustrated step-by-step tutorial features describing a range of more or less obvious, common and useful PC tasks.

Monthly Apple titles

Apple titles tend to carry far less advertising than PC titles. Some PC monthlies are more like phone directories, which can make them unwieldy to read and store. Apple-specific monthlies are much more typical of other magazines.

As befits their readership profile, Apple magazines tend to concentrate on creative and artistic applications. But there is usually plenty for the home and business user too.

MacFormat (Future Publishing)
Covers the full range of Mac software from business to games and creative applications. There is a wide range of reviews, hints and tips and the content is suitable for beginners.

MacWorld (IDG Communications)
A good choice for the professional Apple user. Tends to cover traditional Apple areas of image-processing, DTP and creative design.

Fortnightly Apple titles

MacUser (Dennis Publishing)
One of the more informative Apple titles. It covers a wide range of software, not just the usual graphical and artistic applications, and there is even a 'getting started' section for beginners, although this tends to be aimed at Apple users with some basic experience rather than complete novices.

Weekly titles

MicroMart (Trinity Publications Ltd)
Cheap, printed on cheap paper, it includes some of the best computer bargains around. This is one of the best available sources for cut-price hardware and software bargains. Also has pages of free classified ads.

Internet publications

Internet (EMAP publications)
Internet includes features aimed at both beginners and more experienced users, although the style is always approachable and non-technical. The title is distinguished by its comprehensive directory section, which includes an Internet glossary, full details of UK service providers and a huge selection of Internet locations and services.

InternetWorks (Future Publishing)
A business-oriented Internet title that concentrates on setting up Internet facilities for a medium-sized company, and other topics of business interest. Rather specific and technical for beginners, but can occasionally be a source of useful tips.

.net (Future Publishing)
Includes 'how-to' introductory features. There are useful lists of places to look for software and a directory of ISPs in the UK.

Practical Internet (Paragon Publishing)
Covers a broad range of Internet-related topics and takes a more accessible and less glamorous approach to its subject matter. It is aimed at a general audience and includes a mix of news, comments, tips and suggestions on where to find useful information on the Web.

Web User (IPC)
A fortnightly web-specific sibling to *Computer Active*, offering a similar mix of site reviews, investigations, and entertainment, using *Computer Active*'s 'plain English' approach.

Wired (Wired Ventures Ltd)
Wired is more of a lifestyle and general-interest than a technological monthly, and more than any other it captures the flavour of interactions on the Internet.

Books

It can be worth taking your time to browse when buying computer books, because they can save you money in the long run. Many titles are expensive – expect to pay anywhere from £15 to £50 – but this should be taken in the context of other computer-related training materials. A one-day training course can cost you between £150 and £500, and will not necessarily tell you any more than a book will (although you will be able to ask questions). So good books are a wise investment, and you may find that if you work through a well-written off-the-shelf tutorial you will not need to take a training course at all.

A trip to any bookshop will show that there is an almost unlimited number of titles available. It is impossible to recommend specific titles, as your choice will depend on your own needs and learning style. For example, many computer books for novices take a humorous approach, and some readers respond well to this; others simply find it annoying. The depth of the information presented and the overall layout vary tremendously too.

When starting from scratch you should budget up to £150 for books to get you started, although a basic familiarisation text will cost you £25. This will give you a good range to choose from, and you should be able to find everything you need to master the basics of the subject.

As a rough buying guide points to watch for include:

Style The most effective titles are those that take a step-by-step tutorial approach. Some books take a different tack and are meant as reference works. They may well contain everything you need to know, but it will not be presented in a simple, easy-to-follow way. Unless you are already proficient in the applications covered, reference-style books are best avoided.

Accessibility If you can get to the end of the first chapter without understanding a word – and this is possible, even with some of the titles aimed at beginners – consider another title instead. Some authors fall into the trap of using jargon without explaining it first. This can be annoying and confusing, and does nothing to help you master the subject. An accessible book will make the subject seem easier rather than harder.

Relevance New versions of software are being released all the time, so you will need to check that a book on a specific software title applies to the version you have.

Many computer books are written and printed in the US, and therefore use American expressions. Apart from the culture clash, this can sometimes render information inaccurate. Many Internet books, for example, include lists of Internet service providers. You should definitely look for an English title here, as American lists will not apply. In general, though, most US titles are suitable for the UK market.

Free software Some titles include free software. Check for a description in the book to see whether this will be genuinely useful to you.

Addresses

Business software manufacturers

Although most of these manufacturers can be contacted via email, this is usually reserved for contacting specific employees rather than for general public enquiries. Telephone in the first instance, or try the relevant web site.

Moneysoft Ltd
3 Flanchford Road
London W12 9ND
Tel: 020-8743 9792
Fax: 020-8743 8073
Email: info@moneysoft.co.uk
Web site: www.moneysoft.co.uk

Intuit Service Centre
PO Box 2093
Swindon SN5 8TR
Tel: (0800) 585058
Fax: (01793) 446582
Web site: www.intuit.co.uk
            www.quickbooks.co.uk

Lotus Development UK
Lotus Park
The Causeway
Staines
Middlesex TW18 3AG
Tel: (0870) 6006123
Fax: (01784) 469345
Email: info_uk@lotus.com
Web site: www.lotus.com

Microsoft Ltd
Microsoft Campus
Thames Valley Park
Reading RG6 1WG
Tel: (0870) 6010100
Fax: (0870) 6020100
Email: 2way@microsoft-contact.co.uk
Web site: www.microsoft.com

Novell UK
1 Arlington Square
Downshire Way
Bracknell RG12 1WA
Tel: (01344) 724000
Fax: (01344) 724001
Email: ukresponse@novell.com
Web site: www.novell.co.uk

Pegasus Software Ltd
Orion House
Orion Way
Kettering
Northamptonshire NN15 6PE
Tel: (01536) 495200
Fax: (01536) 495001
Email: mailbox@pegasus.co.uk
Web site: www.pegasus.co.uk

Sage Software Ltd
Sage House
Benton Park Road
Newcastle upon Tyne NE7 7LZ
Tel: 0191-255 3000
Fax: 0191-255 0308
Email: info@sage.com
Web site: www.uk.sage.com

Software602 Inc.
One Independent Drive
Suite 3125
Jacksonville
Florida 32202
USA
Tel: 1-904-356-6020
Fax: 1-904-353-2602
Email: sales@software602.com
Web site: www.software602.com

Tas Software
29 East Street
Epsom
Surrey KT17 1BS
Tel: (01372) 727274
Fax: (01372) 721414
Email: sales@tassoftware.co.uk
Web site: www.tassoftware.com

Health

HSE Books (Health and Safety Executive)
PO Box 1999
Sudbury
Suffolk CO10 2WA
Tel: (01787) 881165
Fax: (01787) 313995
Web site: www.hsebooks.co.uk
For free copies of leaflets INDG36
Working with VDUs and INDG243
Computer Control

PCD Maltron Ltd
15 Orchard Lane
East Molesey
Surrey KT8 0BN
Tel/Fax: 020-8398 3265
Email:sales@maltron.com
Web site: www.maltron.com

Insurance brokers

Association of British Insurers
51 Gresham Street
London EC2V 7HQ
Tel: 020-7600 3333
Fax: 020-7696 8999
Email: info@abi.org.uk
Web site: www.insurance.org.uk/
consumer2/consumer.htm

Burnett & Associates
39-41 Victoria Road
Woolston
Southampton SO19 9DY
Tel: 023-8044 2227
Fax: 023-8044 2210
Email: info@burnett.co.uk
Web site: www.burnett.co.uk

Domestic & General
Leicester House
17 Leicester Street
Bedworth
Warwickshire CV12 8JP
Tel: (08705) 490000
Fax: 024-7664 3322
Web site: www.domgen.com
(Domestic & General offers a
combined insurance and support
service)

Royal & Sun Alliance Insurance plc
St Mark's Court
Chart Way
Horsham
West Sussex RH12 1XL
Tel: (01403) 232323
Web site:
www.royalsunalliance.co.uk

Tolson Messenger
148 King Street
London W6 0QU
Tel: 020-8741 8361
Fax: 020-8741 9395
Email: homebusiness@
tolsonmessenger.co.uk
Web site:
www.tolsonmessenger.co.uk

Internet service providers

America OnLine (AOL)
AOL Ltd
Customer Service Centre
Network House
IDA Industrial Park
Cork Road
Waterford
Ireland
Tel: (0800) 2791234
Fax: (0800) 2797446
Email: Ukgena@aol.com
Web site: www.aol.co.uk

Nextra Cix Ltd
Global House
Ashley Avenue
Epsom
Surrey KT18 5AD
Tel: (0845) 355 5151
Fax: (0845) 355 0010
Email: support@cix.co.uk
Web site: www.nextra.co.uk

CompuServeUK
Customer Services Dept
PO Box 676
Bristol BS99 1YN
Tel: (08706) 000800 (customer
support)
Email: mail@compuserve.com
Web site: www.compuserve.com

Demon Internet
Gateway House
322 Regents Park Road
London N3 2QQ
Tel: (0845) 272 0666
Fax: 020-8371 1150
Email: sales@demon.net
Web site: www.demon.net

Which? Online
Freepost
Hertford X
SG14 1YB
Tel: (0845) 4550370
Email: which@which.net
Web site: www.which.net

User groups

Parents Information Network (PIN)
PO Box 16394
London SE1 3ZP
Tel: 020-7357 9078
Fax: 020-7357 9077
Email: post@pin.org.uk
Web site: www.pin.org.uk

Pre-printed computer stationery

Vista Papers
Nuffield Road
Harrowbrook Industrial Estate
Hinckley
Leicestershire LE10 3DG
Tel: (0800) 616244
Fax: (0800) 716563
Email: sales@vistapapers.co.uk
Web site: www.vistapapers.co.uk

Viking Direct
Bursom Industrial Park
Tollwell Road
Leicester LE4 1BR
Tel: (0800) 424444
Fax: (0800) 622211
Email:
ukimprints@vikingdirect.com
Web site: www.viking-direct.co.uk

Shareware libraries

Atlantic Coast Plc
The Shareware Village
Station Road
Colyton
Devon EX24 6HA
Tel: (01297) 552222
Fax: (01297) 553366
Email: sales@atlantic-coast.com
Web site: www.swreg.org

The Public Domain and Shareware Library (PC)
PO Box 131
Crowborough
East Sussex TN6 1WS
Tel: (01892) 663298
Fax: (01892) 667473
Email: info@pdsl.com
Web site: www.pdsl.com

Support providers' organisation

Computing Services & Software Association
20 Red Lion Street
London WC1R 4QN
Tel: 020-7395 6700
Fax: 020-7404 4119
Email: cssa@cssa.co.uk
Web site: www.cssa.co.uk

UPS and surge protector components

Farnell Components
Canal Road
Leeds LS12 2TU
Tel: (08701) 200200 (sales)
(08701) 200202 (product support)
Fax: (08701) 200201
Web site: www.farnell.com/uk

Suppliers

Maplin Electronics plc
National Distribution Centre
Station Road
off Valley Road
Wombwell
Barnsley
South Yorkshire S73 0BZ
Tel: (0870) 264 6000
Fax: (0870) 264 6001
Email: customerservice@maplin.co.uk
Web site: www.maplin.co.uk

Educational resources

www.bcs.org.uk/ecdl/index.html
Information and some free training
materials related to the 'Computer
Driving Licence' from the British
Computer Society.

www.city-and-guilds.co.uk
Details of courses at all levels at
colleges around the UK. Some
course materials available free on
CD-ROM.

www.key-skills.org
Overseen by City & Guilds, this site
provides free summaries of key IT
skill requirements. (N.B. Details are
in Acrobat/PDF format, so are not
suitable for absolute beginners.)

www.learndirect.co.uk
A government-maintained list of all
UK IT courses, arranged by subject
and region, with prices and contact
information.

www.dfee.gov.co.uk/secondchances
IT information for adult learners,
including information about grants,
scholarships, bursaries and other
possible funding sources.

Others

*Office of the Information
Commissioner*
Wycliffe House
Water Lane
Wilmslow
Cheshire SK9 5AF
Tel: (01625) 545745
Fax: (01625) 524510
Email: mail@dataprotection.gov.uk
Web site: www.dataprotection.gov.uk

*Federation Against Software Theft
(FAST)*
Clivemont House
54 Clivemont Road
Maidenhead
Berkshire SL6 7BZ
Tel: (01628) 622121
Fax: (01628) 760355
Email: fast@fast.org
Web site: www.fast.org.uk

Computers for Charity
26 Hollabury Road
Bude EX23 8JA
Tel: (01288) 361177
Fax: (01288) 361154
Email: cfcadmin@btinternet.com
Web site:
www.computersforcharity.org.uk

Gifts In Kind
Email:
productdonations@GiftsInKind.org
Web site: www.GiftsInKind.org

Magazine publishers

Dennis Publishing
30 Cleveland Street
London W1P 5FF
Tel: 020-7907 6000
Fax: 020-7907 6020
Web site: www.theden.co.uk

Web sites for specific magazines
Computer Buyer:
www.computerbuyer.co.uk
Computer Shopper:
www.computershopper.co.uk
MacUser: www.macuser.co.uk
PC Pro: www.pcpro.co.uk
Maxim: www.maxim-
magazine.co.uk
PC Zone: www.pczone.co.uk

Future Publishing
Beauford Court
30 Monmouth Street
Bath BA1 2BW
Tel: (01225) 442244
Fax: (01225) 446019
Web site: www.futurenet.com

IDG Media
MacWorld
99 Grays Inn Road
London WC1X 8UT
Tel: 020-7831 9252
Fax: 020-7405 0262
Web site: www.macworld.co.uk

PC Advisor
5th Floor
85 Tottenham Court Road
London W1T 4TQ
Tel: 020-7291 5922
Fax: 020–7580 1935
Web site: www.pcadvisor.co.uk

McGraw-Hill
McGraw-Hill House
Shoppenhangers Road
Maidenhead
Berkshire SL6 2QL
Tel: (01628) 502500
Fax: (01628) 770224
Email: uk_queries@mcgraw-hill.com
Web site: www.mcgraw-hill.co.uk

Paragon Publishing
Freepost SWB1565
Patch Way
Bristol BS32 0ZZ
Tel: (01454) 642442
Fax: (01454) 620080
Email: subs@paragon.co.uk
Web site: www.paragon.co.uk

Trinity Publications Ltd
First Floor
Edward House
Tindal Bridge
Edward Street
Birmingham
West Midlands B1 2RA
Tel: 0121-233 8712
Fax: 0121-233 8715
Web site: www.micromart.co.uk

VNU Business Publications
VNU House
32–34 Broadwick Street
London W1A 2HG
Tel: 020-7316 9000
Fax: 020-7316 9003
Web site: www.vnunet.com

Wired
Email: info@wired.com
subscriptions@wired.com
newsfeedback@wired.com
Web site: www.wired.com

ZDNet
International House
1 St Katherine's Way
London E1W 1XQ
Tel: 020-7903 6800
Fax: 020-7903 6000
Web site: www.zdnet.com

Index

software support 180–5
telephone support 39, 109,
181–2, 285
training 34–5, 43, 163, 176–80
SWIFT (Society for Worldwide
International Financial
Telecommunications) 69
switching power on/off 206
system checkers 120

Tablet PC project 193
tape backup systems 152–3, 162–3
TAPS (Trans-continental
Automated Payment Service)
69
task assignment facility 71
tax planners 64
tax returns 18, 61, 64
telephone
ADSL 220, 281
automated system 23, 71
cellular communications 274–5
charges 163
DACS box 219
Internet services 282
ISDN 221, 281
networks and 84
telephone logs 71
WAP (Wireless Access
Protocol) 282
telephone support 39, 109, 181–2,
285
templates 24–5, 29, 54, 57
theft 35, 160–1
trackballs 230–1
training 34–5, 43, 163, 176–80
'turbo' button 206
TV tuner cards 105

undelete utility 120
uninstallers 119–20
Unix 247

upgrades
hardware 108, 136, 144–5, 260,
286
software 41, 130–2, 134
UPS (Uninterruptible Power
Supply) 155–6
USB (Universal Serial Bus) 207,
229, 312
user errors 172
'user-friendly' 34

vapourware 42–3
VAT accounting 18, 59, 61, 62,
63
VAT and delivery charges 163
video clips 16, 52, 54
video recording and editing 16,
30, 105, 107, 232–3
Video-CD system 226
videophone cameras 232
viruses 156–8
voice dictation systems 48, 56
voice mail 86–7, 219
VPN (Virtual Private Network)
84

WANs (Wide Area Networks) 82,
87
WAP (Wireless Access Protocol)
282
Warp 246–7
warranties 147–9, 285
Web (World Wide Web) 53–4, 90,
92, 220, 280
Which? Online 281
Windows emulators 250
Windows operating system
239–45, 311
wireless networks 83, 208, 222,
235
Word 56
Word Pro 56

The Which? Guide to the Internet

It is only a matter of time before the Internet is as widely used as the telephone. As its advantages in communications, shopping, banking, finding information, trading and promotion become universally acknowledged, non-users will find themselves in the minority. With case histories and tips on avoiding viruses, this guide explains clearly and simply how to: get connected; use the Net's vast resources cost-effectively; find information quickly and easily; shop safely; send messages anywhere in the world; set up your own web pages – for fun or to promote your business; access free software plus technical and other help and advice.

Paperback   216 x 135mm   304 pages   £10.99

The Which? Computer Troubleshooter

Do you ever get the feeling that your computer, and all the information you have so painstakingly put into it, is somehow outside your control? By explaining how the computer's 'mind' works, and how to resolve the problem without resorting to expensive computer helplines, this book can help, demonstrating in words and pictures how to complete a wide range of standard tasks without error. It examines common stumbling-blocks, explains jargon, presents examples of ways to use your PC more efficiently, and includes sections on setting up properly, preventive maintenance, installing add-ons, getting online, Internet problems, hardware and software problems, and simple troubleshooting.

Paperback   189 x 246mm   192 pages   £12.99

The Which? Guide to Computers for Small Businesses

Most small businesses can benefit from computer technology, but few can afford professional IT expertise. Questions such as how to produce professional-looking documents, create advertising material, connect with other computers to share information, keep track of sales and client records, and exploit the Internet to increase business are answered in simple, non-technical language, using real-life case histories as examples. Including a hardware and software reference section and guidance for buying portable computers, this handbook offers practical advice on finding training and support, getting free help before buying, avoiding common computer problems, and building your business with e-commerce and the Internet economy.

Paperback   216 x 135mm   352 pages   £10.99

Available from bookshops, and by post from Which?, Dept TAZM,
Castlemead, Gascoyne Way, Hertford X, SG14 1LH
or phone FREE on (0800) 252100
quoting Dept TAZM and your credit card details